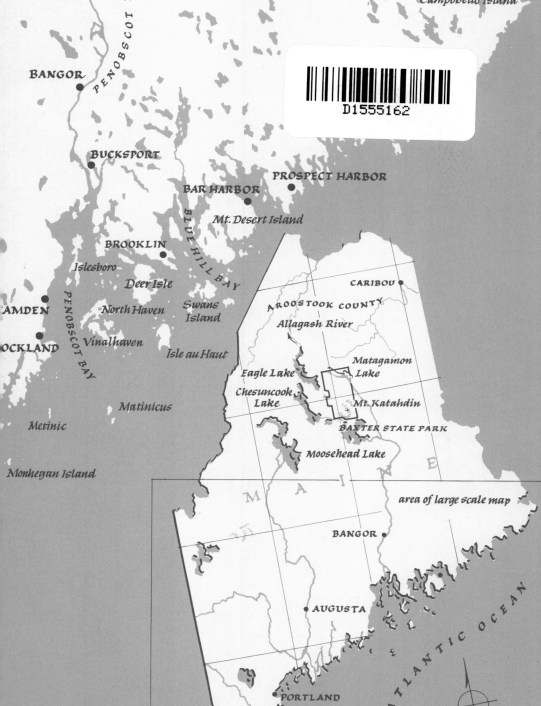

BANGOR

PENOBSCOT RIVER

Campobello Island

D1555162

BUCKSPORT

PROSPECT HARBOR

BAR HARBOR

Mt. Desert Island

BLUE HILL BAY

BROOKLIN

Islesboro

Deer Isle

North Haven

Swans
Island

AMDEN

PENOBSCOT BAY

Vinalhaven

Isle au Haut

OCKLAND

Matinicus

Metinic

Monhegan Island

CARIBOU

AROOSTOOK COUNTY

Allagash River

Matagamon
Lake

Eagle Lake

Chesuncook
Lake

Mt. Katahdin

BAXTER STATE PARK

Moosehead Lake

M A I N E

area of large scale map

BANGOR

AUGUSTA

ATLANTIC OCEAN

PORTLAND

MILES

0 5 10   20   40

Isles of Shoals

MAINE MAGIC

BY
BILL CALDWELL

AUTHOR OF ENJOYING MAINE

SKETCHES BY
KIMBERLY C. MURPHY

BILL CALDWELL

Maine Magic

A VIVID PORTRAYAL OF MAINE LIFE, MAINE TOWNS

AND ISLANDS, AND MAINE PEOPLE...

TOLD BY A MAINE NEWSPAPERMAN WHOSE BEAT FOR

15 YEARS HAS BEEN THE STATE OF MAINE FROM

THE FISHING HARBORS TO THE WILDERNESS LUMBER

CAMPS TO THE SEATS OF POWER AND MONEY IN MAINE...

...HERE IN SCORES OF FUNNY, SAD, MOVING, REVEALING

STORIES AND PICTURES IS THE ESSENCE OF THE MAGIC

THAT IS MAINE

Guy Gannett Publishing Co.

 PORTLAND / MAINE

All inquiries should be addressed to Maine Magic, Guy Gannett
Publishing Co., Congress St., Portland, Maine 04104

The stories in this book appeared originally in the Portland
Press Herald and the Maine Sunday Telegram

Printed by the K.J. Printing Co., Augusta, Maine
Manufactured in the United States

Library of Congress Catalogue Card 79-88015
ISBN 0-930096-03-7   Maine Magic   Cloth
Second Printing

Photos are mostly from the picture files of the Portland
Press Herald and Maine Sunday Telegram, and I give
special thanks to the news photographers who made them.
Charles Merrill, Donald Johnson, Tom Jones, Walter Elwell,
Gordon Chibroski, John Patriquin and Doug Jones. Other
photos are from my family picture drawers.

To Barbara,
Mate aboard Steer Clear,
Mistress of Piper's Bend,
Lover of Maine.

CONTENTS:

I
SPECIAL TASTE OF MAINE
Page 3

II
BRIEF ENCOUNTERS: PEOPLE & PLACES
Page 53

Maine Magic

1
SPECIAL TASTE
OF MAINE

THERE IS A SPECIAL MAGIC to Maine which makes a man happy to be alive here. Happy in himself; happy in his place.

What is this magic? You can see the magic at sunrise, when you wake after a snowfall in the night time and your world is pristine, clean, beautiful. You can see the magic at sunset, when you anchor in Pulpit Harbor and watch the unforgettable, unforgotten magic of the Camden Hills at sundown. You can feel the magic along your spine and inside your head when you stand with a wilderness forest at your back, a lake in front of you where trout leap, and deer drink and no man can be seen and no motor can be heard.

Part of the magic of Maine is her physical beauty. But that is external. In Maine there is more magic; a rare, special fusion between the external beauty of the place and the internal character of the people. They work well upon each other.

This combination of place and people breeds a Maine sense of values, which, when fulfilled, becomes happiness.

This book ends up being about happiness. But it did not set out with such high falutin' ideas.

Indeed this is a book about everyday Maine people and Maine places; about the dawn of days and the moon at night; about hot August days, digging clams at low tide in the mud of offshore islands; and about February days, bright and brittle-cold amid snowfields.

This is a book about small events, the way the world measures events. But it is these small daily events in a man's living and working that taken together add up to happiness — or unhappiness.

Small encounters each day add up to a sense of roots, a sense of truly belonging in the place where you live; and that belonging is an element of Maine magic.

Start a day walking down Main street of the Maine town where you live, and before you've gone a hundred yards, you have a sense of belonging. You wave to Edgar and Pauline Thompson at the gas station; shout to Winty Jacobs in the drugstore; stick your head inside the Yellowfront grocery for a word with Vi; walk by the bookstore, and get a wave from Penny or Ewing; Bill Clark at Clark's Spa, where you get the newspaper, has a word about last night's basketball game at Lincoln Academy; Barbara in the Driftwood shop signals you to bring coffee; so you visit Briggsy in his drugstore, get the coffee, and watch the Greyhound bus stop outside to pick up a couple of passengers headed reluctantly for Boston or New York City. Every few yards on the sidewalk, you swap a word or a smile with more friends, headed to pick up mail in the post office, or to change books with Marjorie at the Skidompha library, or to find a bargain in Reny's Underground. On the street, pickup trucks and cars heading through town may lightly beep their horns as they pass you or somebody inside just lifts a wrist off the steering wheel in that special Maine salute.

Small stuff. But it nurtures the sense of belonging, which is a part of happiness.

At sea, there is an equivalent kind of roots.

Going off the mooring in New Harbor is different than going off a yacht club slip in Greenwich or Marblehead. Freddie Boynton, a topline fisherman, waves from his boat; Cy Morton is out in his beat-up, rickety punt, poling with a single oar off the stern, a trick I've yet to master.

Steaming through the harbor, I see the big Reilly boats, back in from trawling; and Clelle Genthner is working on nets torn last night aboard Four Girls, and he gives us a shout as we go by. By the harbor entrance marker, I spot Manley Gilbert heading home after a short morning of tending traps. I put my motor into "idle" and wait. He comes up at full power, cuts to neutral and swings alongside. We rock on the wavelets, and pass the time of day. He heads in. I head out. Small things. But add them on to others, and a fabric of happiness is in the making.

In newspapering work, Maine is a place that is different. What makes it different are the values. The values this newspaperman writes by here in Maine are different than they were writing in New York, Washington, London, Saigon. When I stare at the empty white sheet in the typewriter here, my news values are different. Here I feel close to the people about whom I write. In the metropolitan cities, in the international - diplomatic - defense - state department beat, the people were all ciphers. The truth was merely the facts you could dig up. The person in your story was a personage — a senator strutting his politics, a justice being pompous in the court, a minister or a secretary of state hiding behind phrases. And if the story was of violence, the violence was a sheeted figure, murdered in a love nest; a young faceless sailor stuffed into a body bag. You wrote your story of war or politics and kept it moving fast, in bright, bloodless sentences.

In Maine, you write about people you know. Indeed, people you respect and often you love. Just telling the facts is too little. You try to show the compassion, hurt, love, rage, warmth, the humanity — the man or the woman, as well as the news items.

Am I getting soppy? Or is this a change of values for the better? And even beyond humaneness, is this today's Maine story about everyday people more important than the latest wrinkle in mid-east negotiations? That 'big' story changes before tomorrow. Nothing is more ephemeral or parochial than the story of what ploy a diplomat pulled at the UN yesterday, or what a senator said to the secretary at the White House dinner last night. But the story of why men go out on a stormy night in small boats to search in a big, dangerous sea for a fisherman who hasn't got back — and whom they may not even like — that story, if you can hit it right, lasts; because, if you hit it right, there is truth and justice and heart in it.

It is a small story. Yet when you get it right, there is a lot of happiness in getting it on paper — and maybe when others read it, they get a moment of happiness too. Maine people write you letters about that, without knowing you, often without ever having written a letter to a newspaper before. So the work brings happiness here in Maine the way it never has in other places.

This is a book about small people and small events in Maine, as the world measures people and events. In the past 15 years I've written about two million words about them. This book is a sampling — an album of snapshots of love.

Go to 30,000 feet for a Maine perspective

ABOARD FLIGHT 127 — Sure-fire cure for pessimists about these United States is a coast-to-coast plane ride in daylight.

Go up to 33,000 feet; spend six hours looking down at this incredibly vast, incredibly dramatic, incredibly beautiful, incredibly sparsely settled nation — and thrill to being a tiny, passing part of this greatness.

Recently I flew on a clear bright October day from Boston to Seattle. I guess I've flown across America 30 times. But it thrills me still. On a daylight trip I sit glued to the window, for hour after hour after hour, looking down and marvelling at America.

I've had to do a lot of flying in my line of work.

I have flown over every major land mass except Soviet Russia and Mainland China. And there is no land in the world so exciting to look upon, so impressive to see, as the United States.

The wild lands west of the Great Lakes enthrall me most — perhaps because I am an easterner.

My spine tingles every time, looking down at the Black Hills of the Dakotas, at the Badlands, at Mount Rushmore, at Yellowstone and Grand Teton and the awesome Continental Divide.

Far, far below I try to pinpoint those places with wondrous names which bring forth floods of spellbinding history . . . Crazy Woman, Big Horn, Virginia City, Snake River, Couer d'Alene, Bearpaw, Glacier Peak.

I find it hard to identify with the big smog covered cities. But every time I see a lone farm in a dry, barren land, a place set out far from anywhere, hard by a bend in a small river — I wonder "What made them stop there, originally? Do the young people go off? Do they come back to die?"

This plane's airspeed is 600 miles an hour. A smiling stewardess passes food and drink. But how did a better breed of Americans first penetrate that land below? What kept them driving on and on? Hope of what lay ahead, the unknown? Or dislike of the known which lay behind?

Maine men led the westering. Many of the first caravans that got through the Continental Divide (and some that did not) were led by men from Maine.

There was, I suppose, some special quality of competence, of ability to cope with whatever came at them, and cope quietly, that made others choose Maine men as leaders.

Today you find that same quality in the north woods, in back country farms, on offshore islands; Maine men able to face emergencies with a calm confidence in themselves.

A fellow can look out a plane window and nourish his soul with the sight of his country.

There is no rhyme nor reason to it. But just looking at this face of the American land as thousands of miles of it go by, gives a new perspective, a new confidence.

Look down at those hard badlands, those high mesas, those terrifying canyons, those rivers — and know that other Americans, only a few generations back took on that country with little but guts and bare knuckles. They made it through. From them sprang Oregon, Washington, California. From the brothers they left back East came the rest of these United States. And between them, they did not number many. Between them, they had no material wealth as we reckon it. Yet it is wrong to think of them as heroes or supermen. They did a lot because they had to do a lot. Don't we?

Inside the cabin, a newspaper lies on my lap. I glance at the day's news. And glance out the window. The news seems petty. Stack it up against what went on out there and it seems silly to take it too seriously.

How serious would it seem to a caravan pushing west to tell them how high the price of milk is? Want to gripe to them about being sick, about how much a hospital bed costs? Want to complain because there isn't overtime pay this week? Go on, tell them how terrible interest rates are!

Later, after I had landed in Seattle, we did a lot more flying and travelling. We criss-crossed the Continental Divide in a chartered plane. We rode jeeps and buses up to lonely mines and far-off oil fields. Ugly things. But in this wild, majestic, fearsome, beautiful country, even their ugliness seems petty, passing stuff.

On the mesa walls, in these rock strewn river beds lies the story of millions of years. I wish I could read geology, to know better what happened in this strong and tortured land. I'm stirred to be an inheritor.

After that wild kind of country, where barely a dozen men live in ten dozen miles, the marvelous handiwork of the city and the industrial towers and the new wrinkles of 20th century technology do not impress very much. Good or bad, they will pass, and pass quickly without leaving much of a mark.

Maybe this is an irrational kind of optimism. But these United States are so big, so glorious, so resilient, that our generation of man will leave little lasting mark for good or bad.

A flight across America induces the same kind of perspective you get in Maine's north woods, alone in a canoe; or in a small boat anchored in an uninhabited cove on a remote Maine island.

This perspective is a sense of being part and parcel of the whole world and all history; a tiny, but integral part of all things; part of the gull flying and the fish swimming and the sun setting and the moon rising and the rock standing, seaweed and mussels clinging to its cold sides, while the wild ocean rolls, everlastingly tugged by the moon and pushed by the wind.

In Maine, you seldom voice out loud a thought like this. But you feel it often.

Maine cove where murder and heaven mingle

HORSESHOE COVE — We have been anchored for the night in this tight little cove on this uninhabited island. There is barely room enough for one small boat to swing at anchor here. When the tides run out, the boulders on the bottom seem to grow bigger and bigger, and reach up and up at you, too close for comfort. That illusion comes about 1 a.m., when you climb out of the bunk to check your anchor lines. By the eerie light of the moon, and the hoot of island owl, and the laugh of a loon, the cove looks smaller, the water looks shallower, the rocks look bigger. And you wish you had slept right through, like Barbara.

But now it is dawn. I have strong coffee brewing. Smells magnificent. That perking sound and the birds' hallelujah to the rising sun are the only sounds. Not even lobster boats are out here yet, hauling traps. The dew-wet world is shrouded in grey mist.

I've got this old typewriter going. The harsh click is a strange sound out here. This typewriter is 27 years old. I bought it in 1952, to use on planes, criss-crossing the country to cover the Eisenhower-Taft fight for the nomination at Chicago.

It is the lightest typewriter I've seen. But it has a rugged steel case, which has taken more punishment than its makers dreamed of. Since that first Eisenhower compaign, this tiny machine has gone a quarter million miles, around the world six times; and punched out about one million words.

Here in the cove, at dawn, it is funny to remember those trips, reported by this machine. But we have been together to wars in the Middle East, nine times to Indochina, mostly Vietnam, but also several times to Laos and Cambodia. I've used this machine in swanky hotels in Hong Kong and in shelled cellars in Quemoy and Matsu, those once-famous, now-forgotten island front lines between then ally Taiwan and then enemy Red China.

The machine has had its fair share of reporting the fleshpots as well as the battlelines. It has banged out words in praise of beautiful women as well as stories of bombings. I can't remember ever replacing the roller over which all these stories of pimps and prime ministers, murderers and mistresses, generals and spies, have been banged out. If that roller were a tape, it might make good raw stuff for an investigation, because not all the stories banged out on it were considered fit to print.

But nowhere in the world have this machine and I ever found a place to work more lovely than the islands of Maine. And nowhere in the world are there men and women so interesting to know and write about as in the State of Maine. Sometimes they are less eager to be found hereabouts; but once found they ring true.

Out here in an empty cove at dawn is a funny time to get sentimental or philosophic. But I think it is offbeat that a lot of my livelihood for so many years came from this simple, beat-up little machine. Yet it had no love, no reward from me. I bought it a few ribbons, gave it a squirt of oil sometimes, and then hit it and hit it and hit its keys. Yet this cheap unloved machine paid for this expensive, pampered boat.

Now I can hear the baby herons from a nearby island, also uninhabited by man. Yesterday afternoon we crept slowly round and round that island, watching and hearing the herons. About 700 of them nest there, in the spruce trees. They are weird to watch, coming in to land on those high branches, long legs stretched out far ahead. The babies in the nests set up a racket as more than a thousand of them screech for food. Until we found this island heronry, I mostly saw herons standing alone, motionless, in muddy coves at low tide, waiting to pounce with their long sharp bills. But on this island I see them in mass, in their heronry. The nests are crude piles of sticks. The female lays from three to six eggs. My Audubon friends hereabouts tell me that most nests on this island end up raising two young herons. The weak ones die, or get pushed over the side out of the nest in the scramble for food. The ground is littered with dead baby herons. The young herons seem big in their nests. But they are helpless for a few weeks, until they learn to fly. When that time comes, it is a comic sight. We will be back to watch those first scary flights. They bring back the cold-sweat terror I felt when my flight instructor climbed out and said, "All right. Fly it yourself!" That, alas, was 35 years ago. I know how those baby herons feel, first time out of the nest, coming in for their first landing.

Rafts of eider duck families are out here in island waters. There are thousands upon thousands. Each colony may number from 30 to 80. These baby ducks, hardly a day old, bring you to laughter, to tears, to applause, to scolding as you watch them play.

The mother ducks form a protective wedge on the flanks and ahead

and behind the raft of babies. Inside the babies cavort. They seem carefree, happy, joyous, learning to swim and feed and quack, and wiggle their tails.

Yet murder is around the bend, here as much as on a city street.

The loon is the goon out here. That laughing loon has a gangster side to his character. He swims near the raft of ducks, then dives down and attacks from below the surface, like a submarine. From underwater he lunges up, snapping to grab and devour a baby day-old duck.

I watch the attack, yelling warnings that go unheeded. Finally, the mother ducks stand up on the water, beating their wings, making waves with their three webbed toes. Then the loon resurfaces, some distance away. The sneaky devil didn't get his baby duck for breakfast. Unlike those helpless gawky herons, these tiny cuddly baby ducks are tough, self-sufficient from the day they are born. Almost from the moment they are out of the shell, baby ducks can run, swim, find food. But when sudden danger comes, the baby climbs right up onto the mother's back. And rides there, while mother paddles like sixty for safety.

The male ducks are not around these days. Poor devils, the drakes have lost their flight feathers. They can't fly. They are molting now. That means they lose all their bright colors, and they are as drab and brown as the females. So the males beat it — they go far out to sea, and set up bachelor quarters where no one can see them, drab and grounded. Only when they grow back bright plumage and get back their flight feathers will they rejoin the females. Then they all fly south to their winter feeding grounds. But here in Maine's islands is where they breed and raise the young.

Funny thing about ducks is that they must oil their own feathers to waterproof them. When you see a duck with its beak up its tail feathers, that duck is getting oil out of its oil gland back there. When it has the oil on its bill, it twists forward and anoints its feathers with it, to protect itself from the cold water. Under its oiled outside feathers is an inner layer of soft curly feathers called "down." Hence the eider-down, used in sleeping bags, parkas, to keep humans warm.

It is now 7 a.m. Back on shore, at this time, I would tune in the

"Today" show. But if you really want to start the day right, start it on a boat in a tiny cove on a remote island watching a raft of eider ducks swim by. Then you know for sure that God is in His heaven; but I bet that Maine is where He'd like to be.

Two years with a nutty Dalmatian

DAMARISCOTTA — Our Dalmation dog called Piper just reached two years old. I never thought she'd make it. That first year or so was rough going. First she ate poisoned meat — and I never want to see a pup closer to death than she was as I rushed her, body shaking violently, face turning black, to the vet and the vet got a needle into her veins pronto. She came home good as new and twice as madcap. Three months later she got run down and dragged by a car. Galloped off yelping and bleeding into the woods, hid there. And I was an hour finding her. What a sorry mess, she was! Torn, ripped, broken. Again a veterinarian performed near miracles. And in a couple of months she was racing across meadows, graceful as a gazelle again. And then, poor beauty — she got spayed!

After a first year like that one, life is bound to be calmer. Piper has chalked up two years now. Her only misadventures since her first birthday have been walking off the bow of the boat into an icy open sea. That startled her. And her first encounter with skunks, raccoons, groundhogs, baby seals, a donkey and a nearby billygoat . . . all these have been side-splitters for us to watch. And pinnacles of such excitement for Piper that her dreams were filled with the noisy and twitching re-enactment of each.

Now Piper is two.

Where do Dalmatians get these crazy quirks? Or are other breeds just as nutty?

For example, what makes this dog crazy for Kleenex? Piper has a passion, perpetual and unwavering for Kleenex.

She'll nose out Kleenex with her wet, cold muzzle, and snitch it out of a coat pocket or a purse; then spend minutes gently ripping it to shreds. She likes yellow Kleenex best. She'll mouth those shreds into yellow little wet wads. And these wads she carries proudly and bestows like gifts, dropping them into the lap of the most pompous, dog-hating guest in the room.

Piper is a secret tissue-chewer. We went out for the evening, and Piper decided to treat herself to a secret binge. In a cupboard, Piper found 24 boxes of Kleenex, bought at a sale price and lugged home that very afternoon. She shredded 12 of those boxes. Let me tell you, 12 boxes of Kleenex finely shredded by a two year old Dalmatian with four hours to kill alone on a Friday night make quite a trail of Kleenex. To know precisely how much, try picking it up.

Where does a Dalmatian learn to like grapes?

About the silliest sight of any day is to see a big dog like Piper mouthing a tiny, soft grape. Still sillier is to see her mouth off the skin, spit out the seeds, then delicately eat the grape.

Where in the dog world did a Dalmatian learn to crack walnuts and shell pecans? This nutty dog has a passion for nuts. On Christmas Day we discovered this secret passion, when Piper discovered and devoured and demolished a great bowl of assorted nuts. She did it by stealing the nuts off a table and cracking them on the floor. Have you ever picked the shells of 123 walnuts, almonds, pecans out of a deep pile rug on Christmas Day after they have been well munched by a Dalmatian — and 17 minutes before guests are due?

I admire and am awed by the sight of primitive instinct at work. I stare fascinated as primitive instinct drives a dog to circle and circle and scratch and scratch before curling up and lying down . . . even on a 20th century rug. I guess some ancient wild dog instinct for inspecting to make sure of safe ground for sleeping is coming into play in a household pet today.

Surely when a dog throws back its head and bays soulfully at the moon, surely that is ancestral instinct that is spooky, blood curdling and admirable.

But Piper never does that. If we go walking on a moonlit night, Piper pays no heed to the brighest or ghostliest moon. She pays no heed to anything except the smells on her turf.

Piper howls only when the sirens go off on TV shows. When the sirens wail on some hospital or cop show on TV, back goes Piper's head; her nose points to the sky; and then up from the deep depths of her dog's soul come long, pitiful, soulful, spooky howls. They are magnificent and we applaud.

But why does the phony sound of fake police sirens on a canned TV show bring out this ancient instinct in my dog, when the moon does nothing?

Two cats and an elderly beagle, now dead, held sway in this household long before Piper arrived on the scene. One is a marmalade cat — a great lion of a fine orange cat. The other is a shy, tiny beauty — a miniature Maine coon cat.

This Piper dog has grown up with these two cats. But everytime that big marmalade cat comes back in the house from outside — and that happens 14 times a day — Piper has to sniff him over from pointed ears to tip of tail, like some customs inspector at the border on the hunt for heroin. The big cat patiently tolerates the frisking. But that tiny coon cat will have none of it. She sits back on her haunches, lifts a fore-paw and bats the sniffing dog right across the snout, sharp claws out at full scratch position. That tiny coon cat is boss over the dog which is 10 times her size and 20 times her weight.

Dogs should have bones for toys. Piper does, putting up with them only because bones are what dogs are supposed to enjoy. In truth, the two toys Piper enjoys are as undoglike as possible; one is an old champagne cork which she carries everywhere and mouths endlessly. The other is a nest of old torn socks tied end-to-end. When Piper has been bathed, brushed, groomed and looks absolutely terrific — she goes out to guests to show off, carrying those gosh-awful old socks to lay on their clean clothes.

Another item this Dalmatian loves to mouth and chew upon gently is your best wristwatch, if you are a man; or a 24 carat gold bracelet if you are a lady.

One day I will get this Dalmatian still long enough to count all her spots. The book says a Dalmatian keeps getting more black spots. Tiny spots grow into big spots . . . that is what the book says. But the only way to be sure is to count them. I don't believe a Dalmatian with 128 or 212 or even 98 spots will ever stay still long enough for me to count them.

I just counted to 68, while Piper slept in front of the fire. Then on the TV set, a siren went off. Now Piper is howling like a wolf. And the spots are still uncounted.

But she got to be two years old. And that is what makes her and me happy right now. But now that she is so big, will she stop trying to climb into my lap and my bed?

A Maine Declaration

AUGUSTA — I'm fed up with hearing people poor-mouth Maine. So here is a Maine Declaration which takes the opposite stance. "Dirigo" — I lead — is the Maine state motto. And here are a few examples to show that Maine is not among the last but is among the leading states of the nation. And has always been out in the lead.

First — these United States began right here in Maine. The first European settlements were on Monhegan. We prospered in Maine settlements while those so-called Founding Fathers were starving down at Plymouth. That first winter it was food sent from Pemaquid, Maine, that kept those Founding Fathers at Plymouth from starving to death. So let's stake out our claim — it all started here in Maine.

Second — let us correct the myth created by the Mercator projection that Maine is a remote state stuck in the distant, frigid northeast corner. Let's consign those old Mercator projection maps to the garbage heap with their anachronistic, deceptive distortions. You know and I know that Maine is south of London, south of Paris, on a latitude with Madrid, Spain.

Mercator was a phony name, an alias for a map maker in the court of a small Flemish prince hundreds of years ago. Yet we still hang his distortion on our school room walls. Down with it! Put up the map of the world as it is today — the Polar projection. This shows Maine where we really are. And, among other things, it shows that Maine is 300 miles closer to Europe than any other spot in the United States. If you own a fleet of ships or planes crossing the Atlantic, those 300 miles can make a huge difference in money with the price of fuel what it is.

Let the truth be heard. Maine is at the hub, not the outer edge.

Third — let's kill the myth that Maine is peopled by country bumpkins who haven't made it into 20th century technology. Facts are that some of the greatest technology is here. One example — American defense. Right now and everyday there are six or seven

Soviet nuclear submarines hiding on the Atlantic deep, ready and able to fire at almost any city in all the United States. These are the most immediate threat to the nation. Who watches them? Who tracks their every move from Murmansk, past Iceland, down to the Mediterranean and across the Atlantic? The men at Brunswick,

Maine — that's who. And if the President needs, in emergency, to reach American nuclear submarines hidden in the deep, close to Russia, how does he do it? He goes through Cutler, Maine — the only transmission station with that capability. What if our most sophisticated nuclear sub needs overhaul or update? Where does it go for expert technical care? To Kittery, Maine. Now add Bath Iron Works and the new frigates into the defense equation; and Loring Air Force Base, the most forward of all aviation attack bases; add in the Early Warning system of the Dew Line.

Put aside military technology. Who invented the first TV tube? A Maine man. The first dry cell battery? Maine again. Remember the Stanley Steamer — about to make a come-back now? Well those Stanley boys got their speeding tickets on the road between Boothbay and Bath.

Want to try for Pulitzer prizes? Maine walked off with nine Pulitzer prizes in half a dozen years. Today much of the finest painting and music making and the best of crafts are being made here in Maine.

This year, Maine led the nation in clean-up of rivers. No state has matched Maine's record of performance. Maine was the first state to revise and update its code of Criminal Justice; to do the same with Banking laws and many consumer protection firsts are chalked up to Maine.

Outside of Maine, people think of this as a male state, where men are chauvinists still and where they must be over the hill and past 50 before they reach seats of power.

Another fairy-tale. On the women's side — the U. S. Congress has 16 women members. In the Maine State Legislature we elected 28 women members. No mere decorations, either. The Maine women are House chairmen of such powerful legislative committees as Appropriations, Business Regulation, Marine Resources, Election Laws.

So much for male chauvinism. Furthermore, the three most powerful voices in Maine are all sopranos. Jean Gannett Hawley is president of the five Gannett daily newspapers and the Gannett TV and radio stations. The president of our powerful and fine competitor, the Bangor Daily News, is another lady — Joanne VanNammee; and the president of Maine Broadcasting System, Channels Six and Two, is Mary Rines Thompson.

Now let's demolish the myth that Maine is for old people.

Start with governors. Republican and Democrat, Maine elected the youngest governors in the nation — with John Reed and Kenneth Curtis. And the only Independent with Jim Longley.

Take state universities. The University of Maine appointed a 21 year old student to the Board of Trustees, and did it when many of the nation's university campuses were aflame with student protest.

A survey of city and town managers in Maine showed most were under 30; and town planners had an average age in Maine of 26. Take the sarsaparilla gang. Some men and women we elect to the state legislature are so young (and look even younger) that they carry ID cards to prove they are old enough to be served a beer in bars near the State House.

The nub of the matter, I think, is that age by itself doesn't count for much in Maine. You can be old and dumb; or young and smart. It is the dumbness or smartness that counts with Maine people — and not age.

Peculiar aspects of a man's character count. One stormy afternoon, the lobster boats stayed inside and the lobstermen sat around a pot bellied stove in a shack on the wharf, talking. Seldom do fishermen say something bad about another fisherman in the harbor unless he is in hearing distance. But this afternoon, one absent fisherman was castigated by a neighbor. I asked what was so bad about him. And the answer was: "The love of Jesus ain't in him. And his feet stink."

When Maine has something good, we hide it

ORONO — Maine is the best state in the union at burying its lights under bushels. If Maine has something good, first thing we do is hide it.

This virtue has its drawbacks. One is that Maine schools don't teach much about Maine. The reason is that no Mainer thought it was a good idea to write a textbook about all the accomplishments of this state.

The last college level text on the history of Maine was published in 1919. Not only is it out of date, but it is out of print.

How many high school students know about William Ladd, Dorothea Dix, Neal Dow? They are all Maine movers-and-shakers of American history. Ladd founded the American Peace Society. Back in 1828 he fought for the principles upon which the United Nations was founded over 100 years later. Ladd was also the nation's first fighter for Women's Rights. Dorothea Dix first led the fight for prison reform, and for medical treatment of the insane. And Dow was the father of Prohibition.

Move to Maine giants in book publishing — G. P. Putnam, W. W. Norton, Ginn of Ginn and Co. First American to publish magazines with more than a million paid circulation per issue was Maine's William H Gannett, whose family still runs these newspapers. They were called "Home" and "Comfort." Cyrus Curtis of Saturday Evening Post, Ladies Home Journal and other magazines, lived at Camden, was born in Portland.

Move to the hot topic today of huge water projects, now being curtailed by President Carter. Maine's Frank Weymouth built the Colorado River Aqueduct in 1896; Frank Crowe of Maine built the Boulder Dam in 1905; Frank Banks of Maine built the Grand Coulee Dam in 1906.

Want to count Maine winners of the Pulitzer prizes? There are a round dozen winners. Six times the Pulitzer for poetry went to Maine. Once for fiction, once for music, once for history, once for newspaper reporting, once as a special citation.

Politics? Maine's year of glory was 1891. Mr. Reed of Maine was Speaker of the House. Mr. Blaine of Maine was Secretary of State. Acting vice president was Mr. Frye of Maine. Leader of the Senate — Mr. Hale of Maine. Chairman of Ways and Means, Mr. Dingle of Maine. Chairman of the Naval Affairs Committee was Mr. Boutelle of Maine; Chairman of the Public Buildings Committee was Mr. Milliken of Maine. And the Chief Justice of the United States was Mr. Fuller of Maine.

The case of the snowshoeing cat

DAMARISCOTTA — We make a funny sight, snowshoeing.

And a baffling puzzle to anyone who tries to interpret our tracks in the snow.

I wear the big, long snowshoes. My wife wears the smaller 'bear paw' snowshoes.

And then there is the marmalade cat, who taps along and doesn't wear any snowshoes at all.

Finally, there is the Dalmatian dog now wholly recovered from that ghastly strychnine poisoning.

We make an odd caravan as we plod our happy way through the woods and along the banks of the Damariscotta river these glorious bright winter days.

Whoever heard of a cat that comes out for a walk with you while you go off snowshoeing? Mine does.

That big marmalade cat of ours is eight years old, and should act wise. Instead he is a soppy, sentimental beast. And snowshoeing appeals to him.

Walking with us in the springtime or the summer or the fall does not appeal to him. Just snowshoeing.

But the cat's feet get cold, when he is out snowshoeing. That fool cat stops in his tracks and turns his orange-flecked eyes upward, meows pitifully and lifts one paw after the other up from the ice-crystalled snow.

He wants a ride.

So the soppy, marmalade cat now climbs aboard the snowshoes. It is a bumpy, precarious ride for him. And tough on the snowshoer.

Try it. Try putting a cat fore, or aft, on a snowshoe and then go tromping off, trying not to spill him.

Every time you lift your leg, the cat's claws dig for dear life into the snowshoe. His back arches. His tail flips frantically, left then right, up then down, acting as a balance rod.

When your foot gets back to the snow again and relishes a moment on flat ground, the fool cat looks prayerfully up at you, seeming to say, "For heaven's sake, don't do that crazy maneuver again! You darn near threw me off!" Then haughtily waits for your next step.

Cowed by the look, you try slithering your snowshoe forward, without any upward movement to rock the cat. In the snow, you now leave a trail which looks like agony personified . . . a long, painful, hesitant stumbling print of a snowshoe in desperate straits.

After three such efforts, you decide you have done enough kowtowing to the cat's cold feet. So you suddenly stomp your snowshoe hard and deep. That will be a puzzlement for Sherlock Holmes. And off bounds the marmalade cat with a dirty look.

His great and furious bound carries him five feet forward. From the impact as he lands his feet spreadeagle in the snow. The result could look like the leap of a tiger or at least a coyote . . .

I've back-tracked over those prints. They are mystifying, even to me, who knows what happened there.

They get even more mystifying when the marmalade cat decides to hell with riding with me. And thinks he will enjoy a smoother trip riding with Barbara. When he hitches a ride with a lady, that cat is ruthless. He usually makes one great leap from the rear; lands where God intended ladies to sit down. This is such a shocking surprise to Barbara that it throws her off balance completely. Wife, snowshoes and cat end up in a messy melee in the snow. Cat disentangles himself and takes a further bound out of reach, where he stalks around the collapsed woman, struggling in the snow to regain her footing.

It is glorious on these brilliant days of Maine's wonderful winter to clamber through the magic of woods silent and deep in hard frozen snow. It is exhilarating and risky to step out onto the frozen river, and try to keep upright as you snowshoe among weird-shaped ice floes, bent and twisted and contorted by the tides running below.

Nowhere does life and the world seem as good as on a bright winter day in Maine. Sit in a snow-cleared spot atop a bold granite boulder, out of the biting north wind. Let the bright winter sun pour down from a pure blue sky and warm you. Let the pure whiteness of untravelled snowfields stretch out before your eyes. Hear the ice floes snap and crack as the tides play below. Watch a hungry gull arch in the sky and effortlessly ride the currents of air — air that is clear, unpolluted, lovely and icy cold. Drink it till your lungs feel young.

Just sit there. And thank God for Maine. And wonder why He made marmalade cats so crazy that they like to snowshoe.

Some very special Olympics at Saddleback

SADDLEBACK — Lori almost burst with happiness and joy when they hung the Olympic medal around her neck. Lori stood on the three-tier winner's stand — gold medal winner flanked by silver and bronze — and her smile lit up the mountainside. Around her, hundreds of her fellow Olympians clapped hands and cheered.

When Lori stepped down, the glorious medal swinging, scores of her friends wrapped her in hugs of happiness.

Lori was one of 300 retarded or handicapped kids who blessed Saddleback on Valentine's weekend for the Special Winter Olympics.

I came to Saddleback like 700 other ordinary people that Saturday, just to ski the mountain. I was wholly unprepared to find hundreds of retarded people all around me, aged eight to 60.

I had never experienced such close proximity to so many retarded people.

To be honest, I must admit that I was at first uncomfortable, embarrassed, even frightened. My initial instinct was to get away and I did — to the men's room.

There, the breakthrough happened. As I stood combing my hair, a guttural shout exploded just behind me. I whirled around. There stood a youngster in distress struggling in fury and exasperation to pull down a stuck zipper. His shouts for aid were not to be denied. I helped him.

When the zipper became unstuck, he beamed. Beamed a smile with more candlepower than any smile you'd see in a year of toothpaste advertising. He let out a whoop that was the finest version of "Thanks, pal," that I've ever heard.

I had done little for him. But he had done wonders for me. He'd released that whole blockage of fear and embarrassment that had me in a mental funk.

I went out onto the base of the mountain and walked over to where Mickey Boutilier was awarding medals to Special Olympics winners. Now I was at ease.

Standing in the crowd, I felt a great current of happiness flooding out from the retarded kids to each of their friends who had won.

That's when I got so infected by the radiance in Lori's face.

From then on, I treated myself to some of the happiest hours imaginable. I stayed with the Olympians as they fell and stumbled on snowshoes, struggled back to their feet and came whooping over the finish line in triumph. Some kids had bodies that could not make it, couldn't coordinate well enough. So another kid flung a supporting arm around his brother or sister and together they would struggle to the finish of the obstacle course.

Nearby, other Olympians went racing and spinning down a fast slope on huge inner tubes and toboggans. And skis. The mountain air rang with joyous noise.

This was a two day affair. Not only did Saddleback Mountain open its arms in welcome but all of Rangeley took these 300 competitors into a warm embrace. They stayed everywhere, in almost every inn and motel, and they all paid their way.

In the hotels, the eating places, in locker rooms and on the streets, other people too, just as I had done, discovered that same wonderful breakthrough with them. Once contact was made, and especially physical contact, all the fear drained out and a new kind of love came in.

There really is a new kind of love awaiting those lucky enough to have close contact with the retarded. You could see it shining on the faces of a hundred "chaperones," and especially among the 44 University of Maine students from Farmington who were around to lend a helping hand. From the TKE fraternity at Farmington, 44 win the chance each winter to work in these Special Olympics.

One of their best jobs is to be chosen as a "Hugger and Kisser." These men stand at the finish lines and they hug and kiss every kid coming across. "Of course, it's right!" says Mickey Boutilier, the schoolteacher from Gorham who is a principal organizational figure in these Olympics. "Look at the Boston Bruins or the Maine Mariners. See how they hug and embrace when one of their team scores. Why not here, with our kids, when they make it?"

On Saturday night comes the Awards Banquet. Then the Victory Dance.

Here is how one hard nosed newspaperman felt when he wrote about it:

"Great as the real Olympics are, moving as the great parade of medalists is in the real Olympics — it is a plastic affair compared to this. The emotion here; the joy, the pride, the happiness here as these kids walk up to get awards and medals is an experience I will never forget.

"I didn't know a 220-pound, six foot, 50-year-old sportswriter who has covered winners everywhere, could get his heart torn out in Rangeley, Maine, watching these wonderful kids."

That's how Bud Leavitt, the outdoors writer on the Bangor Daily News, felt about the affair.

Maine began the Special Winter Olympics here on Saddleback. Until Mickey Boutilier had the dedication and the courage to do so, nobody had dared to let retarded kids out on a ski mountain to compete and revel in winter sports.

Other New England States sent competitors to Maine for the early events.

Now many of those neighboring states stage their own Special Winter Olympics. The first International Special Winter Olympics were held in Steamboat Springs, Colo.

And it all began here on Saddleback. This year the Kennedy Foundation was here again, helping to stage the Maine Olympics.

There is muscle in this crowd too. I would say there is more muscle, more backbone, more resolve, more guts and more bravery in each of these boys and girls than in most of us.

"So it's right we work to pay our own way," says Mickey Boutilier. "The kids here have been salting away a dollar or two a week, from whatever work they do. The tab is $25 per kid, for two nights lodging, 12 meals, and insurance for two days on Saddleback. Basically, they're as independent as anyone, so long as they're given the chance."

How the eagle stole the osprey's meal

BUCKS HARBOR — First, Barbara spotted the osprey. Then moments later, she spotted the eagle, close by. It happened as she stood in the bow of our boat, dropping anchor, just before six in the evening.

For the next hour, until it became almost dark, we did nothing but watch these two giant birds in fascination. And the osprey and the eagle watched each other.

The osprey was closest to our boat. It sat tall and prominent on a dead branch overhanging the edge of the harbor, about 40 feet above the water, ready to hunt for fish.

We had never before seen a fish hawk or osprey so close for so long and at such a head-on angle. He looked huge, as big and imposing as an eagle. With field glasses, we got a scary, close look at the great talons with which it snatches fish out of the sea. The talons looked savage and powerful enough to rip open anything the hawk attacked, including a man's scalp.

This osprey stood almost two feet tall. We were amazed at its whiteness, from this head-on angle. The bird was totally white from under its head, down through its big chest and long body, to its tail.

The eagle was 100 yards higher up the bold cliff, sitting imperiously atop the tallest pine, a throne for the bird that is king of all it surveys.

And surveying its domain was precisely what the majestic eagle was doing. We watched, mesmerized by his savage beak, haughty neck, unbelievable size and imperial immobility. Watching this eagle, there could be no doubt whatever that the eagle is "King of Birds" — and knows it. Yet he is king of more than birds. His size, his majestic bearing, his haughty immobility and his look of fierce disdain were awesome and intimidating to Barbara and me.

We guess he was over 30 inches tall, and when he finally flew in pursuit of the osprey, his wings stretched seven feet across. State officials say that Maine has 120 adult eagles, and 35 young were hatched in 1978.

Down where we humans live, the surface of the harbor near our boat was rippling with jumping fish, thousands of them, about four inches long. Their little bodies flashed silver in the twilight as they made tiny leaps through the air.

The fish hawk went to work. He flew off, vanished among the pines momentarily, and then came back into view, flying higher, soaring now, hunting over the little fish. For a second he would hover, motionless, to choose his target. Then suddenly, he'd drop one wing and do a fast side slip manœuvre which a pilot can only poorly imitate. From that, the osprey would go into a headlong dive, wings tucked in tight; then a split second from crash, the osprey would thrust forward its beak and talons, as airbrakes, splash but barely enter the water, snatch out a fish with its talons, and zoom upward. Back to flying straight and level, it would race away from where the eagle sat motionless.

We kept glasses on His Majesty. That great head saw every move, yet never moved itself. It disdained what the osprey caught. Yet the osprey seemed to suffer from nerves, knowing who was watching. It missed on some dives. Finally a perfect dive and those talons lifted out a fat wriggling fish. Cockily, the osprey crossed the eagle's bow. A mistake. This time, the huge eagle rose. The enormous wings spread seven feet wide, and flapped and closed the gap, coming down hard toward the osprey. Terrified, the osprey let go of its fish. With infinite grace, effortless precision, the eagle snatched the osprey's dinner in mid-air.

A sight in a Maine harbor, unforgettable and unforgotten.

Maine glories in September

Now it is our turn. The best is saved for last.

These last sweet, sun-filled days of September are the beautiful bonus days. They are the bonus paid to Maine people who worked June, July, August, past Labor Day, filling the needs and taking the money of millions of visitors.

Now it is our turn. Now, almost alone in our Maine, we are blessed with the loveliest days of the year.

They've been bountiful this year — these peacock days of late September; the sad, sweet days, treasured and relished one by one like the last sips of the last bottle of a wonderful wine. There is a body to these days, a maturity, a touch of melancholy that spices their joy. A September day in Maine is more beautiful than the finest days of June, July and August.

Midsummer is carnival time — blue skies, hot sun, filled beaches, boats crowding every mooring. The sun bounces to work early, hot in the sky by seven in the morning. And it gallivants across the heaven, staying up late, refusing to bed down for the moon till nine at night. Days of beauty, yes, but long-legged, coltish, gawky beauty. Days which spend themselves recklessly, for in early July lots more summer stretches endlessly ahead. Those are profligate days.

But September days have a transient beauty. Their loveliness is piqued by the astringent nip of fall. In these special days, beginning and end meet. The first of fall and the last of summer blend to create a unique beauty. The last sip tastes the best.

Look back or look ahead at the seasons. Look back to spring. Spring is a brief boisterous moment of exuberant beauty, but shallow. Spring has no past and no future; it lives like a butterfly, lovely, and suddenly gone. Spring does not meld slowly and happily into summer. It leaps across our stage and is gone.

Look ahead to winter. Is there any sweet-sad moment of hello and farewell, as fall blends to winter and the last cold leaves fall dead to the ground? No. Winter races down, hard and relentless, out of the arctic to freeze a sour earth. Then, when finally winter loosens its icy grip months later and spring bounces in, we feel relief. "Thank God winter's gone!" No sadness.

No, only in the benison of September, only in benign goodbye to summer and the glorious splurge of welcome from warm-hearted fall, is this matchless mixture of sorrow and joy.

I think the whole earth relishes this sweet sadness, this gradual transition. Slowly, the leaves change from gaudy green to glowing red and browns and golden yellow. They relish the change, savoring their slow transformation. Not of the brash impetuousness of spring rushing in, bursting out all over; none of the vengeful triumph of winter reaching fast to grab us and hurt us with a brutal storm.

But September's final days move with a special grace. With all their beauty, these days possess a tender sadness. With all the rich majesty of the slow-rolling transformation of Maine summer to Maine fall, there is an intimacy, a very human, friendly warmth to these final September days. It is a change of spirit as much as scenery; a change of temperament as much as temperature.

September air plays lovely tricks. With the breeze from the northwest, distant mountains stand higher and islands seem to rise up and float above the sea and mirages play beguiling tricks out on the sea.

And sound is purer, too. Songs of birds, feasting on rowan berries, waft up from the meadow with crystal purity. Even the night noise of skunks and raccoons rattling in the leaves on the final prowls is loud on the night air of September. The sky is a richer velvet black and the moon and stars seem to glow more brightly.

And then there is the wonder of September wonders. The bright and perfect day when there is no noise, a day so clear and clean and perfect that you can hear the clouds moving and the fish breathing.

These are the best of times.

The fish chowder fracas

PIPER'S BEND — The dispute this morning in this corner is touchy. What is the right way to make Maine fish chowder?

A chowder freak in New York City has sent me six different recipes. "Each comes from a so-called New England expert," she writes. "But you do a column on Maine. So you be the referee. You tell me which is the REAL Maine fish chowder recipe!"

So I raised the question at dinner the other night when we had six friendly, peaceful neighbors at table.

Inside of 15 minutes, I had a chowder war going. These sweet, gentle people were pounding the table, yelling, shouting at each other — all in the cause of chowder.

Now, the night I rashly raised the chowder question followed a day spent in the state Legislature. I thought I'd seen shouting matches up there over a constitutional limit on spending. Those outdid a lot of pig calling heard in Iowa; and that Iowa stuff is good, high class yelling. But I found that neither the constitution nor pigs can hold a candle to chowder when it comes to stirring up a shouting and yelling match.

Up stood one thin, agile lady of 58 years. She leaned across my table, wagging her fist under the nose of a man who has been her friend and neighbor for two score years.

"NEVER EVER spoil fish chowder with salt pork! Never dare do that to any chowder you serve me, Harry!" she shouted. "Why, any pig is too strong to mix with the taste of fish!"

The shocked man rose to the challenge. He came out of his seat, ready to fight.

"Nonsense, Hettie!" he yelled, waving a spoon and banging the table to silence all around him. "Salt pork is a MUST!! You've got to have a pound of salt pork for chowder that tastes right. Really salty, salt pork. Tried-out by itself. You throw off the liquid. Then put the pork in with the fish. Without salt pork, you ain't got fish chowder!"

These two glared at each other. Neither giving an inch.

The others raged over ingredients. They vented vehement voices over whether to use cunners, cod or haddock in a real Maine chowder.

But what almost ended friendships of 30 years was what to do with backbones and heads.

"Cook'm right in with the fish; cook the fish, head, back, tail and all!" cried one chowder apostle.

"Cannibal!" rebutted another. "Throw out that refuse! Only use the meat of the haddock!"

"You're both crazy!" cried the agile, thin lady, who seemed ready to leap on the table to make herself heard. "You must boil the head and backbone separately. Then use the juice as the core, the base of the entire chowder. That's the right way!"

They argued over every item—even over the right kind of crackers.

Pilot crackers? Water biscuits? Sea toast? Plain, round crackers?

I learned my lesson from watching this chowder brawl. The lesson is never to go public with "the right way to make Maine fish chowder."

Instead I am following the wise, but timid, example of Kenneth Roberts. Even at his peak of popularity, Roberts hid behind the skirts, not of his mother, but his sacred grandmother, when it came to stating the right way to make real Maine fish chowder.

So I've told the lady to do as Roberts' grandmother did in her day . . . leave the heads and backbones where they belong — in the garbage can at the fish market.

Then go the simple route; one kettle, one knife, one spoon. Two dozen cunners for small chowder; or good-sized cod or haddock, cut into strips an inch wide, two inches thick, all boned and skinned.

Then cut six onions and six potatoes and a pound of salt pork into small cubes and pile in layers in a fish kettle. Over on the side, put two dozen water biscuits into a shallow pan and just cover with milk.

Then pour off the milk to cover the fish, pork, potatoes and onions and simmer for an hour in the kettle. Line a soup tureen with the moist biscuits and pour the chowder on top. And there you have a real Maine fish chowder!

Sea Smoke: Shrouded beauty

WISCASSET — This morning, the white sea smoke was pink.

Between Cod Cove and Wiscasset, on the northerly side of the road, sea smoke rose off the cove, thick enough to wrap an opaque blanket of white around a tiny islet. Only the top branches of a dozen tall pines showed above the smoke.

Then, in the eastern sky the rising sun climbed high enough to shine over the high ground, and the sun's rays reached out and transformed the white vapor to pink — a tender, pale coral pink.

One mysterious, beautiful blessing of living in Maine in winter is to see sea smoke rising from the ocean and rivers and salt water coves.

But to see it glow pink, to see its opaque whiteness transformed to a translucent pink and then to see the little islet begin to show through the pink vapor was a rare delight.

My car clock showed about 7 a.m. when I pulled over and stopped by the side of the road to watch the miracle of morning sun painting a sheet of white sea smoke pastel pink.

The scene seemed Oriental. Often fogs or sea smoke half-obscuring islands or mainland shorelines seem to be like Japanese paintings. There is a gentleness, a softness, a mysterious smudging of the edges, a mystical distortion of distance on these very special Maine mornings.

As the sun warmed the air, more of the island was unwrapped and revealed through the thinning vapor. As the temperature climbed with the sun, warmth dissipated the white vapor hiding the water. And the climbing sun now touched the water in the cove.

The tide was out. Thin, shallow pools of water lay in the troughs cut in the mud by worm-diggers' forks. These now turned pink.

The islet, fully revealed now, stood amid a surrounding sea of pink, like some heavenly Avalon out of a bygone Arthurian romance.

In a moment, the mystery was gone.

The sun was up full, the sea smoke was gone and there was no more pink vapor left in this slice of Maine. The new day was back to normal.

But the sight just seen stays vivid and unforgettable in my mind.

These sea smokes or white vapors are caused by conditions almost opposite from the causes of summer or regular fog. Fog appears when wind blows warm, moist air over the colder surface of the ocean.

But sea smoke occurs when the first frigid air of winter moves over ocean and river surfaces that have not yet frozen and are warmer than the air above them. Many Maine fishermen swear that in 'white vapor' — sea smoke — visibility is less than in the densest fog.

I've been in 'white-outs' between Pemaquid and Monhegan when the sea smoke blotted out the whole world beyond five feet or less. To me, this vapor is weirder than the worst fog and more scary.

The whiteness is so glaring white, it aches your eyes. There is no boat an arm's length away. There is no sea to be seen. There is no sky. Just glaring, impenetrable whiteness cutting you off from everything and everybody.

The vapor is not so thick as that inland. But as I drove away from watching the islet, the sea smoke on the Wiscasset bridge was so thick that I could not see cars approaching with full headlights on until they were within 25 feet.

That Wiscasset bridge is low and very close to the water. But in the white-out, there was no water to be seen.

On rivers, or close to shore, sea smoke and vapor seldom last very long. But while it lasts, it casts a weird and mysterious beauty over our land. And when washed pale pink in a sunrise, there is no beauty in the world to match this northern phenomenon.

Deer in the meadow at dawn

DAMARISCOTTA — The white-tailed deer came out of our woods early this summer morning.

First the buck came out, and stood at the far edge of the mown meadow. He signaled the coast was clear, then his doe trotted out. Behind her came two fawns, prancing and cavorting.

I stood fascinated, watching from the bedroom windows. The time was 5:15. But I woke Barbara, for she delights in the sight of deer in the meadow.

Their morning stroll was leisurely. At the border between woods and open meadow, they sniffed and nibbled and flicked their white tails. Every few moments the buck would lift his head, stretch his neck, turn and listen in all directions.

Then a decision was made.

The doe and fawns turned back into the woods. The buck struck out in the opposite direction. At a trot, he headed up the slope north-westerly and toward the river. I lost him for a few moments among some trees. Then he emerged into another open field; and he heard my dog bark.

One short, sharp bark from inside the house. Piper, our Dalmatian, had not even seen the deer. She was still half asleep. But she let out her morning bark for her regular morning biscuit. And that did it.

To the buck, the bark was an alarm signal. He stopped in his tracks, lifted his head and listened.

I watched through field glasses. Barbara distracted our dog.

But the buck was wary. Barbara and I passed the binoculars back and forth to each other. Minutes went by. The buck stood motion-less, ears cocked forward, head high. Not a ripple of movement any-where. Neck, chest, back, rump, all four legs — frozen as though cast in metal.

The silence hung on. Then, assured no danger was imminent, the buck moved on.

I kept a weather-eye on the meadow where the doe and her fawns had been. Sure enough, they came back out into the open.

The fawns were very light-colored, their coats the color of sunlight and honey, flecked with spots of white. My guess is they were twins. They played with each other like kids, enjoying early morning hijinks in the meadow. The doe ambled along tolerantly behind them.

They were close now. There is something so graceful and so beauti-ful about the shapes and movements of deer in a meadow that your heart fills with a rush of joyful blood.

They were at the apple tree now. The fawns arched their necks and reached for the fruit. One tried to reach higher by standing on its hind legs and putting its forelegs up on a branch for balance: It was a pretty tableau. We watched the three of them nibbling away, ignorant of their unforgettable grace and beauty.

The branch for balancing broke under the eating fawn. She dropped down in shocked surprise. And the noise scared them all. They raced back across the meadow, hightailing it for the woods and cover. The white tails pointed straight to heaven.

In huge, swift leaps they bounded across the field. A brook and a fallen tree were in their path. They leaped, first the doe, then each of the fawns. The stream and the fallen tree were small, but their leaps were huge — high, wide and handsome. They bounded and leaped far beyond the needs of distance. They seemed to brim with joy in their new day. We hope so. They made our day — and it was only 5:30 A.M.

Wet notes of warm memories

PORTLAND — The door is locked as I write this column for fear a reader or a boss will walk in, take one look and label me crazy.

The entire floor and all table tops are covered with wet, bedraggled sheets of paper from my reporter's notebook. The office looks like a jigsaw puzzle gone berserk.

But it all makes sense. I am in the midst of a salvage operation.

As I climbed out of a low-slung car in a downpour early this morning, a pocket caught on a doorhandle. The cloth ripped. Out into two inches of dirty city rain water fell my reporter's notebook.

In that notebook are my notes on people and stories and interviews made in Old Orchard, Cape Porpoise, Kennebunkport, Wells Beach, Lewiston and Bath.

On this trip, I made all my notes in ink. For years and years and years I have made all my notes in pencil. But this time I was going to be especially neat — no more blunt pencils — and do it all in fine blue ink.

Ink is vulnerable stuff. Drop penciled notes into a curbside puddle and a reporter can decipher what was there. But water does funny and horrid things to notes written in ink. So now I have all those ink-written pages torn out of the notebook and they are hanging out to dry, spread over desks, table tops and radiators.

Gradually, the comedy of it all is coming through to me. Slowly, the pages are drying. And out of those damp blurry pages the faces and voices of the people I saw are shining through.

Drying nicely on the carpet is Cindy. On the radiator above her is Sister Rachel. And that is a strange juxtaposition that has never yet happened in real life. But I think that if real life could imitate my notebook — Sister Rachel and Cindy would enjoy a few hours of each other's company.

Cindy is a beguiling topless barmaid. I hope to tell her story one day soon, so will reveal little here. But Cindy is a Maine girl who ran away at age 17, crisscrossed the nation, learning lots as she went.

She was a go-go dancer in Texas. Then in San Francisco she was about the last of the Flower Children when a kindly lady stopped her, asked if she had run away from home. Cindy said that her home was Maine; and indeed she had run away. "Here is $100," said the lady. "Take it. It is your bus fare home to Maine."

Sister Rachel I met in Lewiston. She is the amazingly likable, competent and undaunted administrator of St. Mary's Hospital there. She told me that 100 years ago, the Sisters of Charity came to Lewiston and soon founded the first Catholic hospital in Maine. It has grown to great size and excellence. The night Sister Rachel and I met for the first time she was opening a "Health Happening" in the Multi-Purpose Center in town.

I lean down to some pages drying midway between Cindy and Sister Rachel. I am delighted by the name and face that is beginning to show through the damp spots.

Here comes Sam Wildes from the lobster and fish dock at Cape Porpoise Harbor. I had a fine talk with Sam there as he sold gas and loaded bait barrels to the lobster boats. The Wildeses have been on

this old Maine harbor for many, many years. A whole part of town down by the water is called The Wildes Section. Sam is a man of close to 65 now and he has seen a lot of strange things happen on that waterfront. But I think that even Sam Wildes would be a bit surprised to find himself drying out on the floor of the Gannett Building, plumb between Cindy, the topless barmaid, and Sister Rachel, the administrator of St. Mary's Hospital.

Here are some pages that are still very wet. But that is appropriate. These are notes from a meeting with Karl Kurz who is living this fall and winter aboard a wooden cruiser built in 1928. She is a 45-foot-long classic Dawn cruiser named "Rubicon" and she is tied up at the slips in the Brendze and Wester yard on the Kennebunk River. Karl, who hails from Machias himself, showed me through his handsome boat which he bought and replanked in places this summer.

At Wells Beach, I spent two fascinating hours with Vander Forbes, father and son. Thin and wiry, strong and vigorous at 81 years, the father began work at Wells Beach over 60 years ago. "I sold fruit from a horse and buggy." Today, this Forbes family are the biggest hotelkeepers on the island. The Forbes story will make a wonderful tale of success the Maine way.

Soon, another 50 pages of notes will be dry. In just a few days of wandering Maine, a reporter's notebook overflows with a livelier, more vigorous, more varied bunch of new friends and stories than a fellow could find on any other beat.

Maine coon cats; are they a Norse import?

PIPER'S BEND — Maine coon cats — how did they get here and where did they come from?

For almost 10 years we have had a Maine coon cat at home. She is a miniature and she has not grown any bigger since she was nine months old. Even at 10 years, the little coon cat weighs only seven pounds. But her fur is so thick, including the hallmark tufts in her tiny ears, that she appears twice her real "bone" size. She is a shy critter with strangers, but soppy and loving with her family, her Dalmatian dog and the senior cat, a marmalade of huge size.

A fancier and breeder of Maine coon cats came to talk with me about them recently. He is Dr. Richard Castner, a professor of Dance at New York State University, who has long family roots in this part of Maine. He is an expert in folk dances. During the bicentennial celebrations, Dr. Castner, an athletic man of about 40, taught militiamen and their ladies how to dance the line dances that were the fashion in the 18th century.

"I am the only living man who has danced the hornpipe on the decks of Old Ironsides," he laughs. A charming gentleman and exotic scholar, Castner is one of the world's six experts on 18th century dances. Couple that with the fact that he is also a front-runner in the breeding of champion Maine coon cats, and you can see why Dr. Castner qualifies as a delightful eccentric in upstate New York, where he teaches dance.

But Castner's talk about Maine coon cats is fascinating, too. He advances a theory that the Vikings brought the ancestors of Maine coon cats to these shores.

"I got bitten with this idea when I was studying in Norway. They have cats there called 'skogkatts', which are dead-ringers for Maine coon cats. These Norwegian cats have the same distinctive heads, the same three coats of hair, the same broad beaver-like tail. The 'skogkatts' go far back in Scandinavian history, and I like to think that Vikings brought the ancestors of Maine coon cats to these shores."

Castner has done some amateur sleuthing in the hope of finding mention of these special cats in the lore of the Mic-Mac Indians.

"So far, no luck. But maybe some of your readers may shed light on evidence that the early Indian had cats."

Another theory, which Castner says has no basis in fact, is that Marie Antoinette, Queen of France, caused coon cats here. "The story is that when she was preparing to escape to the refuge and home provided for her in Edgecomb, her benefactor, Capt. Clough, brought over from France not only some of her furniture, but also some of her cats. In this way, the fleeing Queen, he felt, would be less homesick in Maine."

A third theory is that the Maine coon cats are descended from Angora cats, which came here on clipper ships from Turkey. Castner discounts this idea, saying Angora cats are white and blue-eyed.

A popular fourth theory is that Maine coon cats came from barn cats breeding with coons. "But this is genetically impossible. Even if they had intercourse, a cat and a coon could not produce offspring," states Dr. Castner.

A more genetically feasible fifth theory is that Maine coon cats are the result of barn cats mating with bobcats or fishers. These are "genetically compatible," says Castner, who bases all his conclusions on advice from animal biologists.

But the romanticist in Dr. Richard Castner clings to the theory that Vikings brought the ancestors of Maine coon cats here. "Therefore, I have my champion Maine coon cat sires listed in the Cat Fanciers Association rolls under the Viking name of 'Eric the Red,' father of Leif Erickson."

To get the Cat Fanciers Association to acknowledge Maine coon cats as a special and pure breed took many years of lobbying. The effort did not succeed until 1976. The Canadian Cat Association had long previously listed Maine coon cats as blue-ribbon purebreds.

Maine coon cats grow big and grow old, Dr. Castner said. "I remember my bride, aged 24, being indignant at discovering the family coon cat, aged 29, was her senior. Most Maine coon cats grow big as well as old. They weigh around 15 pounds as a rule, but some get as big as 33 pounds, which is an awful lot of cat."

I have recounted all these theories to Dickens, our little coon cat. She merely arches her back and rolls over to be scratched.

Winging home to Paradise from Gate 28

BOSTON — Thousands of Maine people know it, but nobody in Massachusetts does. There is a part of Logan Airport at Boston that is forever Maine.

It is Delta's Gate 28. This is where the Maine contingent gathers to catch the late afternoon homecoming planes to Portland and Bangor.

Just walk down that mammoth corridor to the departure gates at Logan, and the human temperature changes conspicuously as you come to Gate 28. The crowd is warmer, different than the crowd at any other airline gate.

The people waiting for the Portland plane are human. They talk. They act friendly. They smile. They bust the rule that every waiting traveler must look glum, unhappy, impatient and afraid of contact with strangers. Under the sign which reads, "Portland," people actually seem to like each other.

And they do strange things.

One recent night, when fog, rain and sleet grounded planes, shut airports and delayed every traveler in the eastern United States, dismal, disgruntled gloom blighted every gate except Gate 28.

At Gate 28, you'd think a party was in progress. Clark Neily, the new business-getter for the city of Portland, cut out a new career. He walked among the crowd that had been waiting for a couple of hours and took orders for coffee. Then the big, grinning redhead went off foraging and came back with paper bags filled with cups of coffee. Ever see that happen at any other airline gate?

Bob Marden was there. The Waterville lawyer, one-time president of the Maine Senate, and a terrific man on the trombone, was back from a business day in Washington with his associate Bruce Chandler. "Ike" Lancaster, an establishment lawyer in Portland, with a fine Roman look, was there, chatting with a neurologist from Biddeford's Webber Hospital.

A Camden doctor and a Rockland man who heads Marine Colloids

were there. Scores of semi-strangers. But everyone was chatting and visiting, telling where they had been, and how lousy the weather was, and how pretentious the people were whence they came — compared to Maine, where they were happily heading now.

Of course, the Maine-bound plane was late. Every plane was late this foul-weather day. The men and women at Gate 28 had missed connections, meals and appointments — just as everyone waiting at hundreds of airline gates across Logan had. At those other gates, gloom hung as heavy as the fog outside.

"But this mad Maine bunch is always different," said the airline agent behind the check-in desk. "They're happy. Not just under lousy conditions like tonight, but every day this Maine gate is different. Gets to be kind of a clubhouse; sort of a happy reunion in the Maine crowd. Waiting for the plane to Portland seems to them like waiting for a ride to paradise. Crazy."

He punched more tickets, made more announcements of more delays. I asked why he thought this crowd was happier.

He didn't wait two seconds to answer. "Nuts. They're all some kind of nuts. When I announce, 'Ready to board for Portland and Bangor,' they light up like I'd poured two martinis into each of 'em. . . .

"Funny crowd, the Maine people. Going home makes 'em happier than heading out."

II
BRIEF ENCOUNTERS: PEOPLE & PLACES

Head Tide Church

THIS SECTION 'Brief Encounters' is a covey of friends, a collection of places around Maine. I've picked these few from hundreds of columns which fill many boxes.

It is no fun at all, choosing a dozen or so and putting hundreds of other friends and places back in boxes and returning them to the attic, to sit in the lonely dark, backed against the box of Christmas tree ornaments and my grandmother's old steamer trunk.

Memories unleashed by these old friends are like Chinese fire-crackers, one exploding the next.

For example, the piece here about the glory of garbage at the Kennebunkport dump, triggers the memory of the young skier at Sugarloaf who ran the Groovey Garbage Company there to make money to keep on skiing. In Damariscotta, we had a fancy garbage man named Jack O'Brien, who looked like a Boston Irish million-aire and whose truck sported original art, done by painter Jake Day. You'll meet Jake Day in this section.

The Droggitis family at the Wonderbar in Biddeford triggers memories of the Muskie family, because a Droggitis girl married a Muskie boy. And that triggers memories of visits to the mother and sisters of Senator Ed Muskie, around Rumford, when Muskie was a favorite son running for president. From those splendid Muskie women, I learned about the Polish immigrant tailor, whose son became Maine's governor, and then Maine's senior senator. Putting away the old memories, I get misty-eyed for a moment about *people, too often labelled as waspish, picking a Polish Catholic for governor and senator, and having his son marry a Maine Greek girl, daughter of another immigrant who got here the hard way and also did Maine proud.*

Maine has a richer stream of blood, culture and roots than the Scotch-English protestant heritage, so strongly associated with Maine. French; Armenian; Polish; Slavic; Scandinavian; Lebanese; Greek — all are prominent in Maine life. We just sent the beauteous widow Olympia Snowe to Congress, a Maine Greek girl; our chief justice in the early 1970's was Armand Dufresne, of French extraction; George Mitchell, of Lebanese extraction, was chairman of Maine's Democratic party, followed by Harold Pachios, with a Greek heritage. Tim Wilson, Negro, has headed a vitally important state agency under three governors; and long ago Maine picked a telephone operator from Skowhegan, named Margaret Chase Smith; and she became the most important woman in the Senate, long before the political spotlight was on women.

While looking conservative, Maine has been a pioneer without making waves. With a million population, we've elected 28 women to our Legislature, and many are chairmen of the key committees. By contrast, the 220 million people in the U.S. send less than 20 women to Congress. Maine has long had women judges, women lobstermen; we've had students as Trustees of the University of Maine and named ex-convicts to prison parole boards.

The variety of people, the variety of places in Maine is infinite; and the quality is high. This section touches on only a very few of very many.

Glory of good garbage

KENNEBUNKPORT — Here is the mecca of Maine dumps.

Here is the shrine of that endangered species — The Town Dump.

Dumping is a cherished Maine pastime. Going to the town dump, eyeing its contents judiciously, adding a bit to it, taking a mite from it, meeting old friends and new settlers while we dump our trash is a part of life in Maine.

And it is threatened with extinction. Bureaucrats in Washington and Augusta are plotting to kill off the town dump and replace it with sanitary landfills and treatment plants for solid waste.

The words alone are horrid. Paying for them will be more horrid.

Dumping is as much a way of Maine life as lobstering, deer hunting, franks-and-beans and pea-planting.

A movement is gathering momentum here to get the Kennebunkport Dump named to the National Register of Historic Places.

Edward Mayo, in his waterfront studio, is autographing numbered copies of a limited edition of his new book. "Dump Watchers Handbook," which has a subtitle of "Field Guide to Better Dumping."

It is dedicated to town dumps and dump pickers everywhere. That is a dedication which takes in half the population of Maine.

The scholarly author, Dr. Mayo, is the first man in Maine to receive his D.D. (Doctorate of Dumpology). He wore the D.D. hood and gown when he marched in the graduation ceremonies at Harvard University. The mushy, gaudy colors of his academic hood caused jealousy even among the gaudy hood-wearers from Brown and Harvard. But the sensation that turned the heads of the crowds was the "Eau de Dump," a titillating cologne worn exclusively by senior officials of the Kennebunkport Town Dump.

Dr. Mayo and the numerous executive vice presidents of the Kennebunkport Dump Association are leading a crusade to promote good dumping habits among American families. They speak with feeling

about the town dump as one of the last remaining segments of Americana.

"Retrieval of castoffs, the feeling of amiability and togetherness associated with dumping, and the true community spirit so essential to society is disappearing," writes Dr. Mayo in his Dump Watchers Handbook.

The incentive to make more fine looking trash will vanish, predicts Dr. Mayo, with the arrival of sanitary landfills. These sanitary landfills will compact all trash into one shapeless, characterless, unidentifiable mush. When a family's trash loses its identity, that family loses pride in its trash production. No longer will families vie to produce glamour-filled garbage.

When pride in trash declines, when trips to the town dump die, then conspicuous consumption will die; and recession will walk into Maine along with sanitary landfills.

To keep the spirit of community dumping alive, Edward Mayo, D.D., and his vice presidents in the Kennebunkport Dump Association, stage rallies in York County. Each Fourth of July, amid the tinkle of gin-and-tonics by a swimming pool, a Miss Dumpy is crowned to reign for the ensuing Dump Year.

This trashy lady issues dump credit cards, trash stamps and bumper stickers which boast "this car visited the Kennebunkport Town Dump."

She hands newcomers dump-starter kits as well as trash samplers, as a kind of welcome wagon gift.

If you cherish Maine's heritage, write to The White House, urging that the Kennebunkport Town Dump be named to The National Register of Historic Places.

Wonderbar and the Droggitis Boys

BIDDEFORD — Coming back to the Wonderbar was like coming home to Momma.

Some years ago I spent three days here gathering material for a Sunday feature in the Telegram, and I made my headquarters at the booth in the Wonderbar instead of at the newspaper office.

Everybody I wanted to see came to the Wonderbar. They'd relax over a beer, a coffee or an ouzo while I interviewed them in this great Greek tavern. Nikki Lang, that smart and dashing waitress, would take phone messages for me. The Droggitis brothers who own the place filled me with good stories of old Biddeford. I had a great time.

So I stuck my head back into the Wonderbar when I was in Biddeford recently and suddenly it was like coming home. Archie Droggitis gave me a bear hug.

Then Dimitris (Jimmy) Droggitis came in. He wanted me to drink a glass of Metaxa with him. Yvette Valliere, the hostess-cashier, brought me a sweet slice of baklava, that luscious Greek pastry filled with Athenian sunshine.

Jimmy and I sat in a booth talking for an hour. He taught me about making it in Maine 65 years ago.

"I was born in Biddeford 70 years ago, in August 1907. My mother and father were here on a trip from Greece, and they never went back. After I got born, there was no money for a ticket. Then the next boy came along. Soon there were eight of us. All born here.

"Pappa Droggitis was a shoemaker. I was shining shoes when I was six. By the time I was 13 we needed more money. I pestered the bosses at Saco-Lowell when I was shining their shoes, telling them I had to have a job there. Over 6,000 people worked there then. I got work at 25 cents an hour in the foundry where we poured molten metal. I left school. Worked with huge men — Greeks, Armenians, Turks, Poles and Irish.

"I was street-smart. From shining shoes, I could speak all their languages in slang. So they made me boss after six months and my pay went to $5 a day."

But by age 24, Jimmy Droggitis was dying of TB. The heat, dust, metal and fumes had ruined his lungs.

"I was shipped off to Greenwood Mountain Sanitarium in Hebron," he recalls. "For three years I lay in bed. At night, we slept on cold porches in the open air so some mornings I had icicles on my nose. Then, after three years, a little exercise. After five years, in 1939, I came home. I was 31.

"It was the Depression, and my father went through bankruptcy . . . I was the oldest boy, with seven younger kids. We had to hold on. One man, William Shaw, trusted me. He and the Pepperell Trust backed me, trusted me for $65 a month. No collateral. Just belief in a man's work and his character . . . now I am director of that bank."

Jimmy is the patriarch of the Droggitis family now — though he is a 70-year-old bachelor. "I try hard to keep us all together. The country needs big close-knit families. If a boy or a girl, a brother or sister, ever needs help — first they should go to their family. Our mother held us together. No matter how big and successful we got, she was the boss."

From that bankrupt shoe shop on this site has sprung the Wonderbar, a million-dollar business.

"That's because Biddeford was a kind-hearted place to an immigrant Greek family 70 years ago," says Dimitris. "Now it is our turn, to repay to Biddeford."

Fun for a day: Buy a ticket instead of a boat

BOOTHBAY HARBOR — As a boat owner, let me proclaim this incontrovertible truth: The cheapest, and sometimes the best, way to cruise the coast of Maine is to buy a ticket instead of buying a boat.

The person who rides the sightseeing boats sees our famous coast of Maine from the best seat in the world — from the water in somebody else's boat. He does it at a price that wouldn't buy an hour's gas for his own power boat, or one left nonslip deckshoe for a sailing sailor.

I found these joys because my own boat is out on charter. One day I went fishing on a party boat. Now I have gone on a sightseeing boat. Went out of Boothbay Harbor to Monhegan on a perky classic of a boat called Balmy Days. She takes her 70 passengers cruising an hour and a half on the ocean each way. Left at 9:30 a.m. Got to Monhegan Island about 11 a.m. Walked that beautiful island for a couple of hours, then rode the sightseeing boat again for a little side trip, circumnavigating Monhegan for 45 minutes. Then a nice afternoon cruise back to Boothbay covering about 15 miles in 90 minutes. Price was $14, plus a dollar extra for the trip around Monhegan. And where else can you get a day at sea, and a walk on unmatchable Monhegan for $2 an hour?

I talked with Captain Bob Fish, 49, owner of the "Balmy Days," and half a dozen other excursion and fishing party boats; and with Tom Tiller, the 25-year-old skipper, and with Tom Cromwell, the 20-year-old mate who is a cadet at Maine Maritime Academy.

Their ship, "The Balmy Days," is far older than skipper Tiller or mate Cromwell. She was built in 1932, which makes her a 47-year-old lady now. Charlie Wade, her original owner, and his brother and Mace Carter built her up the Kennebec River in the depths of the depression. Balmy Days and FDR were launched upon the United States about the same time. When Capt. Wade retired in 1973, he sold her to Bob Fish. And Balmy Days is kept in such fine shape that she looks as good as new, even close to the end of her 47th year.

The excursion boat business is a big and important one, not only in Boothbay Harbor, but in Portland and other coastal towns. Fish's fleet alone in Boothbay Harbor (and several other successful boat operators are there, too) carries as many as 1,000 passengers on a hot day in August. His six boats may travel 300 miles on a fine summer day and evening.

Tourists buy the most tickets, but wise Maine people know that a wonderful way to enjoy their state is to get on a sightseeing boat and ride the ocean, get the cool breezes, the sun and the fine salt air. You can do it in Casco Bay or Boothbay; you can do it by riding the ferries at Port Clyde or Lincolnville or Bass Harbor or Rockland. At many spots along the coast, you can enjoy a day at sea for the price of one good dinner ashore.

Some Maine visitors are hooked on this kind of cruising. Two sisters who stay at Spruce Point Inn in Boothbay Harbor for a month every year like to go out with Capt. Fish every fine day for a month. But if Captain Bob is not at the helm, they wait until he is. Another regular is a man who comes fishing two or three times a week during his month's vacation. These regulars have been doing this for 15 years. And when I see some expensive yachts tied up month after month at their slips never venturing out I think the tourists aboard the excursion boats get in more cruising than do some owners of $60,000 yachts.

Bob Fish, like his neighbor and friendly rival, Capt. Eliot Winslow of the Argo and other vessels, grew up on Boothbay Harbor. His grandfather, Jack Fish, worked in the area until, at the age of 70, he retired to Monhegan Island. At age 92, he came back to the mainland, and celebrated his 100th birthday near the harbor. Bob's father, Raymond, began the excursion service from Boothbay to Squirrel Island 50 years ago and more. That old "Squirrel Island Express" has now grown to a six-vessel fleet, which would cost more than $600,000 to replace today and which employs 18 people.

I like to think of the memories people take away. I like to think of thousands in hot cities today, packed in steamy subways, who refresh their souls this day by remembering that day in Maine when they went to sea for a day and walked a treasured island. So never knock a ride on a sightseeing boat.

From Big Bands to Bestsellers

BRUNSWICK — Macbeans Book and Music Store is a special magnet in Brunswick.

That's because Macbeans sells more than $200,000 worth of books and $100,000 worth of records a year.

But few of Macbeans customers know that owner Randy Bean used to be a vocalist with the Big Bands.

In the golden days of Big Band music in Chicago, Bean sang with Hal Kemp's orchestra and with Kay Kyser's band. Bean played a clarinet in the band of the University of Chicago well enough to go off with the football team on trips.

Bean is still a music buff. His bookstore is filled with music — from Beethoven to Glenn Miller. He spends nostalgic moments talking and playing classic jazz with the students at Bowdoin College. At home, the Bean family has its own band.

"My wife Judith, the calligrapher, sings; Oliver, a pre-med student at Brown, plays clarinet or recorder; Hilary, at Wesleyan, plays guitar; Felicity, 10, plays piano, and Vivian, 7, plays the violin and anything she can get her hands on."

Randy Bean, a serious musician, too, sings with the Bowdoin Chorale Group and is chairman of the governing board of the Bowdoin Summer Music School.

I ask why his store is called Macbeans, when Randy's name is Bean. "To avoid confusion with L. L. Bean. We didn't want people searching out a parking spot, coming in and finding we did not sell tattersall shirts, salmon flies or hunting boots."

Macbeans is in Brunswick because Randy Bean's family had a house on Chebeague Island in Casco Bay. "Judith and our kids loved our visits to Chebeague so much, we'd go home to Charlottesville, Va., and dream up ways how to move our business to Maine."

The Beans had been running a bookstore, and Judith had been working in a music store, near the University of Virginia campus.

"We did market research on the best college town in Maine for a book-and-record store. Brunswick was number one; Waterville second; Lewiston/Auburn third.

"So we came to Brunswick and opened Macbeans in August 1969. Took the old Meserve Drug Store; then in 1973 expanded to include the old Troop's Hardware. Now I've got more than 3,000 square feet and stock more than 12,000 book titles and more than 7,000 different recordings."

Randy Bean, gentle-voiced, spectacled, with a graying goatee, looks as if he might be a professor of Greek. He is an innovator who knows the college town market.

"I began experimenting with a used record department 10 months ago. We've bought and sold 9,000 records in that time. If the record is fit to play, I pay from 50 cents to $1.50 for it. One man brought in 60 classical records, and I gave him a $65 credit toward a $250 turntable."

Randy Bean holds up two "used record" treasures he got this morning. "Full recordings of two of Arthur Miller's plays; the Broadway casts of 'View From the Bridge' and 'After the Fall.'

"When the right customer spots these, I'm going to hear a shout of joy . . . I love hearing the shrieks when a jazz or opera fan finds an old record that means a lot, but can't be bought on the open market."

Macbeans is one of the stores in the nation which report sales to the New York Times, and from which the Times compiles its best-seller list.

"But our best sellers are a far cry from theirs," says Bean. "Here in Maine we get a bigger demand for nature books, for craft books and for regional books about Maine and New England.

Maine's taste in records, as well as books, is different from the rest of the nation — as reflected in Macbeans. "We sell $100,000 worth of records a year. But 33 percent of our sales are classical recordings. In the rest of the nation, classicals account for only five percent.

"And we have a strong upsurge in buying jazz. Jazz records amount to 25 percent of our business. And we have strong demand for regional folk music — music out of Maine or New England."

From oil fields to books

DAMARISCOTTA — He is in the last place you'd expect to find him.

The wildcatter, the high-risk oil-explorer from Oklahoma City, now runs the Maine Coast Book Shop in Damariscotta, population under 2,000.

His name is Ewing Walker. Every working day from 8 until 5:30, his big frame is perched atop a swivel stool located behind his bookstore desk. He looks happy and at home in a small town bookstore. With his hornrims halfway down his nose, with his blond-greying hair bookishly awry, you'd guess Walker had been born on a bookshelf. I asked Ewing Walker, the oil wildcatter, how he came to buy a Maine bookstore in 1969

"My brother and I began wildcatting in 1950. Formed Walker Brothers Oil Co. in Oklahoma City, and we ran it for 19 years. Did pretty well. Then wildcatting costs got so high we couldn't afford a dry hole any longer. With oil at $3 a barrel then, even the success couldn't pay for the bummers. So we sold out while we were ahead."

Walker came back to Damariscotta-Newcastle that summer of 1969. "My wife's family had summered here for a lifetime. And Penny first brought me here many years ago. One day I found Miss Mossman was about to sell her Damariscotta bookstore . . . I bought it. All my life I've loved bookstores. And reading is my exercise, as you see," he says patting an impressive girth.

"We moved into my wife's family home, winterized it, and have been here year-round ever since. Now I work longer hours than I ever did wildcatting for oil."

The bookstore has become a mecca in the region. It is a highly personal shop, and it is scoring a success. "We stock 5,000 books. No room for magazines, records or greeting cards. Just books. Books that are right for this (Maine) market."

Taste in books is different in small-town Maine. "The best seller list means nothing here . . . For example, when 'Looking Out for Number One' was second on the best sellers, we sold only one copy — and that was a special order from a city visitor.

"But we sold 60 copies of Andrew Wyeth's book at $60 a copy . . . We have history buffs here. I'm one. So I stock what I like most. For example, we stocked a two-volume history of the Mediterranean at the time of King Philip II. Cost $35. We sold 25 copies of it.

"Poetry I can't give away. We don't get any demand for novels about sex and drugs, or wife-swapping and other big city problems. But I sold over 200 copies of the new 'Audubon Bird Guide.'

Walker sells over $100,000 worth of books a year in this store in a small Maine town. The New York Times gets a report weekly of his sales to use in compiling its best-seller list.

"On some titles I think we sell more copies than any bookstore in the nation," says Walker. "Mostly in Maine books. And children's books.

"For example, we sold more copies of 'Maine Pilgrimage' by Saltonstall than any store. We sold 600 copies of 'Charlie Yorke: Maine Fisherman' over the last four years. We broke records with 'Andre the Seal.' We've sold 1400 copies of 'Enjoying Maine,' our all-time best seller.

"And it's the same with some children's books.

"I sold more copies of 'Bert Breen's Barn,' a children's book by Walter D. Edmonds, than they sold in the Harvard Co-op."

I sit on a deacon's bench in the shop and watch Walker sell. Two local regulars, then three out-of-state visitors, then two teen-age girls bent on horse books; and then two 10-year-olds. Walker chats with them all in a courtly southern fashion. Every one goes out with at least one book — even the 10-year-olds. "I have four who come in and pay 25 cents weekly. They are among my very favorite customers."

After he finished Harvard and served in the Air Force in World War II, Walker's first job was door-to-door selling. "I sold dollar-a-week insurance policies door-to-door at night in Penitentiary Bottom, a tough section of Richmond." That first year Walker led the nation with $800,000 worth of sales. Later came the wildcatting for oil.

I see the soft salesman at work still selling children's books to grandmothers; Maine books to everyone; and making the $70-sale of the new Random House Encyclopedia. "That is 20 of 'em so far," he smiles.

The Oklahoma oil-wildcatter says he has struck the lode he loves most — selling books in Damariscotta, Maine.

An open and shut life; drawbridges

SOUTH BRISTOL GUT — A drawbridge somewhere in Maine is getting ready to open now. Along some river, a boat is blowing her whistle as a signal to open up.

The boat waits, jockeying to hold position while the bridgekeeper goes to work. It can be a tense moment, if a strong wind and tide are working together against you. From the boat you look up watching the bridge tender, gauging the moment when you are safe to move on through the open span.

How you feel about Maine's drawbridges when they are in motion depends on where you sit.

If you are in a car, waiting while a boat goes through when you are pressed for time, you have no love for them. But if you are at the helm of a boat and you get a fish-eye view of the bridge opening for you, it's a different matter. The underpinnings and workings are fascinating. Your ego gets a boost to see the traffic stop and the bridge open in reply to the signal on your horn.

KCM

The process is a ritual which reasserts the ancient seniority of river traffic over road traffic. Boats travelled along rivers long before cars moved on roads, and long before bridges were built. All the world around, where the old laws and old traditions hold sway, new fangled cars and trains — and before them, horses — give way to boats. When the boat wants to move, the bridge must open for it.

There are 15 drawbridges left in Maine today; and the smallest is the busiest of them all. The little drawbridge which spans only 26½ feet of the South Bristol Gut opened 5,393 times in 1976 to allow

6,862 boats to pass between the mainland and Rutherford Island.

The resident expert on Maine's drawbridges is Abel Sirois of the Maine Department of Transportation. Sirois calls off the major drawbridges beginning with Memorial Bridge at Kittery, oldest structure spanning the Piscataquis River.

For the next drawbridge, go off the turnpike down to Dock Square bridge, joining Kennebunk to Kennebunkport. There you'll find a friendly little drawbridge which opens mostly for pleasure boats in summer . . .

The next big drawbridge is the bridge over the Fore River between Portland and South Portland. More than 36,000 cars a day use this bridge, officially the Portland Bridge but nicknamed the Million Dollar bridge after its original cost. When that span is up, complaints pour in from delayed drivers. Last year this bridge opened 1,724 times; and it opens as often in January as it does in July. Last January, 198 boats went under compared to 160 in July. By contrast, the Martin's Point Bridge, linking Portland and Falmouth, almost never opens for boat traffic, which is nil.

Two busy summertime-only bridges help move water traffic into and out of Sebago Lake. The span on route 302 at Naples opened 390 times this July and 350 times in August. Nearby, the Songo Lock bridge let more than 5,000 boats through during July and August.

Heading north, the next drawbridges are across the Kennebec River, which has three: at Bath-Woolwich, Richmond-Dresden and Gardiner-Randolph.

The 3,000-foot span at Bath, built in 1926, used to open 1,300 times a year in the thirties. It is still operated by the Maine Central Railroad, even though only one train a day uses the single track on the lower level. Most people in the cars on top do not even know there is a railroad underneath them.

One of the most beautiful views on the Kennebec is from the drawbridge between Dresden and Richmond. Its operator has a job that is ideal for a man who likes time to think. The drawbridge seldom moves; only twice this June, and thrice a week or so in July. From December, when ice forms, till ice-out in April or May, it stays closed.

A drawbridge already doomed on paper is the Gardiner-Randolph bridge. It opened only once this June, thrice in July and thrice in August. It is being replaced by a fixed high-span bridge.

The drawbridge over the Sheepscott at Wiscasset is another that is seldom opened any more. "We no longer keep a bridge tender on full time duty," says Sirois. "We've asked for a change in the rules, that will require a boat owner to give six hours' notice to get the bridge open."

This 3,240 foot bridge was built in 1931. Its predecessor, a wooden bridge, was lined with benches for the benefit of weary pedestrians. The Wiscasset bridge is showing severe signs of wear and tear, says Sirois, and as soon as $15 million is available, a new high-level fixed bridge will replace it. Already the Department of Transportation has $2 million worth of engineering and site studies underway, to decide where the new bridge should be and where Route One should bypass Wiscasset's crowded Main street.

The two busiest drawbridges in Maine are the ones I know best from my boat. The Southport bridge which spans Townsend Gut at Boothbay Harbor, has been operated for many years by Norman Lewis and his sons. Business is slow in winter — only 23 openings in February this year. But in July and again in August, the Lewises opened it more than a thousand times a month.

Friendship sloops sail home

FRIENDSHIP — The Friendships are sailing home. Tomorrow about 50 gaff-rigged Friendship sloops will be back in Friendship Harbor where they were born. Then on the last Thursday, Friday and Saturday of each July are the homecoming races.

The first Friendships were built here close on 100 years ago. For generations the fishermen of Muscongus Bay used Friendships for lobstering. They paid about $400 for the first Friendships. Now Friendship sloops are pleasure boats; and proud owners pay as much as $40,000 for a new Friendship.

A high point of summer on the coast of Maine is Friendship Sloop Days in Friendship. Go there if you can on Thursday, Friday or Saturday morning of this week. You'll see sights you may never forget.

The parade of sloops around Friendship Harbor is due to begin at 10:30 Saturday morning. The final race of the regatta is scheduled to start at noon.

Hundreds of kids, thousands of parents crowd Friendship (winter population 800) to watch some 50 sloops, sails up, circle the harbor and parade past Robert's Wharf, where each is saluted by a shot fired from a cannon, and her name, her skipper and crew are announced over a loudspeaker. Every entry gets a cheer.

Your ears may be amazed by the skirl of bagpipes. Your eyes may be astounded by the sight of a kilted bagpiper strutting on the foredeck of a Friendship sloop "Eastward." But you will not be hallucinating. The Friendship Sloop Society has its own piper — Donald Duncan. Amid the harbor scene of handsome Friendships sailing by, of kids in prams and outboards, of visitors in power boats, you'll see the piper sailing past, and in Friendship, Maine, you'll hear the skirls of "Cock of the North" and "Scotland the Brave."

There is something about a Friendship that hits you near the heart. Maybe the lines are so simple and sure and honest they hit you with the wallop of truth stripped bare. Maybe it is the history of these

sloops and the fact they are a living part of Maine's everyday working heritage. Maybe it is their jaunty look of confidence and cockiness. And part of the impact of a Friendship must be its name. Whatever causes that impact, the sight of 50 Friendships under sail in parade around Friendship Harbor may bring tears to your eyes.

This is a racing regatta. But there is a lot of nice emotion just below the surface. Proud skippers and devoted crews have sailed countless hours between them to be here.

Friendships are family boats. The crews most often are long-legged, sunburned daughters and flaxen haired sons. And the first mate is usually their mother.

There is a special bond between Friendships. Crews visit back and forth in harbor each night. When the stars are out, the harbor fills with the sounds of oars in dinghies or outboards, of beer cans opening.

The Friendship Sloop Society quietly set up a scholarship fund to help students from the Friendship area. In the last 10 years more than $20,000 has been raised; and $8,000 of it has been given away, and the remaining $14,000 is earning $1,500 a year, to help pay tuition for some Friendship youngster. This is a gesture of thanks to the town.

Typical is the fact that almost no one knows who gets the scholarship money outside of the person who gives the check and the person who gets it. The persons who got the first checks 10 years ago dropped by recently and said, "We got money from the fund when we needed it. So we want to give you some for the fund now."

There is a lot more to Friendship, Maine, than the beautiful boats. Go — enjoy it all.

Happy sculpture in a Maine meadow

WHITEFIELD — At first sight, drivers blink in disbelief. They slow down their cars and look again, at the hillside meadow filled with delightful, unusual sculptures with a touch of humor and a lot of beauty. And then the cars stop, drivers and passengers climb out and look in happy surprise at the sculptures of Roger L. Majorowicz, of Kings Mill, Whitefield, Maine.

Majorowicz is a renowned sculptor in the traditional media of bronze, stone and wood. "But when I bought a Maine farm, I began to see special beauty in abandoned farm implements and machinery, much of it lying in open fields. So I collected it. Brought it to the forge and blacksmith shop I built at my farmhouse. And out of it came the sculptures which I have put in the field across the street from my home," says Majorowicz from his studio in Baltimore, Maryland.

Majorowicz now teaches sculpture for nine months a year at the Maryland Art Institute in Baltimore, spends the three summer months at the Maine farm he bought in 1969.

"Among other things, doing this kind of sculpture in metal requires being a darn good blacksmith," said Majorowicz in a telephone interview. "And I learned welding and forging and blacksmithing as a kid, growing up on my father's ranch in South Dakota. There I had to sharpen plowshares, shoe horses, weld equipment."

After fighting in the Korean War, Majorowicz went to art school in Minneapolis; won two Fulbright scholarships which allowed him to study in Italy for three years, and then he taught sculpture and became chairman of the department at the University of Illinois, 1961-65. For the next 10 years, Majorowicz worked as chairman of the sculpture department in the Maryland Institute of Art, resigning in 1975 to spend more time creating and less administering. He has also taught in Maine at the famous Skowhegan School of Art. "In four more years I hope to retire and spend full time living and working in Maine," he said.

The City of Baltimore has eight major works by Majorowicz and important sculptures of his are in other cities and many galleries across the nation. Reluctant to talk about prices, Majorowicz acknowledges that his big works carry price tags in the $40,000 range. But only Maine has the special "farm sculpture" shown here. Pressed to indicate at least the price range of some of these, Majorowicz estimated something over $12,000 for the Don Quixote. All, by the way, are heavy and imbedded in concrete.

And each is a joy of imagination, whimsey and consummate skill to be seen in Maine meadows.

Jake Day's 80th birthday

STOLEN ISLAND — We went to Jake Day's 80th birthday party, held on a secret island. And the finest wish I can wish you is this: If you live to be 80, may you too be feted on a lovely uninhabited Maine island; and may you too be surrounded by the love of the people in your town; may you too be served with sour mash nectar; kissed by curvaceous young beauties, crowned King of Muscongus Bay, King of Katahdin, King of Damariscotta, King of Jake's Rangers and King of the Children; and may you too enjoy it all as much as Jake Day did!

Jake Day, just in case you don't know about him, is a living part of Maine folklore. Some say he is the descendant of Pamola, the goddess of Katahdin. Jake has been climbing Katahdin, Pamola's mountain, almost every year for more than 50 years. "Last time I went to the top of Katahdin was on my 75th birthday, with that youngster, Governor Curtis. I'd have climbed today again on my 80th, but the blackflies were too bad."

Jake Day has been leading his team of Jake's Rangers, made famous in Ed Smith's books about the Maine woods, through the North country, winter, spring and fall, for years. They have canoed and snowshoed down the East Branch often. Jake's Rangers, that close knit band of druggist, postmaster, garage man, veterinarian, insurance man, doctor, writer (the late, beloved Edmund Ware Smith), plus a Supreme Court Justice (William O. Douglas) have built more campfires, caught more fish, canoed more white water, played more poker, told more lies and had more fun than any band of men since Robin Hood.

Painting, of course, is Jake's life and livelihood — painting the Maine he loves and knows so well, and painting those fantasy animals of his which people the toadstools and live in the lichen and play politics in their burrows. Jake left Maine for a few years to work with Walt Disney out in Hollywood. Even in that glitter world, Jake left an unforgettable, unforgotten Maine imprint — Bambi, the white tailed deer was his creation.

Then, of course, there are Jake's Christmas windows. For years these windows in Jake's home were filled with carved figures of his fantasy animals. Those windows drew crowds of children from all over Maine for generations. Every Christmas the little children came by the hundreds after dusk, climbed up on the small benches Jake placed for them, and pressed excited noses against the frosted panes; and revelled and gurgled at the wonderful Christmas worlds which Jake's mind had seen, and Jake's hands had carved for their joy. Now those windows are gone from Jake's house and are in the Farnsworth Museum at Rockland, for future generations to pleasure in. The winter snow outside Jake's home will no longer be pressed with footprints of a thousand children with magic in their hearts, thanks to Jake.

But back to Jake's 80th birthday . . .

At ten o'clock on the best Sunday morning of the year, a happy invasion fleet of a dozen boats assembled at the Lucy B. wharf in Round Pond Harbor. There, more than 80 of Jake's friends, family and grandchildren were assembled, secretly. They boarded the waiting boats in relays. And the boats sped them out to a secret island in Muscongus Bay, debarked them and sped back to fetch more people. By 11 o'clock, the wharf was empty again. Then Jake's wife, Perk Day, and a couple of close friends drove down from Damariscotta to take Jake out for a sail, some mackerel fishing, a quiet birthday picnic — he thought.

Out they went into Muscongus Bay, among the islands where 70 years ago Jake rowed and paddled as a boy . . . Those lovely islands with the grand, stirring names . . . Louds and Hog; Indian Island and Killick Stone; Wreck Island and Jones' Sea Garden; the Devil's Elbow and the Devil's Back; Marsh and Cow, Cranberry and Otter, Black and Harbor Islands. Half a century and more ago, Jake had explored every one. Except one. The one which, here, we will call Stolen Island.

When Jake and Perk hove to near Stolen Island, close to 100 people, from waddling two year olds to teen-agers to those fat and fifty, to some three score-and-ten, poured down to the rocky beach to hail Jake and show to him their love for a wonderful neighbor and friend on his 80th birthday.

We crowned him on a rock, with the salt spray wetting him down nicely from behind, while more spirituous waters flowed in front. Grandchildren clambered over him. Bikini-clad girls, who'd been in diapers when first they climbed on Jake's lap, kissed him. Sons and grandchildren, nieces and nephews, even dogs, brought presents to pile on the rocks beside the man Maine loves.

From a driftwood mast a tattered, homemade banner flew, proclaiming Jake the King of all he surveys.

Out from picnic baskets came food made with loving hands in the finest kitchens for miles around. Feasts were spread upon every ancient, sun-baked, sea worn rock. The sun shone. The bright lobster buoys bobbed in the cove. Stomachs were filled. Toasts were drunk. The energetic ones left to walk the rocky perimeter of the pine crested island. Sailboats came sailing by, waving. Powerboats came by, tooting a foghorn in salute to Jake, King of Muscongus Bay. Slim teenagers found a grassy meadow, and snoozed in the sun. Matrons and patriarchs mightier in the midsection reminisced. Young boys looked with love into the eyes of young girls, and tried to imagine being 80 years old.

The sun sank. The tide changed. The boats began departing. With cheers and waves from shore, Jake left. "Stolen Island" soon was clean and empty as it had been before the happy invaders first set foot on its shore. Gone was a day that will live forever . . . a taste of Maine love for a good neighbor in a good Maine town.

May you live to enjoy such an 80th birthday!

Larry Epsling; spirit triumphant

PRESQUE ISLE — Larry Espling is one human being who truly lights up the world.

When Larry, 35, got his B.A. at the University of Maine, 1,500 people in the hall stood and cheered, clapped or sometimes wept.

Larry Peter Espling is a man whose body is wracked by cerebral palsy but whose spirit soars. If the Olympics included categories for triumphant spirit, then New Sweden, Maine, would be lining the streets to welcome home a gold medalist.

Larry Espling is a victim of severe cerebral palsy of the spastic kind. He suffered birth damage, says his mother, Charlene Espling, whose own indomitable spirit deserves another medal. Larry, she says, could not manage to sit upright for years. He could not manage to walk in any fashion until his mother and father took him to the Spears Hospital in Denver after he had turned ten.

Time and again, experts advised Larry's parents that he was so severely physically handicapped and retarded that he should be placed in an institution.

They rejected such advice.

Charlene Espling, a school teacher herself, taught Larry at home. When she had to be at school, Larry's father, Peter, and his sister acted as tutors. Later teachers from the school system serving New Sweden taught Larry. Larry, himself, read hungrily.

Early in Larry's life, Peter and Charlene Espling arrived at a decision they would not hide Larry or his cerebral palsy. Larry, himself, had an outgoing personality and despite the difficulties, he enjoyed meeting the outside world. "He's a stubborn Swede and there's nothing that can dent his determination," says his father proudly.

By the time he was 20, Larry had shown himself, his teachers and his many friends that his mind was bright, hungry, restless and insatiable.

"Listen, you could go to college if you really wanted to," said one close friend. And Larry set his heart on just that.

He was 20 then and it took another 10 years to get there. By the time he enrolled at University of Maine, Presque Isle, as an undergraduate, the university was more apprehensive than he was.

Just getting around in an Aroostook winter is not easy even for the able bodied young. Larry, leaving home at 30 for the first time, took an apartment in Presque Isle, sharing it with a student who was legally blind. Together they got to classes on time everyday in every weather.

It took Larry Espling five years to graduate.

Simply writing a class paper was an obstacle of giant proportions. His hands shook so much and were so misshapen that he could not use a pen. So he had to learn to type.

First he had a guard built over the keyboard of an electric typewriter to prevent his jumping hands from hitting keys by mistake.

He demonstrated his technique for me. Reaching out his shaking right hand with forefinger extended, he uses his left hand to steady it and push it down on the proper key. He has to use the strength and tension of both his arms for every single letter he strikes.

In class, Larry didn't mind asking and answering questions.

It took a long while for Larry Espling to get out an answer or a question. Often, teachers and students could not understand his enunciation. So Larry patiently and without embarrassment, would restate the answer or question; time and again, if necessary.

It is not easy for Larry to talk; it is not easy for people to understand what he says. But then when you grasp it, your heart may leap with joy.

Larry's remarks are packed with humor, frequently about himself. He has one of the most infectious laughs, one of the most heartwarming smiles in Maine. It blazes out suddenly like a shaft of sunlight into a dark corner.

Larry laughed and smiled often as he told about growing up, about learning to walk and talk and type and catch a bus. Now he, himself, is a Big Brother, helping another handicapped youngster.

One incident I shall never forget happened as we were walking down a campus path to where our cars were parked. Larry fell. Fell suddenly and fairly hard, just ahead of me. His mother let out a quick, fearful cry. Larry just looked up, beamed, made a funny crack and held out a twitching arm to grasp a helping hand, then stood upright and dusted himself off. As they drove away, he turned, waved and flashed that crinkled, beautiful grin.

Now I've met Larry, I understand why 1,500 fellow-students gave him a standing ovation when UMPI president Stanley Salwak handed him his bachelor of arts degree "awarded with distinctions."

They were cheering Larry. They were shouting, clapping, weeping with joy at this clear evidence of how high the spirit of man can soar when the test is tough.

"This one, indomitable man," says Salwak, "had more impact on the whole campus than anyone else in his five years here."

Larry stood up, waving his diploma, his lean, angular face beaming a smile to light up the world and saying to the 1,500 cheering people, "Thank you — thank you, thank you everyone!"

Dr. Currier McEwen; Irises and arthritis

BRUNSWICK — Erect, silver-haired and, above all, happy, Dr. Currier McEwen, 76, stands amid his 9,000 irises.

The blossoms run down to the sea at Harpswell Sound, heat-misted, sun-lit and lovely on a hot summer day. He is dressed in khaki work shirt and pants, covered by a huge, faded green apron. From a cavernous pocket in the apron, he pulls out a school exercise book and with a stubby pencil writes an entry.

My shadow falls across the page, and he looks up smiling. "I'm Currier McEwen — expecting you. This book is my stud book, where I keep track of the genetics of all the hybrids I'm raising. Come, I'll show you what I'm working on today."

To botanists, Dr. McEwen is a world-famous authority on growing and crossbreeding iris. To the medical world, he is "Doctor Arthritis — foremost authority and leader in rheumatology research and treatment for 40 years. For 34 years, he was dean of the medical school at N.Y.U.

More than this, Currier McEwen seems to have the happiest retirement of any man in Maine.

His formula seems to be doing more valuable, fascinating work in a day than many younger people do in a week, or sometimes a year.

As the world-renowned medical expert on arthritis, Dr. McEwen now makes his headquarters at Brunswick Regional Hospital, 13 miles up the road from his 9,000 irises. Here, McEwen frequently sees patients for 12 hours a day. He spends equally long days as an arthritis consultant in Mid-Maine General Hospital at Waterville; and again at Togus Veterans' Hospital and Augusta General Hospital.

"Then one week a month, we get our northern exposure," says the doctor. "On Sunday morning early, Mrs. McEwen and I set out on our regular drive from Brunswick to Fort Kent — 345 miles. Arrive Sunday night and start our week's work in Aroostook and Washington counties."

By the time the McEwens are back home again they have driven close to 1,000 miles; have helped more than 50 patients in hospitals at Fort Kent, Calais, Caribou, Houlton and Presque Isle. Except for the visits of Dr. McEwen and his therapist, Cindy Toutant, Maine people north of Bangor have not had a specialist in rheumatology to treat them, relieve their pain and give them hope.

At no charge to the sick and lots of travel, McEwen spends 14 days in his normal retirement month treating arthritis sufferers. The other 16 days he spends working long hours with his 9,000 irises. In his idle time, he goes sailing, plays tennis or plays the role of father-and-grandfather to the 17 members of his family visiting each summer.

McEwen, here among his beloved irses, seems happy, serene, un-hurried. I follow him through row after row of his hybrids of Siberian and Japanese irises.

He pulls a magnifying glass from his apron pocket and examines the inside of a purple bloom, "just making sure a bee has not polli-nated it before I get there. If he has, I can see the yellow pollen he's left behind." He hands me the magnifying lens. On one flower I see the telltale pollen; on the other the virgin white, is unstained.

"I'll prepare this one for tomorrow." McEwen takes tweezers from his apron and pulls out the stamen, or male breeding part, of the iris, and buries it among the petals, so it will be handy for use tomorrow. McEwen then folds all the petals of the wide bloom up onto each other, plucks a leaf stalk and uses that like string to tie the bloom into a tight bundle. "Now, no bee can beat me to it. And I put this hat on it to keep off any rain," says McEwen, slipping a plastic sand-wich bag over the spectacular iris.

He reads from his stud book, matching the number on the stake by the flower to the number in the stud book. "This is among the best of my re-bloomers. My stud book shows eight blossoms at first bloom-ing; then 26 more blooms a month later. So I'm cross-breeding this specimen." Most irises bloom once, for a few days only.

Dr. Currier McEwen bends down into his garden of 9,000 irises, and sifts a handful of soil through his fingers.

"Not a drop of fertilizer. We just bulldozed out the wild bushes, ploughed the ground. It has nourished over 50,000 iris plants and

day lilies. But this soil grows rocks, too. We've dug the ground over six times and each time got more rocks than ever."

Linking the soil at Harpswell to Dr. McEwen is a long and loving bond. "I'm 76 now; and I came here aged three months, to that house across the street. My sister has it now. My grandfather was a founder of the Auburn colony down here on Harpswell Sound — a good 100 years ago."

Dr. McEwen retired as dean of the medical school at New York University in 1970, after holding that post since 1935. "We began the now famous Rheumatology Study Group in 1932, when I was assistant dean. Started on a shoe-string, just a couple of us.

"But when I left in 1970, we had 30 fine doctors in the study group and a budget that was bigger than all the money for the entire School of Medicine when I went in as dean. We ran nine rheumatology clinics in New York City, seeing tens of thousands of arthritic patients yearly."

Piled on tables at McEwen's grey-shingled house on Harpswell Sound, two tables of research papers vie for his attention. One table is piled with arthritis research compiled over five years, from 16 hospitals across the nation. Dr. McEwen will write the definitive analysis of the findings.

On a nearby table is another McEwen manuscript. "I'm writing a handbook on iris hybrids for the American Iris Society. And my wife has left files filled with the genetic records of all the most successful hybrids we've developed."

McEwen says he became a "nut about irises" by accident. "The postman made a mistake. On a snowy January day in 1955, he mistakenly left some beautiful catalogues about irises and day lilies at our house in Riverdale, just outside Manhattan. I read somebody else's mail and got bitten and sent for plants and joined the Iris Society. Soon I started experimenting with hybrids. Here I am 23 years and hundreds of thousands of irises later, still iris-crazy."

But the dominating force in McEwen's so-called "retirement" is helping Maine patients, doctors, hospitals and therapists treat arthritis.

"When I retired to Maine in 1970, the state had only three rheumatologists. Now we have 13 or 14, but still none north of Bangor."

McEwen's father, a doctor, too, suffered so severely from psoriatic arthritis that he had to give up surgery. "I had an instinctive drive to find out more about treating, curing or preventing the disease.

"After graduation from medical school, I went to work from 1928 to 1932 in the Rockefeller Institute. Then as dean of NYU Medical school from 1935 to 1970, I had a special interest in all rheumatology research.

Today, McEwen says, "the toughest problem still is rheumatoid and osteo arthritis. We don't know yet the cause or the cure or the prevention. But I have no doubt that inside 10 years we'll know the cause. Once we know the cause, we'll get the cure; and finally we'll know how to prevent it, which is the most important job."

McEwen's twin avocations of arthritis and irises meet and join in a medicine called colchicine, made from the root of a crocus plant.

"This is the drug that can stop the ghastly, indescribable pain of gout. And it is also the drug I inject into iris plants to change their genetics. It transforms a diploid cell into a tetraploid — four chromosomes instead of two."

Dr. McEwen leaves to keep a date with his sailboat and his grandchildren for crew.

Deer Isle breeds America's Cup winners

DEER ISLE — Somehow, we won the America Cup races in 1977 without Deer Isle men aboard the Courageous.

With the little 12-meter boats they race in the America Cup these days, they can manage to win without Deer Isle sailors. A softer breed of crew can manage the smaller sails.

But back in the days when America Cup contestants were boats 130 feet long, and carried 13,000 square feet of billowing sail, and had 25 feet of keel reaching down into the ocean — then Deer Isle boys were needed to win the races.

We lay at anchor a few miles out from Deer Isle listening to radio reports on how Ted Turner skippered Courageous and her 11 amateur crew to a 4-0 victory over the Australian challenger in the 1977 America Cup races.

Down in the cabin, we had recent issues of the Deer Isle weekly Island Ad-Vantages, edited by Nat Barrows, an able advocate for Maine fishermen. And this weekly ran a series of articles on Deer Islanders and the America Cup races at the turn of the century.

Deer Isle boys won those races. Capt. Fred Weed of Deer Isle came home to the island and picked the entire 22-man crew from Deer Isle boys to man the "Defender" in the 1895 America Cup races.

Of course, they won.

And Deer Isle knew how to celebrate as well as how to win yacht races.

In 1899, Sir Thomas Lipton, that great sportsman, who made

his money in tea trade and so was not recognized by the snobbish English yacht clubs, sent a challenge from Dublin. Lipton sent over the Shamrock — first of many Shamrocks — to try and win the America Cup back for the United Kingdom.

That time the American syndicate answered Lipton's challenge with a new boat — Columbia.

Once again, Capt. Fred Weed came home to Deer Isle to hand pick the crew of 22 Deer Isle boys to man her. Again, the entire crew hailed from Deer Isle.

Sir Thomas Lipton's 'Shamrock' took the early lead.

But the Deer Isle boys came from behind and beat Shamrock in 1899.

How much pay did they get?

The Deer Isle boys got $45 a month, and officers were paid $2 a day, or $60 by the month. Every man got a $5 bonus for each race sailed.

This year, 11 amateurs, instead of 22 professionals, crewed the Courageous, a boat of about 40 feet, compared to the 130 feet of Columbia and Defender.

But even without benefit of Deer Isle boys, Courageous won.

With that good news under our belt, we rowed the dinghy ashore to explore Camp Island, one mile south of Deer Isle. This is one of those very special island jewels which fill the sea between Stonington and Isle au Haut. We stood on a small point at Camp Island, and looked at all those other lovely islands, their green crests of pine, their granite shores and inland ledges, and watched the great sails of seven cruise schooners moving majestically among them. This is one of the loveliest sights in all the world; and it is sad that not one Maine person in a thousand has a chance to enjoy it.

The Indians must have loved this spot. A big point of land on Camp is entirely made of clam shells, thrown there by generations of feasting Indians. Millions of clam shells are piled many feet deep. We lie there in the sun dreaming of the feasts staged on this idyllic spot long before white settlers sailed in.

William Eaton and his three sons were the first white settlers to sail into Deer Isle — more than 225 years ago. The Eaton name is everywhere on Deer Isle still — from lobster pounds to garages. The Greenlaws came to settle on Deer Isle that same year of 1762. Today, Capt. Reggie Greenlaw runs his famous sight-seeing boat among these islands.

One of those early Greenlaws suffered a terrible terror. He was captured in the Revolutionary War and, at gunpoint, was made to climb to the top of the mainmast. There he became a human target. His captors fired, to see how close they could graze him. The experience drove him to insanity.

Fishing here was so good that population grew from those first settlers to more than 2,217 people before 1830. And those Deer Islanders liked their rum. When the temperance movement hit Deer Isle, the men staged a liquor riot. A tiny island off Stonington is called Rum Island. John Marin spent six summers painting some of his finest water colors there. He knew there are few places in all the world so beautiful. Beauty, plus rum, plus good fishing led to ripe old ages. In 1884, more than 100 Deer Islanders out of a population of 3,000 were past 70 and still busy. And 26 of them were between 80 and 100 years old.

Little wonder they came to Deer Isle to find men to win the America Cup races.

Relaxing way to ride a tide

DRESDEN MILLS — I went ice fishing for the first time and came to this conclusion: The ideal ice-fisherman would have been W. C. Fields.

Sitting in an ice shanty, administering internal fortitude to himself while a tiny smelt nibbles (maybe) somewhere under two feet of ice — that's the kind of sport he would have relished. A classic movie would have been a day with Fields finding happiness in a smelt shack.

I'll kid nobody about ice fishing. I know zilch about it. But now I have succumbed. I put away my skis and snowshoes last weekend

and went to see what makes ice fishing and smelt shacks so popular with so many Maine people.

I found out that almost all ice fishermen have this in common: they are friendly and they're crazy.

After that, the ones I met on Eastern River and then on Damariscotta Lake fall into these major categories.

Ice fishermen who fish.

Ice fishermen who drink.

Ice fishermen who drink and fish.

Ice fishermen who visit around.

All categories seem to have a tremendously good time.

First I went to the smelt shacks. You've seen them by the hundreds on Maine rivers and lakes each winter. They bear a striking resemblance to that early American style of architecture that use to grace each back yard. But these have no half moon; they have a chimney instead. And these are sometimes painted red or green, or perhaps even tarpaper black.

This year the bureaucrats embraced smelt shacks. The commissioner of the Maine Department of Marine Resources wrote owners, "The new law makes it unlawful to place any shack used for ice fishing on the tidal waters unless the owner's name and address are painted or otherwise clearly marked on the outside with two-inch letters."

So now when you walk among a colony of smelt shacks, you know who is inside.

Some smelt shacks are comfortable family camps on the ice — a small-scale equivalent of a summer or hunting camp. These belong to the fanatics who go fishing every weekend from January 1 until ice-out or the end of March. The family places may be equipped to include bunks, a stove, well-stocked cupboards, radio, books and cooking gear. They'll have kerosene lamps — unless they are close enough to shore power to run an electric cable inside.

There are shacks you can rent by the tide, day or night. On a fine weekend when the smelt are running, these shacks go like hotcakes; often they are booked many weeks in advance.

Mostly the rental shacks are taken by Maine families or groups of friends who make ice-fishing and smelting an important part of enjoying winter. They like to cook up a mess of smelts, fresh caught and fast-fried; they like the fun of a day on the ice; but a few times a winter is enough for them, so they rent rather than build.

To see this kind of rental operation, I went to Morris Quintal's Smelt Camps on the Eastern River, between Dresden bridge and Richmond bridges.

The rent is $4 per person per tide. Quintal has 32 shacks, some for two to four people, others for six or eight.

Four dollars each gets renters the shack and a stove complete with wood. There will be some seating, probably a wooden box or two, and rectangular holes about a foot wide against the long sides of the shack. From poles suspended over these holes hang lines, lots of them; half a dozen or more for each person. Worms are used for bait and are supplied as part of the rent.

At Quintal's cabins, you get electric light, too. The light is for the fish — not the fishermen. It hangs down near the opening in the ice, and its illumination is supposed to attract smelt.

Families and groups of men together arrive by pickup truck and car. They unload vast quantities of food and drink and move into the shack they've rented for the tide. Almost immediately they go visiting. Winter fishing is a neighborly sport. Fish a while, drink a while, visit a while.

If the smelt are biting, one shackful of people can haul in 200 to 300 on a tide. If it's a bad day, the catch may be less than a dozen.

I met a group from Connecticut who have been coming here together for a long weekend each February for the past 10 years. Bill Cable, their old-timer, says they work together in a hinge factory near Beacon Falls and they fish together year around. "Ten years ago we read in Outdoor Life about smelt fishing here at Quintal's camps, and we've come for 10 years in a row," he says. They stay at the Dresden Inn, take two shacks and fish both tides for three days and nights.

A Maine foursome has taken the shack next door. They are George Savage and Jack Hyde from Augusta. Guy LeClair from Sidney and Ned Beit from Hartland. "We come four times a winter," says George.

They are old friends of Morris Quintal, who began with one camp 14 years ago and now runs his 32 shacks 24 hours a day through the season with the help of his three sons.

We stand in the shack around the fire and watch them pull in a few smelt. They bite very gently and the haul-up also is gentle, for the fish are small. "Pull too hard and you lose 'em, or their heads come off," says Quintal.

They tell the story about the beer-laden fisherman who fell through his own cut in the ice and swam to the lighted hole in the shack next door, where a lot of serious drinking had been underway for hours. Poking his head up out of the ice, he looked through their lines and politely asked, "Fish biting?"

Quintal laughs at the old tale then talks about the economics of the ice-fishing business. It costs him $150 to build a small shack, $250 for a big one. Eight years ago he ran electric lights to each shack. "But I still carry fire insurance," he says pointing to a burned-out shack. "It's not so bad as in kerosene days. But sometimes a party that's had too much beer and not enough fish gets careless."

We leave Quintal's and the tidal river and drive to Crescent Beach, a state park on Damariscotta Lake. In summer, people swim and canoe from this beach. Now they drive out on the ice, which is at least 20 inches thick.

The crowd is different here on the fresh-water lake, where they are more hopeful of catching togue, trout and pickerel as well as smelt. Here there are almost no shacks. Mostly we meet family groups fishing from pickups or cars, people who come almost every weekend, grandparents to grandchildren. "We fish winter, summer, spring and fall. If it swims, we try to catch it," says Ben Lizotte.

Roy Miller of Thomaston is out on the lake with his eight-year-old granddaughter. He fishes while she drives his snowmobile around the lake. "We love fishing all year long," he says. "Now the wind here is cold. But look at my new contraption." He shows a portable shelter on runners, made of brilliant red canvas with plexiglass windows. "I made the frame from pipes. A tentmaker did the canvas; for me. And it makes fishing a lot more comfortable."

Next we meet the John Lemar family from Whitefield. He is a huge man, as big as a bear inside his snowmobile suit. His welcome is tremendously friendly. "Have some hot coffee . . . Have some chop suey." His wife is inside the comfortable heated camp they keep on the ice. Lemar, a carpenter, says they go fishing as a family year round. "Between the five of us here today we have 25 ice holes — the laws allows five each, and the bag limit is five fish per head, a combination of salmon, togue and trout. We try for the two-quart limit per person of smelts. No such luck today."

Lemar and his wife and grandchildren are laughing and content. "Not many fish," he says. "But where could you find a prettier day or a nicer way to spend it?"

Waterville Opera House alive again

WATERVILLE — Ghosts — beautiful, talented, out-rageous — lend haunted enchantment to the dark stage of Waterville's 1900 Opera House.

It is midday. Outdoors sunlight is bright and the world is real. Here on stage, the light is half-dark and the world is peopled with wonderful ghosts.

"Tom Mix and his horse entered the stage through this door" says a voice off in the wings. It's a man's voice with an English accent. "Remember Tom Mix, the great cowboy in the first big white hat?" . . . . . . My memory reels back, back, back, to silent movies on Saturday mornings when a nickel got me a balcony seat to heaven — and Tom Mix and his horse. . . What was that horse's name? Tony?

The voice from the wings speaks on. "Tom Mix came to Water-ville and performed on this stage. The Waterville Opera House was a regular stop for the top travelling shows — opera, plays, vaudeville and politics."

The voice and its body emerge from the wings. They belong to Dr. Antony Betts, a London-trained medical doctor who now lives in Waterville. Betts is president of the Waterville Opera House Improvement Association, which has spent $30,000 for the restoration of Waterville's historic Opera House.

Betts, brown-eyed curly black-haired amateur actor, musician and director strides center stage and shouts into the empty theater.

"Teddy Roosevelt spoke and shouted and beat his breast on this stage. The great Rough Rider was on the stomp here for votes. . . And some of the greatest American voices sang from this stage. Marion Anderson loved to sing in this Opera House. She said the acoustics in the Waterville Opera House were the best north of Boston — and better than many halls in Boston and New York."

Dr. Betts leads the way up steep steps to control panels and plat-forms high above the vast stage. "We can fly scenery from 20 stations. We can stage the most lavish operas here. I got those new nylon ropes for moving scenery from a boatyard. Where else but in Maine would a boatyard suppy a theater?"

Betts takes me from darkened balcony down to the orchestra pit. All the way, this theatrical pathologist recites the amazing history of this remarkable Opera House.

"There are 995 seats; and not one with a bad view of the stage. No posts and no pillars to block your view. See how the balcony slopes two ways? Down to the stage, and in toward the center from the sides? Note those Royal Boxes. They face into the audience and not to the stage. They are for performers and not spectators. . . Now in the orchestra seats you see the sharp pitch again. The back row seats are far far higher than the front row. Perfect view from everywhere. . . Here in this pit you can accommodate at least a 30-piece orchestra. All designed before cars really came to Waterville."

Dr. Betts leads me to the last row. "If I whispered on stage you'd hear every syllable clearly back here. No theater built today could match these acoustics."

Fred Jobber, the City Hall janitor, is waiting for us. He too is nostalgic. "They showed movies here when I was a kid. I'd pay a nickel for popcorn and 10 cents to see the show." He flicks a series of light switches. The harsh light exposes cruelly the tawdriness of bygone glories left untouched too long. But in his mind's eye Dr. Betts has already spent the $30,000 refurbishing this rare and lovely theater.

"A lady expert from Massachusetts Institute of Technology was here. She said there are nine coats of paint on the walls. The ceiling used to be all pale blues and golds, heavens with angels flying in them. She told us how it used to look here when the theater opened in 1901. And that is the way we will restore it. . ."

Dr. Betts describes how the stage will look with its new rich red velvet curtains; how the boxes will look with their handsome new upholstery; how the foyer will be stunning in palest green, backed with ivory and gold. How new carpets will transform the scuffed stairs and worn corridors. How new lighting will bathe the performers in kind but dramatic pools of illumination.

Then janitor Fred Jobber locks the padlock and we are out of the

KCM

dream of the theater past and the theater to be. The theater is upstairs over City Hall. The big brick building in the heart of downtown Waterville is a fine example of the multi-purpose civic structures
built in Maine at the end of the 19th century. Waterville's City Hall
and Opera House was designed in the Colonial Revival style by
George G. Adams of Lawrence, Mass. and built between 1897 and
1902.

   "Senator Ed Muskie, with roots in Waterville, got the Opera House
listed on the National Register of Historic Places. That opened the
way for us to qualify for these matching federal funds," explains

Dr. Betts. "But Waterville's a town crammed with enthusiasm for plays and music and performing arts. Long before any federal money came our way, Opera House volunteers came down at night and did the hard dirty work. The barber shop singing groups came en masse and washed the foyer walls, singing joyfully in four-part harmony to the swish of brush and pail."

Waterville citizens are making their Opera House live in new splendor and resound with new talent.

UPDATE; The rejuvenation is almost complete. Raising $10,000 in Waterville, getting a matching $10,000 in federal funds, the Opera House has now been beautifully restored, repainted throughout; and new red velvet curtains on stage and in the auditorium are in place. With the Opera House now booked solid throughout the year, the City of Waterville has rewired the theater, and installed an elevator for the handicapped, which also transports scenery. "Our productions are sellouts," says Dr. Betts, "and we'll soon be able to afford new lobby and stair carpets, as in the glorious days of 1900."

Perham's: Home of Maine gems

WEST PARIS — Purists call them "minerals."

But those beautiful pinks and purples, mauves, and greens beneath the earth of Maine excite me too much to call them by such a mundane name as "minerals."

To me they are gems — gems lurking in the Maine ground.

If you are a rock-hound then you are too much of an expert for this column from an amateur. But if these Maine gems are outside your ken, now take my suggestion . . . stop in one of Maine's fine rock and mineral stores and enjoy the world they will open up for you.

The most famous is Perham's at Trap Corner, West Paris.

Count on spending close to an hour browsing among its thousands of stones, including beautiful amethysts, aquamarines and tourmalines mined at quarries here in Maine. You'll enjoy a fascinating family store.

Stanley Perham had begun swapping and trading rocks and minerals when he was 12 years old. Then in 1919, he opened a small store here. It is world famous now, and is operated today by Mrs. Perham and their daughter, Jane Perham Stevens, who is a graduate gemologist.

They tell me that more than 90,000 people visit Perham's in a year.

And once you have visited it you may come away with more than a Maine stone or two. You can come away bitten by the rockhound bug.

Perham's encourages you to go and dig your own. The store owns five quarries which they keep open especially for collectors. Ask at the store and they will even give you maps together with hints of where to dig for what and it is all free.

Among the quarries owned by Perham's are the Harvard quarry, the Waisanen quarry, the Whispering Pines quarry, the Nubble quarry and the Willie Heikkinen quarry.

If those magical names do not bring your prospector's blood to a boiling point then savor these tantalizing descriptions and let your imagination do the rest . . .

"Harvard quarry was first prospected about 1870 by George Shavey Noyes; operated in 1917 by Harvard; in 1942 by Arthur Valley; and since 1958 by Perham's.

"It is noted for purple apatite, green tourmaline, black tourmaline, garnet, beryl, quartz and cookeite.

"Also taken from the Harvard quarry are amethyst, cassiterite, zircon petalite, columbite gahnite (green), spodumene, scheelite, vesuvianite and leidolite."

Try this: "At Whispering Pines quarry one may find rose quartz in two- to 10-carat sizes; and orange quartz, smoky quartz, black tourmaline, muscovite mica and star quartz . . . "

Then there is a spicy smell of danger in the line, "Willie Heikkinen quarry has a great deal of fluorescent hyalite and is ideal for night collecting . . . A 10-foot beryl, three feet thick, was found here."

Or there is the more practical monetary side as stated in connection with Nubble quarry. "During the war this quarry furnished the highest grade mica mined in New England . . . an estimated 750,000 pounds was taken out."

Got your picks and mining hammers ready?

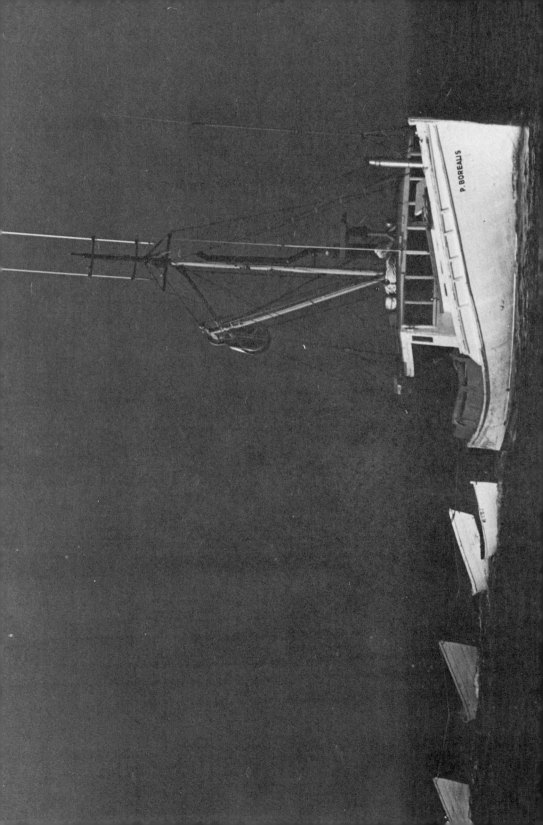

III
CRUISING IN
STEER CLEAR

Seine boat and dories

I MIGHT AS WELL admit the truth at the start: I would rather be out on Steer Clear, our boat, heading for a Maine island, than anywhere else in the world.

I'd feel more confident about my sanity if that were an overstatement. But it is the truth.

Manley Gilbert in New Harbor, where Steer Clear is moored, probably diagnosed the sickness right. After watching me slave over this so-called pleasure boat, Manley sculled over in his punt from his lobster boat, came alongside and asked 'Do much boatin' as a young man?' 'No,' I answered. 'Never owned a boat till I moved to Maine.' 'Figures,' replied Manley. 'Any man who waits till he's past 40 to own a boat, or to take a wife, is likely to spoil 'em with too much care and kindness.'

Steer Clear is 25 years old now, old enough to qualify as a classic boat. She had turned 12 when we bought her from Robert Porteous; we've cruised her for 12 summers and this will be her 25th summer in Maine waters. To celebrate, she is being spoiled with more love, more care, more money than ever. Why not? She gives a lot. The log shows about 60 days and 40 nights spent aboard most years.

Steer Clear is a 30 foot Bristol, powered by twin Palmer engines. About 98 per cent of her life underway, she ambles along at eight knots or less, sipping rather than guzzling gas. But if necessary, she can sprint at 17 knots and outrun most foul weather headed her way. She is good in a sea, easy to handle and since she draws less than three feet of water, she is fine for gunkholing into hidden coves.

She has two features that are special. First is her poor man's flying bridge. Instead of the top-heavy, high-up standard flying bridge, Steer Clear has hatches over the helmsman and navigator positions; the hatches hinge back flat onto the cabin roof, and we hang two strong canvas slings up there. And from there we operate the boat; head and shoulders out in the sun and air. I steer with my educated feet. Second feature that is great for cruising is that her entire cockpit and aft deck become one big, enclosed, warm room at night. At anchor after sunset, we drop these canvas curtains, with big plastic windows and transform more than half the boat into a dry, warm living room with a view. The curtain stores on the cabin roof and it takes 90 seconds to button-up for the night.

I should apologize perhaps for all this detail about a boat. But to us this boat, and the places she takes us to, are a huge part of the magic that is Maine.

She is a work boat too. For 12 weeks a year, Steer Clear is often my office. I keep a typewriter and radiotelephone aboard, and cameras — the tools of my trade. And I work in the world's best office. Here are a few pieces written from that office.

Damariscove Island, where this nation began

DAMARISCOVE ISLAND — We are out among the islands, where this nation began. It is night now. The wind has dropped; and the sea is now so calm in the cove where we are anchored that the stars shine back up out of the ocean as well as down from heaven. The only night noises are the laugh of a loon, a primeval sound by the shore of a deserted island; and the sound of small waves breaking on the rocky shore and of the tide gurgling among the boulders. Lean over the side of the deck and run your hand through the ocean and the sea comes alive with flashes of fire — the phosphorescence miracle. There is a beautiful word for the tiny sea creatures who cause this light to shine in the cold ocean; the name is notilucci. That, too, is as old and primeval as the laugh of the loon.

We are anchored in a cove on the eastern shore of Damariscove Island, about six miles to sea from the center of Boothbay Harbor.

This island is where white man's America began. Long before the Founding Fathers ever set foot on Plymouth rock, this Damariscove Island was a flourishing port, the first commercial settlement of consequence in America.

Today Damariscove is a deserted island. Even the Coast Guard abandoned its station here in the winter of 1959. Now Nature Conservancy owns a part of it; and Chester A. Chase of North Whitefield is listed as owner on another piece — bought for a song when the Coast Guard left, I'm told.

But this unsung place is where our nation began. Here are the roots of America, and almost nobody realizes it.

The Mayflower sailed into Damariscove Harbor long before she sailed with a load of 102 pilgrims into Plymouth. The famed Mayflower was a fish transport before she went on charter to haul pilgrims. And Damariscove was her prime port of call, years before she sailed to Plymouth. The crew knew Damariscove as a friendly port. In fact, the Pilgrims' records show, the Mayflower and her cargo of pilgrims came by Monhegan and Damariscove Islands "to take some coddes before sailing on to Maffachufetts Bay," in 1620.

The year the Mayflower and her small sister ships arrived with Pilgrims, no less than 32 European fish transports came to load up with salt fish in Maine waters in the Monhegan-Damariscove area. Records show that seven English ships averaging 180 tons came into Damariscove Harbor alone, to load fish from these shores.

Today we raise a rumpus (rightly so) about the foreign fishing fleets. But more than 355 years ago, 32 foreign fish transports, comparable in mission to the Soviet factory and mother ships today, were taking Maine fish back across the Atlantic.

Before sunset we rowed ashore in the dinghy and took a walk for an hour or two along animal paths. The island is only two miles long; and a very narrow waist in the middle divides it almost in two. The land is almost barren of trees now. Sheep ate the vegetation down to the roots. A hundred years ago, Damariscove was covered with a dense growth of fine evergreens. The northern half of the uninhabited island is called Wood End still but barely a tree grows.

We walked to the southern, seaward end. We watched the seas surge and break ominously over rock and ledges at the harbor entrance. On the chart they are called, appropriately, "The Motions." In 1620 and earlier, charts were scarce and less detailed than today. But this is the same harbor where voyagers and traders and fish transports from Europe came to anchor, chart or not.

Historian Charles K. Bolton in his book "The Real Founders of New England" wrote about Damariscove Island. "Here was the chief maritime port of New England. Here was the rendezvous for English, French and Dutch ships crossing the Atlantic. Here men bartered with one another and with Indians, drank, gambled, quarreled and sold indentured servants."

This evening the harbor is empty. Only life here are eider ducks, with their flotillas of babies, and black-wing gulls threatening to swoop and eat them — and that laughing loon. The only remnants of buildings are remnants of the recent Coast Guard station. But we stand by the harbor and envisage what must have been here 380 years ago. To service those fish transports such as the Mayflower, there had to be wharves, derricks, salting sheds, houses, stores, taverns, and a boatyard or two for repairs. Sailors being what they are, they surely found other livelier pleasures here on Damariscove after the long Atlantic crossing.

Of all this, nothing remains. Ancient records show that Captain Humphrey Damerill set up the first trading posts here about 1600. And to supply those fish transports, scores of fishermen along the coast from New Meadows river to the westward, to the Georges river to the east, must have brought their catches here to sell. In the diaries of his 1614 voyage hereabouts, Captain John Smith writes about Damariscove.

The roses are in bloom now. And the story is that these sweet smelling roses came from France, planted here almost 380 years ago by a French trader. Not far from the old harbor is an inland fresh water pond, bright with lilies. In the marshy places of the little island we find cranberry bushes. The land is blood-red in the fall when the cranberries are ripe and red.

Long before those Pilgrims stepped on the Mayflower, pioneering English families were settled here and along the nearby coast. They prospered. That first hard winter at Plymouth, 50 of the 102 pilgrims, the so-called Founding Fathers, failed to survive. So Governor Winslow of the Plymouth Colony sailed here, to Maine's Damariscove Island to ask the fishermen for food. And those tough, roistering fishermen of Maine fed the pious starving Pilgrims for free.

Now, from the little deck of "Steer Clear," we look at Damariscove Island where we walked before the stars came out. Nobody else is here tonight. We share the island with the laughing loon and the nesting birds and the ghosts of the men who began these United States. But down in Plymouth, the Maffachufetts promoters are getting ready to sell thousands of more tickets to gullible tourists to view the Plymouth rock where the Maffachufetts version of Founding Fathers stepped ashore.

Balderdash, Maffachufetts! It all began here in Maine — on Damariscove Island.

Low tides are the loveliest

DEER ISLE — Low tides are the best tides, I think. The lower, the better. Among the islands, low tides give you more rocks to climb, bigger beaches to walk, scores of tidal pools to explore. Low tides give you a rich smell of salt-soaked seaweed. Low tides give you clams to dig and mussels to collect for supper. Low tides give you a chance to look at the bottom of the ocean and to marvel at what grows there, deep under water about 20 hours out of 24. Low tides reveal a world that lies hidden except for those brief hours when the tug of the moon pulls down the seal level here by twice the height of a man.

A jar filled with vivid purple-blue heather stands by my typewriter as I write this piece in the stern of Steer Clear. Barbara picked these sea flowers at the last low tide. They are as bright and vivid as any flowers in the flower beds at home. But they grew 12 feet underwater at high tide.

In the same jar are grasses greener by far than the lawn at home. These, too, grew 12 feet underwater. There is a lovely garden growing under the hull of my boat. My anchor may be set now in a flower bed of infinite beauty which will bloom and die unwarmed by the sun, untouched by the wind or rain, unseen by a human eye.

But there is another side to that thought which is not so nice. Under the hull of my boat are also enormous rocks and hills of granite ledges bigger than houses. When the tide goes out around the islands, you can see the terrifying landscape over which you may sail at high water.

On some small islands, the rock ledges exposed at low tide are bigger than the entire island you see at high tide. The pines and the meadows and the beach from which we swim may seem, at first, like the whole island. But at dead low tide, you begin to see that they are only a tiny fraction of the island — just the icing on the cake.

Low tides have been given a bad name, largely by people who live beside polluted rivers or dirty harbors. For when the tide goes out, the dirty truth is revealed. The skeletons in the closet (Davy Jones' locker?) are there for strangers to see.

But this column is in praise of low tides, the lower the better. Watching the tide go out beside a little island is like watching a fascinating, revealing, slow, long striptease. Inch by inch, foot by foot, more loveliness is uncovered. But, unlike a striptease, the island is never bare, never totally exposed.

The island goes down hundreds, maybe thousands of feet deeper; and its rock, its ledges, its underwater sea gardens may stretch out for hundreds of acres, never to be seen. The retreat of the sea, measured as a striptease, drops only a pair of shoulder straps.

Yet, a wondrous new world is exposed to enjoy and explore for a brief hour or two until the pull of the moon brings back the sea to cover up that secret world again.

The most mysterious rhythm of the universe, to me, is the way the ocean tides trail the progress of the moon with tireless precision. The pull of the moon on the waters directly below it, raises the level of the oceans there.

At the same time, a greater gravitational pull is exerted on the earth as a whole than on the waters on the far side of the earth from the moon. This results in a high tide on the two opposite sides of the earth at the same time and low tides in the two intermediate quadrants.

Twice a month, the moon, the sun and the earth are in line — at new moon and again at full moon. Then the tides respond to the combined pull of moon, plus sun, and the result is we get higher high tides and lower low tides.

These are called "spring tides." But they have nothing to do with the season. When the moon is in its first and its third quarter, the tidal forces oppose each other and we get especially low tides then. These are called "neap tides."

When the boatyards are launching, they do it on spring tides. If you beach a boat on the high spring tides, you may have to wait two weeks before the next spring tide will float her.

While tides rise and fall in regular cycles everywhere on earth, the range between high and low tide varies hugely and depends on the basins and bays and inlets of the coast.

Tides do not rise or fall at a steady pace. In the first and sixth hours the change is only about 1/12th of the range; only 2/12ths in the second and fifth hours and speeds to 3/12ths in the third and fourth hours.

Another rule of thumb with six-hour tides as we have in Maine is that the tide will be high when the moon bears true east; low when it bears south.

But the tide that reveals the most beauty and the worst of the rocky dangers to a boat — is low tide. For the best of sights and the strongest of smells, my vote goes to the much-maligned low tide.

Barbara the beachcomber

MERCHANT ISLAND — Barbara, my wife ashore and first mate afloat, is a beachcomber. Beachcombing is a polite word for what ails her. The truth is, she is hooked beyond hope on picking up every piece of rose glass, heart shaped stones, stones with white rings around their middle, multicolored chunks of granite, black hulks or basalt and soapstone.

Going ashore with Barbara on small, uninhabited islands is back-breaking work. We anchor Steer Clear in deep water, and row ashore in the dinghy with just a bucket, a clam rake and a pail for berries. But as soon as we beach the dinghy, I discover Barbara has performed her bag of tricks. This is the trick whereby the one canvas bag, in which she was supposedly carrying lunch, towels and swimsuits, contains nothing but other canvas bags.

"You can skinny-dip, then dry in the sun like a cormorant," she says. "I need the empty bags for my collections." Head down, she starts combing the beach. So much interests her that her rate of progress is one mile in two hours. Her clock is not time nor tide. It is the capacity of her tote bags, her pockets, my pockets and her hat.

When all are full, we row back to Steer Clear and sort out the latest load of island loot.

The collecting and sorting process is adding new dimensions to our enjoyment of the Maine coast. Through it, we are learning a little about the rocks of the islands, and the mud which holds our anchor secure, and the history behind them. It is heady stuff. The rocks picked up on the beach a few hours ago may be 10 million years old.

This paradise, called the coast of Maine, was 400 million years in the making.

The how and the when Maine was made is written in the rocks. But to read that writing in the rocks takes the knowledge of a geologist. I wish I had one as part-time crew, who could read aloud the fascinating, incredible, story behind the rocks of Maine. I carry a few books as a substitute.

Rocks on these peaceful island shores were torn from the throats of volcanoes. Fiery, violent explosions ripped out the very innard of the earth and hurled it through space till it fell, sizzling, into the sea. Molten granite, so hot it ran as a liquid, created the ledges on which we lazed in the sun after lunch today.

Far downeast by Quoddy Head, where sunrise first touches the New World, the rocks are dark gray, dark green or black. They are massive and unfractured, quite different from the layered, striated rock in Penobscot and Casco Bays. In my new geology books, these black, massive rocks are called "gabbro." But look at gabbro through a magnifying glass and the seemingly solid rock is revealed to be a mass of interlocking crystals, white and green, black and gray.

I've learned from the books aboard, that the white crystals are called 'feldspar.' And when I chased down 'feldspar,' I found experts define it as a mineral composed of oxygen atoms tied together by atoms of calcium, sodium, aluminum and silicon. The dark crystals are pyroxene, again oxygen atoms, but this time tied together by atoms of magnesium and iron.

Until Barbara began collecting these rocks, I thought of them just as rocks. Now, I am learning that this gabbro is 'igneous' rock. This simply means related to fire, as in the word ignition. But the fire involved with these rocks was molten lava from volcanoes, cooled now for millions of years.

Rocks change in the mid coast of Maine. They change from these massive, black, solid seeming 'igneous' rocks downeast to the rocks and ledges that seem built up in layers. And now I have learned that they are just what they seem to be — layers of rocks, built up one layer at a time. Each layer is made of mud or sand or volcanic ash. The experts call these 'sedimentary' rocks, because millions of years ago they were sediment on the sea floor.

Above all, and everywhere, there is granite. Maine must have dozens of kinds of granite, above and under the water. Granite is an igneous or fire rock, like gabbro, which rose at huge heat out of the

belly of the earth, and slowly cooled and solidified on the earth's surface.

But where gabbro is mostly black, granite in Maine is often pink, gray, black or pepper and salt. A look at it through a magnifying glass shows why. This time the crystals include pink feldspar, rich in potassium; quartz, which shines like glass mirrors; and specks of black mica; and specks of white calcic.

All along the coast, especially in Penobscot Bay and the Muscle Ridge Shoals, you can go ashore at several islands and see the huge granite quarries. Millions of tons of Maine granite were taken out from these islands. Maine granite built Grant's Tomb, Grand Central Station, the Kennedy grave, thousands of federal and business office buildings. Now, alas, the new buildings are made of glass and cement.

Geologists say an ancient and very high mountain chain ran along the Maine coast 300 million years ago. Much of it started on the ocean floor, and worked its way up. It is all coming full cycle now. The granite atop Mt. Desert began as sedimentary rocks on the ocean floor. Now streams on Mt. Desert are eroding that same granite and returning it as sand and clay back to the ocean floor, millions of years later.

Erosion over 200 million years has transformed the mountain range to rolling upland. What were once the valleys of ancient mountains are now the great bays — Casco, Muscongus, Penobscot, Blue Hill, Frenchman, Machias.

The advance and retreat of glaciers thousands of feet thick gave the Maine coast its wild and rugged beauty. The last advance of massive ice in the Ice Age began in Maine 40,000 years ago; and the last retreat of ice in Maine was only about 10,000 years ago. The ice was thick enough to bury Mt. Desert. As the glaciers melted, immense boulders and fine, mucky rock "flour" were left behind. That "flour" is the muck into which boatsmen today sink their anchors. It is great holding ground. But the same kind of mud is found 100 miles inland and at altitudes of 100 feet, far up Maine rivers. The same kind of black, muddy clay is found near the coast 200 feet down in the ocean bottom; and also 200 feet high above sea level. Clearly, say geologists, the Maine Coast must have been flooded by the sea after the last ice retreated to heights almost 200 feet above present sea level.

Due to my wife, the beachcomber, I get thoughts like these when I look at the rocky coast of Maine. Begin by picking up rocks and, suddenly you are delving into history 300 million years ago.

Cruising this coast of Maine is more than running a boat.

Weather lingo

PORTLAND — In Maine we talk a lot about weather — and for good reason. So we've developed a special language concerning weather. Some of it is earthy, better said than printed.

But here are a few weather words that warrant a bit of description.

WEATHER BREEDER. When we get an absolutely beautiful day in Maine — clear, sparkling, cloudless so you can see forever — some old curmudgeon on the wharf moans in my ear "Nice enough today, Bill, but watch it. She's a breeder . . . Any day as good as this is a weather breeder, you can be sure." And he grunts and looks gloomy. The worst is just over the horizon, he says.

He's right too. The earmark of a "breeder" is perfect visibility.

When you can see a distant buoy or a faraway lighthouse clearly, when you can look out from Pemaquid Light and pick out the roofs of houses out on Monhegan Island, you are likely to get clobbered in the morning. You are in "a breeder."

Maybe there is good meterological reason for this. But I'm inclined to think it is hairshirt morality. The Puritan streak in Maine clings. When we have one absolutely perfect day, we fear there may be hell to pay. We'll make up for it with a stinker tomorrow . . . And so the old curmudgeon on the wharf, looks dourly at the gorgeous, clear blue sky, the perfect visibility and says: "Watch her, Bill — she's a breeder!"

SNOW EATER.   This one you hear in the longest week of winter
— the last days of February and the first days of March. Sometime
in that week there comes a wind shift. Warm air blows in from the
south off the ocean. It brings wet fog with it; a misty drizzle, and
warmish rain.

And that weather is called "a snow eater." It eats away at snow
drifts, demolishing them faster than sunshine. In some spots a "snow-
eater fog" will melt the snow down completely; and poking up at the
bottom is the first tinge of green. That is why a snow eater in late
February is like a kiss from a pretty stranger.

LINE STORM.   This mean kind of storm hits when the March
and September equinoxes arrive. A gale out of the northeast comes
ripping down the coast, and drives the rain so hard it slashes at
you head-on. Instead of falling vertically, rain comes at you in a line.
Another quirk of a "line storm" is that it can begin and end along a
defined line.

One of my grudges about line storms is that they seem to hit at night. We go to bed with the rain coming down in torrents and a moderate wind blowing. Then, just as the first deep sleep comes, crash go the shutters and bang goes that loose chair flying across the porch. A line storm is here. You get up to close the shutters, you get drenched recovering that chair. The wind climbs to gale force. Slamming down hard from the northeast, it drives the rain straight out flat at you in a straight line. The rain stings as it hits. Out of the black, wet night, a miserable drenched cat appears, whinning. You need to tie a splice in its tail to keep it from blowing out to sea.

Line storms find cracks in a house the way a dentist's drill finds nerves in your tooth. As you head back to a safe warm bed, you see the line storm is driving water through the window caulking. Time for towels. You see the gale is forcing rain through a roof peak. Time for buckets. You know that by morning, some small boats in the harbor will be stove up on the rocks.

Then dawn comes up like a happy lamb. The worst line storms spawn a beautiful child. When that mean gale out of the northeast backs around to northwest, it gives birth to a bright day of peacock blue and warm sunshine.

It's just the reverse from the fine summer day that turns out to be a "weather breeder," with a sting in its tail.

But they are good words. "Weather breeder." "Snow eater." "Line storm." They are words with a rough, wild music to them.

Magic at Loud's Island

LITTLE HARBOR — Cecil Prior, born on Loud's island more than half a century ago, came down from his meadow when he saw Steer Clear coming into the island harbor. We waved. And Cecil called out, "Be glad if you lie on my mooring." He jumped in a skiff and came out to lend a hand, tying a nylon pennant through the shackle at the end of the heavy iron chain he uses for mooring his lobster boat.

Cecil and his wife Elizabeth live in a big, white farmhouse atop the hill from their fishhouse and float. Cecil, a fair-haired, blue-eyed islander, can do every chore on land or sea that faces a man with no easy access to stores, garage, plumber, electrician, boat mechanic or carpenter.

Cecil went to the one-room schoolhouse on the island; his mother was the teacher. In those days, 17 families farmed and fished from here year-round and built a church and kept a fine community store. For hundreds of years, farming and fishing families had flourished here.

The Indian chief Samoset had his headquarters on this island, which was known as Samoset's island, then as Muscongus, now as Loud's, after an English naval officer who settled here about 1750.

Cecil and Elizabeth stay on Loud's longer than anyone. But they leave in the fall for the mainland. The island is empty these winters, every house closed, every person gone. There is no school on Loud's, no postoffice, no store, no phone (except for a line strung between some of the island homes).

Yet life on Loud's is looking up. Summer people, from away and from Maine, have repaired and restored the simple, handsome homes that used to be lived in year-round. But, thank heaven, no roads or new houses have been built.

Even so the long and greedy arm of state government has reached from Augusta. The assessor paid a visit and property taxes quadrupled. Island people wonder why. State government does not provide one single, solitary service.

On Cecil's mooring, we sit in the cockpit of Steer Clear, having a sundown drink with Cecil. This is one of the loveliest tiny harbors along a coast of lovely, tiny harbors. And nowhere have we enjoyed more interesting bird-watching.

Swallows by the hundreds do acrobatics in the evening air around our boat. They must be right on target because no mosquitoes bite us while this squadron is overhead.

There are two types of swallows — barn and cliff — and they swoop and dive into and out of our boat's cockpit. Their aerial acrobatics are incredible. But the special beauty of this Little Harbor evening is the soft grey light. The sky is overcast without being sullen and the air is wholly still. No wind ripples the water; it is flat calm, lead-colored.

Then comes a shower. It is so quiet here that we listen to the raindrops hitting the sea, the noise building as the drops come faster until it sounds as if God is pouring a pitcher of water slowly over Muscongus Bay. Then the sky lightens and the rain and its noise stop.

A pair of great blue herons flies majestically into the cove on evening patrol. This pair moves back and forth. I have never before been able to watch so many heron landings and take-offs at such close quarters. This evening these two are flying so close to the water that the tips of their enormous, slow-flapping wings seem certain to touch, but do not.

On some of these short hops one heron is clearly a flight stylist. He stretches his long neck far, far out ahead of his wings and his long legs far, far back. His body looks like an arrow flying to its mark.

Long-legged, they stand almost invisible against the sea-wet granite. One keeps its neck outstretched, almost two feet of neck. The partner sinks its long neck down between its shoulders, standing hunched like a loafer on a street corner.

It is almost night. And at this time of fading light, there comes a sudden luminosity close to the sea. Lobster buoys glow and look larger.

The white hulls of two skiffs in the cove and the white hull of "Free Rider" — Cecil's lobster boat — also shimmer in this last light.

The gulls and herons and swooping swallows hurry home for the night. And the silence in the cove grows silky and sweet; even the sea seems noiseless here.

The moon rises late tonight. And when she comes, she peers down dimly through leaden clouds. But light enough gets through to turn this grey ocean into a miracle of silver sheen.

Two loons swim in the path of the moon, big in their arched backs and lovely in their flowing necks. They separate; and then they cry their eerie call to each other.

That laugh of the loon in the moon path carries a spine-chilling mystery and a haunting beauty in its ghostly sound. In the far distance across the flat sea, a dragger steams out for its night's work. I can see its lights moving; and barely visible are the low silhouettes of the seine boats it tows, piled with net.

I close the boat for the night and go below to my bunk to read awhile. Tucked in a sleeping bag, in the little cabin of a small boat gently rocking on the tide brings a diminution of the world to a few square feet. Two inches from my ear is the hull and washing at the wooden hull is the mysterious sea. Wavelets make a soothing, comforting sound. Maybe that noise from the vast, cold ocean outside the thin hull should be scary; instead it is a familiar, reassuring sound, linking a man back to the sea where all life began.

Sleep comes fast in a boat, after a day of motion and salt spray. Sleep in a narrow bunk, zipped into a sleeping bag with a dog as foot-warmer and a gentle rocking by the waves is somehow more deep and real than sleep in a king size, soft-sprung bed with smooth sheets. But it ends at first light.

Going topside to watch the dawn of a new day come to America is a special part of waking on a small boat in an island cove. On a little boat there is nothing to getting up early. One step from the bunk and you can reach a night-cold peach; one step more and you have your hands on a thermos of hot coffee; one more step and you're up on deck. Sitting there, watching the sun climb up out of the Atlantic, seeing the first light kiss alive the myriad small night-dark islands, is a peculiar joy to Maine.

The joy is tinged with smugness, too; for this sun you watch rising is touching this Maine coast first of any land in the United States. Minutes later, even hours after you have looked this sun in the eye, millions of other Americans will be seeing it rise over them.

Here by the island, the world is silent and suspended in stillness. Even the wind sleeps. The sea is flat, mirror calm. Then like a waking man, the wind wakes as the light of the sun strengthens. Soon a slight ripple of breeze is creating ruffles on the surface.

The climbing sun reaches in among the branches and lights the night-blackness of the island pines, waking the birds in trees and on nests at the edge of the sea. The first birds sing; the first eider duck mother leads the first flotilla of baby ducks out for a swimming lesson and morning feed.

Soon your ears prick to that most special of Maine's early morning sounds — the sound of a lobster boat. No sound in the world is like that of a lobster boat engine across water; it races, slows, then idles as the trap is hauled; then races in a surge of sound to the next trap, slows, idles again; and soon you hear the racket of the blaring radio or CB turned up to full volume over the engine noise to keep the fisherman company on his dawn rounds.

People who do their world-watching from a porch miss the greatest unending pleasure of world-watching from a small boat, swinging on its anchor or mooring. As the boat swings, a new slice of world comes into your range of vision. New islands; new buoys of different colors; new gulls swooping; new ducks with new sets of babies; new rocky shores; new ledges jutting out of the sea; new lobster boats hauling new traps.

It is 6 a.m. All the world is awake and stirring now; birds in full song and speedy flight; the breeze blowing in growing vigor; lobstermen by the dozens out hauling; sun now being seen by millions.

Gone now are the magic moments of feeling as if you are the only person witnessing the birth of day in an island cove. Now the spanking new day belongs to everybody; but, as you go below to dress, you are glad that you knew this day when it was just a pup.

In Maine, sharks bask, don't bite

ABOARD STEER CLEAR — I've got a 'poor man's flying bridge' on my boat, and the other day I spotted shark's fins from it. So I have boned up a little on sharks in Maine waters. Since "Jaws", the sight of a shark fin causes consternation. But the only record I can find of a shark making a fatal attack on a swimmer in New England goes back to 1936. That is 43 years ago and that happened in Buzzards Bay. As far as Maine waters go, there seems to be no record of a shark ever even attacking a human.

At first glance the shark I spotted seemed huge, as long or longer than my boat, which is over 30 feet. I could see the dorsal fin and tail sticking up out of water, and a calm sea was just breaking over its grayish brown back.

We were very close. Maybe 40 or 50 feet apart. I thought the shark would submerge when it heard my engines. Then I thought I would submerge when I realized how big the shark was. But instead the shark stayed basking in the sun, and I cut my motors to slow, put the boat in neutral, I calmed down. I guess the shark never was in the least perturbed. And as I looked at the big beast, I remembered a recent talk with Helen Barlow, and I hung around the shark, watching.

Helen Barlow sailed across the Atlantic in a sailboat built by her husband. She said that out in the vast Atlantic in that tiny boat, she felt a kinship with anything else that was alive out there. She said "I never tried fishing because we had food enough. And I didn't want to kill anything else alive out there. I felt close to them, a kind of kinship to the fish. Even sharks." If Helen Barlow, a small and gentle and lovely woman could feel that way about sharks way out in the Atlantic, I decided to play it cool with this one close to Maine. So I sat watching for 10 minutes.

I think now that it was a basking shark. That is the biggest shark around these waters, and grows as big as 50 feet, according to the shark experts. It is gentle and harmless. The enormous fish eats only plankton. Such teeth as it has are tiny. In colonial times, it was hunted for its oil. The books I consulted report that as much as 600 gallons of oil was taken from a single basking shark. The oil was used for lamps.

Fishermen catch sharks in their nets, and wish they hadn't because they thrash around and rip holes in expensive twine. On Aug. 12, 1976, Capt. Genero Balzano, on the dragger Gerry & Joe, hooked a 300 pound blue shark 15 miles off Cape Elizabeth. These blue sharks are fish eaters, and this one was trying to get at the dragger's haul of fish. Balzano caught it on a six strand rope, and took an hour to bring the 300 pound fish alongside.

Smaller blue sharks are often caught by handliners fishing for groundfish off the Maine coast. They are a lovely blue color, shaped like a streamlined cigar and run up to 15 feet. Again, no record of a blue shark ever bothering a swimmer.

Three other kinds of sharks swim in Maine waters. Smallest is the dogfish. My wife is always catching dogfish by mistake. She hates them so much that she is getting afraid to put a drop line over for fear of hooking dogfish. They come in enormous schools. When you catch one and throw it back bleeding, the water gets thick with its brothers and sisters who come not to help but to dine.

In Europe, they eat dogfish. In fact those famous 'fish and chips', so enjoyed in England, are mostly dogfish. A great fleet of Norwegian fishing boats catches millions of pounds of dogfish for the English market every year. But in Maine, we cuss and throw them back. Now a British-German firm is in Maine, buying these three and four foot sharks, called dogfish, and paying a nickel a pound. Some days they buy 8,000 pounds or more. The bodies go to England for fish and chips. But the bellies go to Germany. Twenty years ago another firm bought about $25,000 worth of dogfish at Orr's Island for use in high school biology classes. And 20 years ago, you got a pile of dogfish for $25,000.

And then we find the mackerel shark in Maine. They are a bit bigger than dogfish, going about six feet long. It too is a fish eater, never known to have bothered a swimmer. Thousands are caught here. And they taste good enough to be sold as swordfish. But it is a case of men eating sharks.

The one shark to worry about is the white shark. This is a man eater, with saw-edged cutting teeth. They are mostly 20 to 30 feet long, and are often mistaken for mud sharks or cow sharks and makos.

The records I have read show that a white shark 17 feet, 6 inches long was taken in 1957 at Cutler in Little Machias Bay. It got caught in a fish weir, and the men who discovered it shot the beast. Before it died it did plenty of damage to the weir and to a fishing boat. Reports say that this shark towed a 32 foot fishing boat for a half hour. When they opened up the shark's stomach, three full grown harbor seals were found inside. The seals had no external wounds. They had apparently been swallowed whole.

I have found no record detailing encounters with man eating white sharks in Maine waters for the last 22 years. But I have heard fishermen tell about sharks caught in their nets. I have seen sharks washed up on a shore, dead. And I know harpooners who have harpooned sharks, and wish they hadn't. The shark can be a strong, tireless beast, so powerful that he will pull a boat for miles, even with a barb stuck in him.

The five kinds of sharks that get into Maine waters give birth to live young — not to eggs. Baby sharks are called pups. A mother may give birth to a whole litter of shark 'pups', each about two feet long.

This is all I know about sharks in Maine. And I have no plans to get first-hand, close-up knowledge.

T - H - U - M - P in the night

ABOARD STEER CLEAR — It was a bad night. We pitched, rolled, careened and swung wildly on our anchor. And we did it at the worst of times — during those scary, lonely, never-ending hours between 1 and 4 a.m. And in the worst of places — a narrow cove on an isolated island. Totally unpredicted winds gusting to 30 miles an hour funneled wildly into this tight cove.

But even through wild gyrations, it is possible to sleep on a small 32-foot boat.

It was the T-H-U-M-P on the hull, at the waterline on the bow, that unnerved me.

You wake up smartly and worry hard in a small boat on a rough night when there is a sudden, repeated, unknown banging on your hull. Your ears play detective, trying to identify the sound, trying to pin down its exact location. But the harder you listen, the more the banging sound seems to move. Wherever you move, it moves to the other side.

I time the T-H-U-M-Ps. Every 45 to 60 seconds, something raps the hull. What? No collision noise. We're not hitting ledge or rock; we are alone in the cove — no boat could blow down on us, pulling its anchor. No lobster pot was close enough to be hitting us. Unless one had broken loose in the high wind, had come up against our hull and got stuck and was out there, mean and vengeful, thumping, rapping, banging at the hull in these lonely, scary hours of the night.

I'm a chicken sailor on nights like this. I hate the thought of climbing out, going topside, bucking the wind on a slithery deck on a plunging boat and peering through the wet, wild wind for some damn pot. Finally, I do it. Barefooted, in idiotic pyjamas and a yellow slicker, holding a flashlight in one hand, holding on for dear life to the bucking boat with the other hand, I inch my way forward to the pulpit, overhanging the choppy, wind-driven sea. For a sickening second, I envisage the final absurdity — falling overboard, when not even my sleeping dog knows I am out, prowling around in this miserable night.

Out on the pulpit, holding the handrail so tight my knuckles are white, I bend far out over the sea, and shine the flashlight beam down the length of the hull. Both sides. Then deep into the water. Bouncing all the while like a toy.

No pot. Nothing. Nothing banging my hull. I retreat back to my warm bunk, prepared to sleep through the gyrations. I close my eyes.

"T-H-U-M-P." Again. And again. And again. No sleep possible with that unknown rapper at my hull, banging away by my ear.

This time I tear apart the rope locker in the hope some abandoned saucepan got loose up there. Nothing but 200 feet of soft, noiseless rope, that is now piled in a snarling mess around my feet.

T-H-U-M-P. That damnable banging keeps up. This time I search every locker for the culprit. It is 3 a.m. now. The boat is rolling and pitching wildly. The T-H-U-M-P keeps thumping. Out from every locker comes stuff I haven't seen for years. Now the boat looks like a jackdaw's nest. The aftermath of a rummage sale. No culprit uncovered. And then that T-H-U-M-P bangs again and again on the hull. Sounds ominous at 3:30 a.m. What is hitting us a hundred times each hour?

Cussing every word I ever learned on every waterfront, I hoist myself outside again, into the foul, wet windy night to look again. Bigger, heavier, stronger spotlight this time. Nothing to be seen. Back inside. And T-H-U-M-P. In my head I see beautiful images of that comfortable, non-bouncing, non-thumping bed back home, and wonder why I ever got hooked on boats.

Sleep is impossible. Only another noise can drown out that ominous T-H-U-M-P. I turn on the marine radio for the weather. The forecast has at last caught up to the fact that a high-powered wind is blowing out here. Then comes the kicker . . . at 4 a.m.

"Urgent notice to all mariners . . . " Mesmerized, I listen to the calm voice, speaking from an earth-bound, warm, dry, safe room. I hear that voice read the urgent notices to mariners. They concern fishing vessels overdue and unreported, on their way from Canadian to Maine waters. One is 59 feet long with one crewman aboard. I think of him, way offshore, imagine him struggling. And that picture shrinks my unknown thumping and bouncing and bucking to nothing. I am safe on an anchor that is holding tight. An hour later, I pick up the radio news that a yacht has sent out **MAYDAY** signals — distress and SOS calls. A Coast Guard plane on routine patrol had heard them, answered and is flying overhead until ships rescue the crew adrift in their lifeboat.

I suffer their horrors secondhand. Seldom does a boatman let his thoughts stray for long in this direction. But the seed is planted. And because dawn is coming now, I feel secure. So I make coffee and sample books in my small ship's library. I read a bit about rescues and life-saving, comforting myself that today we have it easy.

One book, "New England and the Sea" reports that the very first life-saving service for mariners in these parts was the Humane Society of Massachusetts, organized in 1786. There was no way of rescuing drowning sailors from a broken, sinking boat at sea. So instead, they built shelters, stocked huts with food, brandy, blankets, on desolate shores and tiny islands, where shipwrecked men might land by life-boat or by clinging to wreckage. By 1841, the Humane Society had 16 such stations between Martha's Vineyard and Newburyport.

Thousands of small ships plied these coasts. What few lighthouses existed had only candles. No buoys marked ledges. No radios forecast storms. How many sailors died? How many ships were lost? There was no federal lifesaving station anywhere in New England until 1850, when the first was established at Watch Hill, R. I. Finally, in 1871, Congress earmarked $200,000 to fund a life-saving service, and ordered the Secretary of the Treasury to employ "surfmen at such stations and for such periods as may be necessary."

By 1873 Maine had five stations. Some were manned by volunteers in foul weather. Some had surfboats weighing about 1,000 pounds, lined with cork for buoyancy. In 1878 Congress authorized the issuance of gold and silver medals as awards to those heroes who risked their lives to save others in peril on the sea. Were 100,000 lives lost? I find no records. But the one seaport of Salem had 400 widows of lost sailors. I can find no authoritative tally, but many thousands were lost at sea along these coasts.

Greatest loss in one night was in the Portland gale of November 26, 1898. That wild night sank 141 vessels and took 456 lives.

The amount of shipping in these waters in those days is hard to envisage now. For example, records from the Bangor harbormaster show that within two hours on July 14 in 1860, 60 ships arrived in Bangor. That year, 3,376 ships anchored in Bangor and, of course, the same number left.

Add the traffic at Maine's other major ports. And Maine had 13 ports big enough to be federal customs districts. The nation had 90 customs districts; and the Maine port of Waldoboro, now a little town and no longer a port, ranked fifth in 1860 — just behind the big four of New York, Boston, Philadelphia and Baltimore in tonnage owned. And these were the years when there was no life-saving service by the federal government anywhere along our nation's coast.

Now it is full daylight. Even so, I cannot find what caused that frightening thumping in the gusty night. But by day, all things look better. Except perhaps the image of the perils of those Maine sailors of earlier days. One freak accident that ended without tragedy is the strange case of the six-masted schooners. In 1901, there were only two six-masters in all the world — the George W. Wells, built in Camden and the Eleanor A. Percy, built in Bath. One summer night off Cape Cod, these two collided with each other, suffered severe damage, but made port.

I put away my reading of wrecks and storms after reading the terrible tale of the seal hunters. In 1829, 13 New England sailors hunting seals were captured by cannibals near the Fiji islands; and all but one was eaten. The survivor returned to tell the story and never again put to sea.

But what — or who — went T-H-U-M-P on my hull all through the night?

Mackerel in, fireflies out

MUSCONGUS BAY — When the fireflies are out, the mackerel are in.

When lightning bugs flash their taillights at dusk, mackerel are ready to bite.

After work these summer evenings, men and their wives and kids head for their boats and the bay. The word travels fast when tinker mackerel are schooling.

Hit 'em right, and you get five fish at a time on one rod.

Mackerel lures — white and red feathers — come five on a string.

And when your boat trolls through a school, every rod out may pick up five mackerel at once.

The other night I saw a lobster boat with five rods out, and inside two minutes all five rods reeled in five fish each.

The same night one boat with four fishermen aboard came back to harbor with 85 mackerel. They fished only for two hours on the evening tide. No sooner had they tied up to their mooring, than a smaller boat came into harbor with a man and his wife aboard. They had 35 mackerel.

"We had an arm-breaking time of it," said the wife. "We hit into a school of big fish. All from one pound to almost three pounds."

She held up some whopping samples. "Get four or five of those babies on the line at the same time and you've got a battle on your hands. Boat one lot, throw out again, and right away you've got another batch of five more. It went on like that with us. After a half hour we were tuckered out and had to come in."

When the mackerel are schooling and hitting there is no waiting between strikes.

Haul five fish — beautiful, silver and blue, and strong and fresh — into your boat and they almost unhook themselves.

In less than a minute, you have all five off the hooks and into the keeping bucket. There is no bait to put on — you just toss the five mackerel flies-and-hooks over the side, let out your line and keep trolling slowly. If you are still in the school, you will have five more in a couple of minutes.

If there are only single fish around, it is often better to jig for them. The mackerel jig we use is a simple, stainless steel jig, two inches or so long, with a hook built into. Trolling this behind the boat about 50 to 70 feet, we jerk it with a swift wrist motion every few seconds.

I'll never forget the hot summer night some years ago when our whole family went out mackereling. Not only did we hit an enormous school of tinker mackerel, but we couldn't get out of it.

Our kids were about 16 years old then, and had friends along. They refused to tire of hauling in these splendid, handsome fish. When we docked, we filled gunny sacks with tinker mackerel. My son was determined to make a pile of pocket money by hawking them.

But the trouble is that, if you hit a school, so do two dozen other boats; and everyone is out peddling their catch. The bottom drops out of the mackerel market with a thump. Suddenly there is such a glut that not even your friends can take any more.

But that night we had a determined mackerel salesman for a son. He got his mother to drive him around half the county. It took so many hours for him to unload the hundreds of mackerel that the car smelled like a boat for the entire month of July that year.

Tinker mackerel under a pound make the finest eating. I know of no fish to beat a fresh-caught, fresh-cooked tinker mackerel. They are quick and easy to clean and to cook. (Clean them on board, and feed the gulls, before you dock.)

Cook them whole, and as simply as you can. Fry 'em, or broil 'em, or bake 'em at 350 degrees for 40 minutes in milk. Use salt pork fat, or butter.

Cook 'em as they came out of the sea; or roll 'em in a mixture of flour and cornmeal. Don't spoil by seasoning. Salt and a flick of pepper is all you need.

There is no nicer way to spend a summer evening in Maine than going mackereling. We troll our own special beat, between New

Harbor Dry Ledges past Chamberlain, past Brown's Head and past the Rachel Carson preserve, and down the channel between Round Pond and Loud's Island.

To relax on the boat, to sniff the pines and the salt sea, and watch the gulls and terns dive, and see the lovely islands stretching off to Monhegan, and then to catch a mess of mackerel to boot — that is the finest kind of summer happiness.

Awesome to behold, that whale

MONHEGAN ISLAND — We saw and heard a whale blow off Monhegan Island the other day. The sea was flat calm and a thin white mist hung like a half-transparent curtain from sky to sea. There was no wind, no noise, no other boat near. It was a time of doldrums.

Then we heard the noise. A weird sound, close to a loud rush of air out of a huge truck tire. Or like a gust of wind trapped momentarily in a blow hole which found the opening and gushed out with a WHOOOSH. On an empty ocean it was a scary, alien sound.

Barbara and I heard the noise at the same moment and turned together to face the direction whence it came. We were just in time to see the water spout and the huge blunt-domed gray head breaking the surface. Transfixed, we watched in silent awe. The huge shape submerged, leaving only ripples on the flat sea. Then those smoothed out. No sign was left of the momentous sight or sound.

This was no "blackfish." This was a full-scale whale. But what type, or how large, neither of us could say. Each year a number of whales are spotted and reported off the Maine coast. The College of the Atlantic near Bar Harbor is keeping a record of these sightings.

Maine has never done much in the way of whaling. We had a short and unsuccessful fling at it when the money went out of fishing, at the end of Mr. Madison's war. Under the treaty of 1818, Maine fishing boats lost the right to fish within three miles of British dominions.

They couldn't put in to Nova Scotia to get needed bait, find shelter, do repairs, or take on food or water. The Maine fishing fleet dropped down from 10,000 tons to a mere 760 tons. To encourage its rebuilding Congress upped the bounties and subsidies for new fishing boats. Tonnage quickly increased to a record 11,000 by 1820.

To make quick money, the Wiscasset Whale Fishing Company was formed in the 1830s. Maine men had seen with envy the huge profits reaped by whaling fleets out of New Bedford, Nantucket and Provincetown. So the Wiscasset syndicate bought a hull being built on the Hitchcock ways at Damariscotta, fitted it out as a whaler, christened her "Wiscasset", and sent her hunting under the command of Captain Richard Macy.

Three and a half years later she came back to port with 2,800 barrels of sperm oil. Out she went again for a voyage of two and a half years, and that time she came home with 900 barrels of sperm, $6,517 in cash, and 150 pounds of coffee.

Discouraged, the whaling company sold the "Wiscasset." And that was about the sum total of Maine whaling.

But in nearby Massachusetts whaling was a multimillion dollar business. New Bedford alone had 329 whaling ships home-ported there in 1857. Sailors in the fo'c'sle got a pittance — maybe $200 after a four-year voyage and terrible living. But owners and captains made profits of 100 per cent and more on a single voyage. Whales paid for many of the most extravagant ship captains' houses in New England.

A New Bedford negro named Lewis Temple was the master blacksmith who developed the best of all whale harpoons — called The Temple. He did not grow rich, however.

Harpooning a full grown bowhead whale in those days was like bringing in a "gusher" oil well today. One 50-foot whale might yield 8,000 gallons of oil. Whale oil lit the oil lamps of the world; was the best lubricant for machinery; kept lamps burning in lighthouses. Whale oil fetched a dollar a gallon some years.

But whaling killed men, and the ice of the Arctic killed ships. In 1865 the Confederate raider Shenandoah burned 25 whale ships caught helpless in the Arctic ice, according to whaling authority Paul Giambara. In the winter of 1871, 33 more whaling ships were crushed by Arctic ice and abandoned where they were trapped. More than 1,200 in crews escaped, helped by Eskimos.

American whaling had a short, spectacular heyday. The discovery of petroleum in 1859 and the marketing of kerosene for lamps killed the demand for whale oil. The last whaling voyage out of New Bedford was made by the schooner John R. Manta in 1927, 52 years ago this month.

But magnificent whales are still seen and heard as they swim, awesome and majestic, along the coast of Maine.

IV
GUNKHOLING, LOBSTERS & FRIENDS

Bass Harbor Light, Mt. Desert Island

THE WORLD *looks different when you come in a boat. And when you come in a boat, people on land treat you differently, usually are better, than if you come by car or plane. Especially if your boat is small and you run it.*

So half the fun in cruising Maine in a small boat is in going ashore — ashore on remote islands; ashore in small fishing harbors; ashore in gunkholing coves where you must creep, slowly, slowly, watching the depth finder, with a look-out forward.

Even as I write these words, sitting by a typewriter far inland, my mind's eye fills with the islands, and I feel that wonderful twinge of anticipation a boatman feels when creeping into a new island cove, searching for the right spot to drop anchor.

Even the names turn me on. Brimstone. Otter. St. Helena. Wreck. Cranberry. Butter. The Blessed Islands.

On the snowy day I write these words, I hear the soft shouts from helmsman to mate on the bow; I hear the anchor chain being paid out, then the signal to back down on the scope, and set the anchor in the mud, hard. I can feel Steer Clear sway and grab hold, then swing with the running tide, till she points steady into the breeze and hangs firmly on her anchor.

I feel now, that moment of exquisite peace; the moment of no noise, no motion, of feasting your eyes on the magic island for this night. With luck, there is warmth left in the sun, and time to stretch out and bask in it while you drink down hot, sweet tea or cold, foaming beer.

Next, the moment of rowing ashore in the dinghy, choosing where to beach the little boat and trying to hold onto Piper, the Dalmatian, always over-anxious to leap, swim and make her beach head. Then, the exhilaration of exploration; or the sweet nostalgia of coming back to the island you found and loved three summers past.

And, of course, the friends, the people on the islands, in the boats and boatshops, in the harbor stores. There is something extra special about picking up these friendships exactly as you left them summers back when you headed out to sea.

So, come do a little gunkholing . . .

Boat Doctor; Merritt Brackett

NEW HARBOR — Say the name, "Merritt Brackett," in harbors from Rockland to Gloucester, Mass. and you'll likely light up fishermen's faces.

They'll smile and cock their heads a moment to freshen their memories, and then they'll tell the story of how Merritt Brackett got them going again — out fishing, out making a dollar — when nobody else could.

Along the coast of Maine there are thousands of men richer and thousands more powerful than Merritt. But I don't know of a name that lights up more faces or a name that triggers more stories tinged with gratitude than the name "Merritt Brackett." Few men earn that kind of monument, no matter how rich or powerful they grow.

Merritt Brackett heals sick boats.

He is more a boat doctor than a marine mechanic.

He has a bedside manner with a sick engine that makes those critters want to get better and run.

Fishermen laid up with a sick engine in a strange port first try to do the repairs themselves. Then, they call in local mechanics. When their motor still fails to respond, they finally go to the wall telephone at the end of the strange wharf and call up Merritt Brackett in New Harbor.

They describe the symptoms, rather like a mother describing a fever, upset stomach and dry throat in her child to the family doctor on a Sunday night.

At the other end of the phone, Merritt listens and asks about tell-tale signs. He talks about that engine as though he were bending right over it, taking its temperature, counting its pulse and probing its fuel lines or water pumps or listening to the thrum-thrump-thrump of its cylinders firing.

Merritt is a long talker. He takes his time and plenty of it. He asks kindly questions about old weaknesses he has treated before in your engines. Finally, out of his vast experience with thousands of other engines which he has doctored, Merritt prescribes a temporary treatment for yours.

"That trick may get you home if you go slow and easy. And soon as you get back in harbor I'll come to your boat," he says, signing off.

If the boat was far off and in serious trouble and his fishermen friends couldn't get out of harbor to make their living, then Merritt would go to them. He'd get the "sick call" sometimes when he was sleeping. He'd wind up saying, "I'll be along by daylight."

Then at two or three o'clock in the dark of night, he'd dress in his dark green work-pants and shirt, put on his long, peaked cap, fix a lunch, swing a heavy box of tools into the back of his pickup truck and head out on a drive of three or four hours, to tend the sick boat in a distant port.

Merritt was down on my boat recently, diagnosing an oil leak between the reverse gear and the engine block, which new seals have not stopped. He did what repairs he could out on the mooring.

"She'll go OK, even if she leaks a little. Try using the regular engine oil instead of transmission fluids in the reverse gear. It'll work fine and will do better if it still leaks up into the engine."

I guess I knew that already. But when the word comes from Merritt, it is like getting the word from your trusted family doctor. You feel better and the worry is off your mind because your own trusted doctor looked you over and told you his verdict face to face.

Merritt Brackett turned 60 some years back. He started doctoring engines as a kid here. An uncle gave him a broken-down roadster about 50 years ago. "I got it to run. Painted it up grey and red. Had no mudguards. But it was a sporty hit at school."

For half a century since then, Merritt has doctored so many cars and later on so many thousands of boat engines that he knows the family history of 'em. He will sit on your boat working and tell you about similar ailments in engines of other boats in the harbor. "Harry had same kind of trouble two boats back. Had the same trouble, too, with the boat Percy had down in Round Pond . . . "

Merritt may take a 10-minute break and sip a cool beer and talk about boats with similar aches and pains and the remedies which

worked for them. He fixes your boat, teaches you new ways of looking for trouble and curing it, and gives you a bit of boat history, too.

Portland harbor has its Charlie O'Reilly; Bucks Harbor has its
Steve Bridges; North Haven has Jim Brown; other harbors have their
special boat doctors. And New Harbor has its own very special Merritt Brackett.

Like the old family doctor, these boat doctors are a vanishing
breed. When they finally go, the Maine coast will remember them
and miss them for a long, long while.

Why Canadian bait for Maine lobsters?

NEW HARBOR — The lobster boats were idle. It was a good day for lobstering. But the boats were not out. The fishermen stood talking on the wharf.

"No bait. The trucks from Canada didn't come with our bait. So we can't fish today."

Maine lobsters are being tempted into Maine traps with bait from Nova Scotia. Redfish. The redfish bait costs $27.50 a barrel this summer, for which the Maine lobstermen get only a skeleton — the head, backbone and maybe the tail. The rest of Canadian redfish are in the supermarkets, where they are sold as Ocean Perch fillets. But for the skeleton left after the ocean perch are filleted, Maine lobstermen pay up to $27.50 a barrel. And a serious lobsterman with 300 traps to bait, will put two barrels of bait aboard his boat. There goes $50 and more. Now add the price of gasoline or diesel fuel to keep him running all day and then add the cost of his helper, or sternman, and it costs a Maine lobsterman about $100 a day, just to leave the mooring.

Add to that the monthly payments on a $60,000 new boat, fully equipped, which is about the price of a modern 36 foot lobster boat equipped with depth finders, radar, hydraulic hauling gear, VHF and CB radio and powered with a big Detroit diesel. The top-liners in most fishing harbors have lobster boats of this caliber.

Most lobstermen do their work from older boats with a Chevy or Olds engine converted to marine use; and they go fishing in the fog without the benefit of radar and VHF radio. But bait and gas and traps cost everyone the same high price.

The wooden traps run to $15 each nowadays and the new metal traps are up to $27 each. Multiply that unit cost by the 300 or 400 traps a serious lobsterman owns, and it adds up to a cash investment in traps and potwarp (the rope that links the trap on the bottom to the marker buoy on the surface) of over $7,000. "In a storm you can lose 50 traps overnight — and kiss goodbye to $700," says a lobsterman stuck on shore because he can't get the redfish bait he wants.

There are 8,000 licensed lobstermen in Maine. Perhaps 4,500 of them are full time year round fishermen. And researchers at the Marine Resources laboratory in Boothbay Harbor say that 60 percent of the lobster catchers in Maine prefer redfish to bait their traps. "Maine lobstermen bought over 10 million pounds of Canadian redfish a year to use as bait," says the Marine Resources staff.

Maine lobstermen have strong, but different opinions about their bait. What is one lobster catcher's favorite is the next lobsterman's poison.

For example in New Harbor, lobstermen will use only redfish. As for pogies — they'd stay ashore rather than bait with pogies. But five miles away, in Round Pond, other fishermen fishing the same Muscongus Bay swear by pogies. Go east to Washington County and lobstermen there won't use either redfish or pogies. They use bait bags. This means that instead of putting a fish head, spine and some meat into the trap as bait, the Washington County lobster catchers may use herring, mackerel or kajaks — fish which crumble, and so must be painstakingly "bagged" in small net bags and then put into the lobster trap as bait.

Redfish used for lobster bait by Maine fishmen is a smallish fish usually 12 to 18 inches long, with goggle eyes and spiny fin rays and it is caught in the colder waters of the northwest Atlantic.

Clarence Birdseye of Gloucester, father of the frozen food industry, was the first man to sell redfish commercially with success. He used it during the 1930's in his first quick-freezing process.

The color of the fish runs from pink to flaming red, and that color alone makes it a stand-out in the gray, cold Atlantic. But the redfish has two other unusual traits; first it bears its young alive, not as eggs; and second it may be one of the longest-living fish. A fish which weighs two pounds and is 15 inches long may be 11 or 12 years old. Whopping big redfish weighing 30 pounds and measuring 40 inches long may be over 50 years old.

When redfish are netted and hauled up to the surface they are ugly. As they are pulled up from the deep the pressure changes causes their already grotesque eyes to pop out and their internal organs often rupture. This is why you don't find fresh redfish on sale in fish-markets. But the meat on them is firm, white and suited for freezing. The fillets are marketed as Ocean Perch. They are also a prime ingredient in frozen fish sticks and fishburgers and fish sandwiches and in the miniature fishballs sold in supermarkets as cocktail nibbles.

Everyone who has watched barrels of redfish bait being hoisted onto a lobster boat knows well its rank, rich smell. On the ocean bottom it smells and tastes delicious to lobsters. The price of this bait stays high because fish meal plants also use the redfish carcass for making fish meal. Their demand keeps up the price of the carcass. Thus Canadian redfish are a good cash crop. The meat on them is sold for frozen fillets. The carcass is used for making fishmeal and for catching lobsters. This is why thousands of Maine lobstermen pay $27.50 a barrel for the leftover head and backbone. And why on some days there is no truck from Nova Scotia bringing the redfish bait to Maine fishermen.

The hard heart of the issue is this: Why must Maine depend on Canada for bait, especially when Maine's rival in the lobster market place is Canada?

Dr. Spock: Long man in short boat

NEW HARBOR — The gangling man with gray hair, hornrimmed glasses and shorts had rowed ashore from his little sailboat to negotiate a shower for his wife — the hot freshwater, tingling, soap-and-shampoo shower that seagoing wives pine for.

The man was Dr. Benjamin Spock, 75, and the shower was for his second wife, Mary Marogan, 35.

The Spocks do hair-shirt cruising. Although Dr. Spock's book, "Baby and Child Care," has sold about 29 million copies in 30 languages, the boat he sails is a little 23-foot sloop that is more than 21 years old.

I asked if he felt cramped in the tiny forward cabin as he squeezed his own 6-foot-4, 185-pound frame and his wife of some 21 months into it.

"No," he said. "When my first wife of 50 years, Jane, and I were cruising in it, we had a third bunk installed for our son. When there were three of us, quarters were cozy."

Spock's tiny sloop has been poking in and out of Maine harbors very inconspicuously for years. I saw him three years ago in New Harbor when he sailed in with Jane. Then there were some dark mutterings against his presence by the fishermen and boatsmen on the wharf. That summer, Spock, the beloved baby doctor, was more closely identified with the Boston 5.

Spock has been tried and convicted in June 1968 of conspiracy to aid, abet and counsel young men to avoid the draft for the Vietnam war. Then in 1972, he had run for president of the United States as candidate of The People's Party.

But in 1978, time had healed most of those rifts, and Spock was again welcome in New Harbor.

For instance, a red-haired young man driving a truck filled with potato chips, stopped and called out, "Are you Doctor Spock?" The truck driver lit up like a 1,000-watt bulb when Spock said "Yes" and came over to exchange handshakes, sending his best regards back home to the driver's wife.

It's easy to spot the boat of the world's most famous baby doctor. It has strange looking — but practical — canvas-and-plexiglass curtains over the cockpit.

"I spent two years worrying about how to enclose that cockpit, so we could have more living space protected from rain and fog on our tiny boat. About 20 years ago, I drew up the solution — three hoops, supporting three zippered sections of canvas and plexiglass for windows," Spock explained.

"I had a sailmaker run it up for me. And it is still in good shape 20 years later. Replaced just one frame of plexiglass.

Spock says he retired 11 years ago as professor of child development at Western University in Cleveland.

"I keep this 23-footer here to cruise Maine. And in the Virgin Islands, I keep a 35-foot ketch for cruising there. Have to have a bigger boat there so more air can circulate in that hotter climate."

Between cruising in both places, Benjamin and Mary Spock live in a new home they built facing a remote lake in her native state of Arkansas.

"You know my young wife, Mary, never set foot in a sailboat on saltwater until she married me, a year and a half ago. Now she loves it. But what she wants most right this minute is a shower."

And the tanned, happy, healthy man, looking 15 years less than 75, jumped in his dinghy. You'd never guess close to 100 million babies had been raised according to the dictum of this sailor, scrounging a shower for his bride in New Harbor.

Power of Maine tides

EASTPORT — All along our coast, the scars are there, still open, still aching.

Thousands of us saw the terrible killing power of high water and high winds. In February, 1978, our big storm wrecked a full $15 million worth of property hereabouts. Whatever man can make in a lifetime, a tide can destroy in an hour.

When you look at all that destruction, you begin to think again about how to harness that force to useful purposes. Making energy for us, perhaps?

How much energy could a giant tide produce?

Well, a nice, well-behaved tide moves four billion tons of water into Passamaquoddy Bay every day and night.

Want more? Something bigger?

Then go farther down east to the Bay of Fundy. When the tides rush in between Nova Scotia and New Brunswick, the weight of the water that tide moves is beyond comprehension — at least by me.

Those Bay of Fundy tides move 200 billion tons of water in and out twice each 24 hours.

A nice gentlemanly tide at Calais is 22 feet. For landlubbers this means that a spot where you can stand with water to your ankles at dead low tide will be covered by 22 feet of water at high tide.

South in the city of the Superbowl at New Orleans, or at the super-port of Houston, the tide is measured often in inches; maybe five, maybe 10 inches.

But Downeast at the Bay of Fundy you'll find the biggest tides in all the world, about 50 feet.

Terrifying as the power of these tides can be, the comings and go-ings of a tide can be a great comfort. Stand on a piece of our coast and be comforted by the infallible, absolute, unchangeable regularity of the rise and fall of these huge tides. So certain is their coming and going that books are in print now which show the time of high and low tide in Portland 25 years hence. And they will be right to the minute, say the Navy officials who publish them.

Each day the tide arrives 50 minutes later because the moon, 238,000 miles away, rises 50 minutes later as we see it. When the distant moon is full, the tides are highest; and when the moon is new the tide again is at its peak height.

Twice a month, at new moon and at full moon, the sun, the earth and the moon are in line. Tides respond to the pull of both sun and moon, and we get higher high tides and lower than normal low tides. These are called spring tides — no matter in what season they occur.

In the first quarter and third quarter of the moon, the tidal forces of sun and moon oppose each other and this results in tides which are lower than average high tides and higher than average low tides. These are called neap tides.

A boatman along the Maine coast can benefit by these rules. The moon, assisted by the sun at new and full moon, picks up a wave and carries it westward along the shore from the Bay of Fundy. High water is 30 minutes to an hour before the moon crosses the meridian. The water, released by each previous wave, runs east to join the next one coming, so the tidal current in general runs east on the flood and west on the ebb. It is a sound rule-of-thumb, but there are many exceptions; for instance the tide ebbing out of Blue Hill Bay runs east across the Bass Harbor Bar; and off Two Bush at the entrance of Penobscot Bay, the current seems to run west constantly; and in Saco Bay, the set seems to be northwest on both ebb and flood.

Stand on any piece of coast and watch the tides. And be comforted that no force is able to alter their predictable rise and fall by so much as a minute. Whether war breaks out in the Middle East, whether there are earthquakes in Iran, whether Carter runs for another term, whether you make a million or go broke — none of these things will have the faintest effect on the time of the tide at your feet.

Glory in the morning

ATOP BUTTER ISLAND — I have been watching a
new day being born. From the top of Butter Island in Penobscot Bay,
a man can see all the miracle of creation.

Look east and you see the sun rising out of the Atlantic and the
first rays kiss the top of Cadillac Mountain on Mount Desert Island.
A new day has dawned over the United States; and like all new days
in America, it began here on the coast of Maine.

The lovely light spreads quickly. Island after island after island
lights up and wakens. The dark green island pines which had been
reflected black in the flat, calm sea are touched by the sun. They
change color to a lighter, livelier green; and the wet black island rocks
turn bright gold and the reflections in the calm ocean become a rippling mixture of greens, yellows and gold.

Now the sun suddenly hits a lobster boat, out hauling early. And
those first brilliant sun rays transform that work-stained hull for a
magic moment into startling scintillating white. You hear the beat of its
engine, carried for miles across the empty sea. The only other noise
in the world is the sound of two gulls squabbling and a young osprey
squeaking for breakfast in a soprano too high for so big a bird.

Now the whole bay is filled with the new day. All traces of dark
night have been miraculously washed away from sea, sky and islands
in the few short minutes I stood atop Butter Island, watching a new
day being born.

Raspberries grow wild and wonderful here. I eat a handful cold
from the night and spiced with the morning. Pivot on your heels,
and spread out through 360 degrees below you is a miracle of creation
as that makes joy and amazement and gratitude run through your
veins. Dozens of Maine islands appear before you in all directions.

There is Duck Harbor Mountain on Isle au Haut; Sargent and
Cadillac mountains on Mt. Desert; look north and you think you can
see fire-scarred Mt. Katahdin, the early day is so clear. Look land-

ward and marvel at how the sun is painting the rolling Camden hills with astonishing hues.

The whole day is here now. The miracle of standing alone, atop an island, watching a perfect new day be born, is over. You climb down the steep paths.

The smells of morning are sweet and strong. Wild bayberry mingled with wild roses and the salt sea air; there is a wondrous smell to breathe deep and hold in your lungs; and breathe again to remember.

The "Steer Clear," our small blue boat, looks so tiny and frail, resting on her anchor line in the cove far below.

Down on the beach, I drag the dinghy noisily across small rocks, into the cold ocean. The thought of a skinny-dip is enticing; but that sea is bone-chilling cold from the night.

I row out to my boat, slowly, and on the way I see a shag dive, catch his fish; and that cormorant seems to have a silly grin on its face as it sits on the water, with a flat fish drooping and squirming out both sides of its beak — and slowly the bird swallows breakfast. Aboard, I put bacon in the pan, and soon that fine open-air smell of smoked bacon cooking fills my hungry world.

The islands along the coast of Maine are where our nation began. Here the first explorers made their first landfalls. Imagine the shouts of joy aboard those small, wet, cold ships when the crew saw the first sight of land after crossing the Atlantic.

These islands were the first centers of trade and fishing, hundreds of years ago. Then they became fine farm communities, too.

This Butter Island, for example, used to have a flourishing year round population. It had a town called Dirigo. It had a school, church, post office — even a summer hotel. But now nobody lives there. Nobody farms there. Only cellar holes mark their passage.

But today's owner, Thomas D. Cabot of High Street, Boston, has put small metal tags on some of the trees along the shore. The tags state that this is the Avelinda forest. And the owner hopes you will enjoy its beauty. He asks that you do not smoke, that you build no fires and that you leave the island as clean as you found it.

One man-made sight is still firing my imagination. In a tiny clearing, 30 feet back from the beach, I found a table, made like a tiny raft. It stood only 12 inches off the ground, was two feet wide and three feet long. In its center was a small piece of orange carpet. In the center of the orange carpet was a circle of grey stones. In the center of the stone circle was a vase, and in the vase was an offering of wildflowers, now dead. Did some one have a little dinner party seated here? Or did someone build it as a kind of altar?

Keeping lobsters back is tricky business

DEER ISLE — Keeping lobsters is a tricky business, about as risky as playing the stock market.

And you keep lobsters for the same reason you play the market — to make money. To win, you buy low, sell high.

Right now there may be a million pounds and more of lobsters being kept in pounds along the Maine coast. Maine has the pound capacity to store six million pounds of lobsters.

A big lobster pound is a fascinating place which relatively few people ever see.

Essentially, a lobster pound is a live stockpile of lobsters kept in a contained area and sometimes given controlled feedings. In this way, a pound for lobsters is a bit like the fattening up, grain feeding yard for beef cattle. The idea is to fatten up the lobster too, and thus get far more money for a fatter lobster than you paid for a thinner lobster.

But if you can make a pile, you can just as easily lose your shirt running a lobster pound.

For example, lobsters can and do escape in large numbers. Overnight, you can get a mass escape of maybe $10,000 or $20,000 worth through an undiscovered break in the 'wall,' out of sight, far below the water line.

Lobsters are cannibals. The strong eat the weak.

Lobsters get sick. Disease can spread like wildfire among them, and can kill off all the profit overnight.

A disease called redtail is the dread killer. Some pound owners have lost more than half their stock in a season from redtail. That means losing half their money.

Pollution can kill lobsters. A bit of oil on their gills spells sudden death.

If the incoming tide fails to mix new oxygen with the old water deep down at the bottom of the pound, the lobsters lying on the bottom may die, asphyxiated from lack of fresh oxygen.

But, of course there is the good side, the money making side to keeping a lobster pound.

If all goes well, you may buy at 90 cents a pound and sell at $1.90 or more.

If you do this with 100,000 pounds, you have made $100,000. Stated another way, you may have laid out $90,000 to buy lobsters in the Fall and taken in $190,000 or more for the same lobsters in February.

On Southport Island, there are two lobster pounds, one with a capacity for 150,000 pounds, the other with a 100,000 pound capacity.

At Friendship, there is a six acre pound that can hold over a quarter million pounds of lobster. (This pound got hit catastrophically in November 1963 by an oil spill.)

Other big pounds are at Milbridge, Hancock, Hewlett Island, Boothbay, Deer Isle, Vinalhaven, Small Point.

There are two dozen or more pounds in Maine with capacities from 50,000 up to 450,000 pounds.

The biggest is the old Consolidated pound at Hancock, with a capacity of almost half a million pounds.

Together, these kinds of lobster pounds have a total capacity for holding 4.3 million pounds of lobster.

In addition, another million pounds can be held in big 'cars,' which are huge crates floating in harbors which hold about 1,000 pounds each.

Then there are tanks of circulating water in which another 850,000 pounds of lobster can be held for serving up immediately to customers.

Robert Dow, of Maine's Department of Marine Resources says the two biggest seasons for holding vast quantities of lobster are in spring and fall.

"In late spring, pound owners may buy heavily from Canada. Their lobster catching season ends by June. So in May, Maine dealers may stock up and hold those Canadian lobsters to serve to tourists in July."

Lobsters kept in a pound can be better controlled, so that they are the more desirable 'hard shells,' available when most Maine lobsters are 'soft shells' and shedders. So as hard shells, they bring a premium price.

"Next big holding season is to buy heavily in the Fall, and hold and fatten the lobsters for sale in March, when the price is highest and the catch is scarce because of foul weather," says Dow.

Lobstermen themselves often hold back their catch till the price goes up. They have crates, each holding 80 pounds, which they may tie onto their moorings. Sometimes it works well, and they can hold to sell on a rising market. Other times, they wish they'd sold at any price. For example, Fred Boynton of New Harbor recalls the day he was down in the harbor and a friend came along wanting 35 pounds of lobster for his little girl's birthday party. "I went down and hauled a crate of my lobsters. Found a few dead. So I hauled my other crates. Found 200 dead in five crates. Well, it had been awful calm down there with no wind or circulation, and there was a lot of seaweed caught around the float and I think they smothered for lack of oxygen. The only other thing I can figure out; one of those draggers came in yesterday foɪ water, and of course his cooling water discharge was going overboard right near my crates. It's possible he heated the water up. Well, we repacked what we had left and towed them off to a mooring in the middle of the harbor, and we're watching it carefully now."

Lastly, there is the human predator.

It is known that some scoundrels in outboards come into a strange harbor in the nighttime, which they have 'cased' in daylight. They cut loose some crates, tow them to a cove nearby, empty them and steal another man's livelihood.

Along the coast, that is a dangerous game. And not many fools risk trying it.

But 'keeping lobsters,' hoping the increase in price will more than offset losses in the pound, is the Maine coast version of 'playing the stockmarket.'

Loons, shags and sandpipers

ABOARD STEER CLEAR — Seven loons are laughing, diving and fishing, within 100 feet of where we are anchored in Muscongus Bay. Never before have we seen so many loons at once, so close.

The loons came very early this morning. They were fishing here at first light. And first light today was thin, watery, ghostly. A mere glimmer of sun vainly trying to brush away the white cocoon of fog that swathed the world.

A westerly wind blew and moved the wraiths of fog mysteriously across the mirror-flat, steely-surface of the sea. Out of this eerie white vapor came the wild cry of the loons laughing. For a moment, it sounded like the cry of the world at birth.

Then as the loons laughed again and again, crying back and forth to each other, they overdid it. The eeriness was laid on so thick and the fog was so ghostly, that it all seemed like the spooky sound track out of a bad movie.

That was when the birds drifted into sight on the current. One by one, they hove into sight until all seven of them were in a tight circle. As they fished, some would disappear under the water. Sometimes only one or two would be on the surface. Then five. Then none. Then seven. Then three.

The young loons seemed a soft, pearly gray. The adults were black necked, with black backs flecked with a checkerboard of white.

Whenever I aimed my camera, half of them would duck. When I lowered the camera, all seven would surface, glance my way, then duck again as I tried for a picture.

These loons, I think, are out here on salt water only for a summer holiday. They do not nest here, where a receding tide can leave 100 feet of dangerous ground between nest and water.

Loons cannot walk on or fly from dry land. They would be too easy a target for predators out here. So they build their nests at the edge of fresh water lakes. When danger threatens there, they can just slide out of the nest into the lake.

Once on water, they are fast-swimming experts who can dive to safety, hide far below the surface for a long time and swim out of sight to surface far from the spot where they were sighted. But, happily for boatmen, the loons like to summer out by the islands.

The smallest seabirds are my favorites. I admire the ospreys, which look like small eagles. The cormorants — or old black shags — are the hallmarks of the Maine coast, sitting atop buoys, wings held out to dry like so much laundry.

I can't imagine why God made a seabird which is underwater half its life without putting any oil into its wings. The poor shag's wings just will not dry as do the oily wings of all other seabirds. And the gangly herons, standing one-legged and motionless in quiet coves, are yet another hallmark of the Maine coast. At Wreck Island, in Muscongus Bay, I admire hundreds of herons nesting high in the trees.

But my favorites are the tiny birds. I love to see them scamper on spindly legs for food on the flats at low tide. They are the sand-pipers and the phalaropes. There are 30 kinds of sandpipers in North America. As a rank amateur in bird watching, I know only a few. The spotted sandpiper, with thrush-like spots, is teetering around everywhere, bold as brass. The cunning sanderling plays tag with the waves, racing out on tiny legs as each wave recedes, grabbing some invisible speck of seafood on its trailing edge; then as the next waves come in, the sanderling wheels and races just ahead of it up the beach. There is something funny about this tiny seabird working to keep its feet dry.

But the one I love best has the least lovely name. It is called the semipalmated sandpiper and has dark legs that flick along at such speed they seem to be a gray blur. They are no bigger than a sparrow — except for those long spindly legs. They have a kissing cousin called by the delightful name of the least sandpiper. These have yellowish legs. And there is no prettier sight on a beach at low tide than the sight of these lively, lovely, delicate, tiny seabirds racing on matchstick legs across wet, food-filled sands.

Mountains under your hull

ABOARD STEER CLEAR II — We are cautiously poking our way deeper into the cove. The 'flasher' on the electronic depth finder reports 20-22-18-14-19-20 feet of water under the hull, and we drop anchor. We'll be safe here for the night. Tidetables show a nine foot drop from high water, as we anchor, until low tide six hours hence. Even then we'll have a safe 11 feet of water under us.

We are just off George's Harbor, tucked in behind Allen island, sheltered from the southerly wind. Just over the bow, on a hill at the shore, is a granite cross. The stone cross marks the spot where George Weymouth landed in 1605 from this same cove, and held the first Protestant church service north of Virginia.

Settled on the anchor, dug in firmly, long rode out, I think about Weymouth and his crew anchoring in this same spot, 374 years ago. No depth finder for him. No compass like mine, either. No chart to show the rocks and shallows; no buoys to mark the ledges that will rip out the bottom of a boat. Some boats of the early voyagers were only twice as big as mine. But they came across the Atlantic to unknown, uncharted coasts and explored. Weymouth's chart from Monhegan to Kennebec is astoundingly accurate, even compared to the newest issue by the Coast and Geodetic Survey.

We row ashore in the moonlight and stand by the Weymouth cross, thinking about that crew and their vessel anchored here long, long ago. Our wish is that someone from that crew somehow knows that down here in 1978, somebody is standing where they once stood, marvelling at their seamanship, which got them here safely — and back again. We will go back on board, turn on the VHF and get tomorrow's weather, speak to other ships and friends on shore by telephone. Tidetables tell us their essential facts, other tables reveal the current and drift here, and charts tell us all the hazards. Those amazing voyagers had the stars and a lead line and perhaps the best seat of the pants known to mariners.

Was ignorance a bit of bliss, too? They knew not what was under their frail hulls. The depthfinders of today can tell us not only if there are five or 5,000 or more feet under us, but a good Maine fisherman can tell whether the bottom is muddy, rocky, sandy or mountainous. He can read the printout from a depthfinder, so he knows each nook and cranny, each hill and valley, each flat pasture down there as well as he knows the countryside around his home on shore. He knows the spots the fish like best.

The most fantastic map of the Atlantic floor that I have seen hangs on the wall of the admiral at Brunswick Naval Air Station. He uses that three dimensional map of the ocean floor to find submarines, not fish. He knows the mountain passes and gullies where Soviet subs hide and wait.

The biggest mountain range in the world lies out there, under the Atlantic ocean. It is 10,000 miles long and 500 miles wide, reaching from Iceland to Antarctica. Near the Azores, the ocean floor is 20,000 feet— almost four miles — down. Then the wild mountain range races up to the top of the ocean; breaks surface and rises on up and up to Mount Pico, in the same Azores, towering 7,613 feet above the Atlantic surface.

I've sailed those innocent, tropical blue waters between the Virgin Islands and Puerto Rico; lolling in the sun, it is scary to think of the Brownson Deep under you, reaching 30,432 feet down, close to six miles of ocean deep.

Weymouth and the early sailors knew none of this terrifying knowledge. The ocean on which we sail happily and confidently in such small boats, is the world's biggest cover-up. We call our planet Earth, but, in fact, 70 per cent of it is Ocean. Under our ships are mountains higher than the Alps and the Himalayas. But until the invention of sonar, we hardly knew the ocean as anything but a vast watery plain. You could put Mount Everest into it, and lose it — covered by a mile or two of ocean.

Not far off the coast of Maine lies one such incredible mountain. It rises up out of the Atlantic Abyss into what is called the Slope of Newfoundland. On the ocean charts, you can see the depths changing from 13,482 feet to 9,000 and then to 6,000. Then in a few short miles these underwater mountain peaks get higher and higher until they form that huge plateau called the Grand Banks. Here is such a range of high mountains that the ocean is only 500, to as little 100 feet deep, and sometimes less. Here are the richest fishing grounds in all the world.

The Atlantic, like all other oceans, has three main parts to it. The Continental Shelf; the Slope and the Abyss. The Shelf of all the oceans in the world amounts to only about seven percent of the ocean and it is shallow, with water averaging only 432 feet deep, whereas, the mean depth of the oceans is 13,000 feet deep. The drop-off on the Shelf — really land covered now by ocean — is so gradual that a human eye could not detect it. The change in depth is, on average, only 15 feet in a mile.

But it is on this small amount of Shelf that most of the fish and plants of the sea live. They can flourish only where sunlight penetrates strongly enough for photosynthesis, needed for most fish and plant life. In murky inland waters, you can barely get enough sunlight at 25 feet deep to see by; but in clear offshore waters the depth of photosynthesis can be as much as 400 feet.

The Shelf turns into the Slope. Here are terrifying cliffs, escarpments, precipitous gorges, jagged mountain peaks higher, steeper than most on land. But even the slopes amount to only 15 percent of the ocean; the rest is the Abyss, a name signifying the dark, silent, unknown, alien world that man has never been able to penetrate — yet.

Sitting peacefully at anchor on the surface, it is hard to imagine that mysterious, alien world, where there is total darkness, total silence, far beyond the reach of sun. No rage of the storms on the ocean surface can cause a ripple down there. Down in that blackness, pressure is said to be seven tons per inch. Can any weird animal possibly lurk and live down there with that weight on his neck?

But down there may be the secrets of our world. Scientists who probe the ocean abyss with seismic soundings report that much of the bottom core is covered with soft sediment. These scientists say that sediment is miles thick, and they estimate that it takes 2,500 years for one inch of sediment to accumulate.

This most mysterious ocean remains man's ultimate challenge, as it was the first birthplace of life on earth.

Days of the 25-pound lobster

HEWETT ISLAND — Last night we anchored and slept in a small cove off a small island in the Muscle Ridge Channel. Mid-September until early October can be the best time of all for cruising the Maine coast. The days sparkle, fog is short lived, the air has a nip.

You have most islands and coves to yourself. There is wine in the sea breeze. You can see forever across Penobscot Bay. And the other cruising boats are pretty well gone. Last night we were alone. Or almost.

Ken and his family came out to their summer shack. Ken is one of the few lobstermen who move out to live and lobster from the islands in the summer. The summer shacks are simple, basic shelters, and the youngsters grow brown and strong before returning home by Labor Day for school.

Last night, as Ken's lobsterboat came chugging in to the harbor, we waved, shouted greetings and watched them unload. They carried their bundles up the grassy path to the shack, from which the kerosene lamp was soon sending out its golden yellow glow.

"We're here just to clean her out for winter," Ken told me as he sculled in with a single oar off the stern of his dinghy. "We'll batten down, close up and go ashore again for good tomorrow."

After awhile, the kerosene light in the kitchen goes out. Briefly, another goes on in the bedroom — the only other room in Ken's summer place. Then that goes dark.

It is now almost 10 p.m. The wind is down to a soft breeze, southwesterly — just enough to ripple the moon's sheen on the empty ocean. I go on deck. There is no sound here. No birds make night noises on the little island. The only thing we hear is the lap of waves, kissing our hull, and the gurgle of the tide running in and out through the rocks of Ken's wharf. Not that everything is still: I can see the lights of draggers working out beyond Hurricane and the White Islands.

I go down to the cockpit and turn on a lamp to read a pamphlet about Maine lobstering 100 years ago. I found it recently in that treasure house of old books — L. Berliawsky of Camden. Mrs. Berliawsky has reprinted from Scribner's Monthly Magazine of 1881 an article called "The Lobster at Home in Maine Waters," written by W. H. Bishop, and illustrated with a dozen wonderful drawings.

According to Bishop, the traps and the lobsters were both bigger and heavier than they are today.

"The traps have the appearance of mammoth bird cages. Each structure is four feet long, two feet wide and two feet high," wrote Bishop in 1881. "The bait used is a cod's head or a row of cunners arranged on perpendicular hooks within. The lobsterman has 150 such traps covering a circuit five or six miles in extent . . . A lobsterman with his dory filled with a pile of these curious cages ventures far out to sea, often at no little personal risk."

I look over at Ken's 36-foot diesel-powered boat with its hydraulic gear for bringing in traps that are smaller and lighter than those described by Bishop. I think of those Maine lobstermen in dories and sloops, hand-hauling heavy traps up from 100 and 150 feet. Traps that were weighed down with rocks — and heavy lobsters.

According to Bishop, writing in 1881, "A mature lobster should measure without the claws from one to two feet long and weigh from two to 15 pounds . . . Lobster have been taken as heavy as 25 pounds. At South Saint George, below Rockland, hangs the claw of a lobster which in life weighed 43 pounds."

In those days of 1881, lobster smacks travelled from cove to cove and harbor to harbor, buying lobsters. One smack came to buy the bigger lobsters, bound to market in New York and Boston mostly.

The other smack-buyer came from the nearby lobster-canning factory. Canned lobsters were a huge Maine business then. One canning company, alone, had 23 different canning plants along the coast. Bishop describes some of their operations:

"The canning factory opens at one end to the sea and the wharf. Two men bring in squirming loads of lobster on a stretcher and dump the mass into coppers for boiling. Dense clouds of steam arise, through which we catch vista of men, women and children at work.

The boiled lobsters are thrown into carving tables. Men with knives separate them into constituent parts and then the meat is put into cans. The first girl puts in a suitable selection of parts. The next weighs it (one or two pounds). The next forces down the contents with a stamp invented for the purpose. The next puts on a tin cover with blows of a little hammer. They are carried to the solderers who seal them tight . . . then they are plunged into bath cauldrons and boiled . . . "

Solderers made top money, says Bishop, being paid $12 to $15 a week. The girls got no more than $3.50. "Yet, even at this price, a respectable class of female labor is engaged. This is not so remarkable when the wages of school-keeping have been reduced to $2 a week."

Nine-tenths of the canned lobster was sold to foreign markets.

A law in Maine then, prohibited the canning of lobsters, except between the first of March and the first of August.

As soon as lobster-canning stopped, the canning of sweet corn started. The corn-factories and the lobster-factories were owned largely by the same companies. Some felt they got the lobster-canning season law passed so they could have a ready supply of solderers. Bishop quotes a local informant as saying: "It ain't in the interest of the lobster, nor yet of the public. The factory owners wants the sawderers down to Freeport and Gorham for cannin' the corn — that's how it is; and they don't want no one else a-goin' on with cannin' lobsters when they ain't at it."

In a hundred years, these offshore islands haven't changed much. Nor have the pet peeves of Maine lobstermen — that too many traps are out, that prices are too low, that the big dealers rig the prices to suit them. But lobsters keep right on being caught in almost the same kind of traps — and taste as good as they did almost 100 years ago.

Goodbye to summer love

NEW HARBOR — Her mooring is empty now.

The white and blue styrofoam marker bobs alone on the cold grey water, and no boat will come. The nylon pennant line streams out on the tide, waiting and available for a boat hook to reach out, snag her and tie up. But the Steer Clear will come no more this year.

My boat has gone up the railway.

It is a mean and brutal end to a wondrously lovely summer, which Steer Clear has given.

The faithful boat with strangers board her, is towed ignominiously toward shore, and jockeyed onto a great cradle, half hidden in the water. Safely in the wooden-armed cradle, a steel hawser is hooked, like a bridge, to each side of the cradle; and the other end of the hawser is on a winch, mounted on a truck in the boatyard. The brute strength of the truck is put to work; shouts and waves are signals from boat to truck. Slowly inch by inch, then foot by foot, finally yard by reluctant yard, Steer Clear is pulled up out of her natural element, the water, and hauled up the railway onto dry land. High and dry in the yard, she is manoeuvred to the line of boats where she will winter; then, final shame, she is shoved sideways like a crab to the slot where she'll sit, swathed in dank cold tarpaulins until the sun of April comes again.

Putting a boat away is a miserable time to a cruisingman. To me, seeing that boat go up the ways to dry land signals an ending more final, more significant than the Times Square clock and the Times Square balloon at midnight, New Year's Eve, signalling year's end. Maybe this is because there is no crowd. There is no band playing Auld Lang Syne. No champagne corks pop. No kissing. Just the wet hull of a boat dripping as she is hauled out.

Perhaps owners of summer camps and cottages feel just as miserable when they nail boards over windows, throw sheets over furniture, pull down blinds to lock out daylight for months ahead, slam shut the doors and turn the final key.

You can't put your arms around a boat or a cottage and kiss 'em goodbye, and thank them. So you turn your back and walk to the car, start the engine and roar away, brutal farewell.

Goodbye to summer love. On, on to the new joys of November in the fall woods, and then the ski slopes of winter. Can a person be loyal to a boat? Faithful to a cottage?

The last days aboard are sweet memories of Indian summer. Parting with Steer Clear was gentler this year. We brought her up river in October. In our last small ocean cruise, we left New Harbor, rounded Pemaquid and then decided to turn out to sea a while; and went past the white surf breaking at Thrumcap, past the underwater outcroppings of the Threads of Life, magical name for islets. We ran out seaward, past The Hypocrites, and blew the horn at Ram Island Light. From now till May, we shall see the beam of that light at night only from a bed on shore. We make a final visit to Damariscove Island, and drop anchor and walk that wild old land where first settlers walked and salted cod and waited all winter long for a sail from England to arrive with springtime. Then late in the afternoon we turned toward land and for two hours cruised slowly up the Damariscotta River. Much of the river looks as it must have looked 300 and 400 years ago, when Indians paddled up this same river from the islands, heading to winter camps. Damariscotta is the Indian word meaning 'river of many fishes'. Huge, heaps of oyster shells left hundreds of years ago by Indians testify to the feasts and revels they enjoyed along the river bank.

Near the Damariscotta town dock, we tie to a friend's mooring and unload. Unload so much stuff that we fill a station wagon three times, before the boat is bare. Sad work. Each item is spiced with summer memories. The wooden picnic basket that almost got left on the summit of Isle au Haut; the boat cushion stained from sun oil on a hot day on the ledge at St. Helena. A rod — brings back the flash of the tuna that threw the hook. I pack the sky map, splotched with salt spray and back to vivid life come the magic nights when velvet heavens sparkled with a million bright stars; and the sea was so still at a remote island that the reflection of every star stared up out of the ocean to its twin in the sky.

Goodbye summer love.

V
ON THE JOB IN MAINE

G ET A MAN or woman talking about what they do for a living, and I'm the world's best listener. As a result, hundreds of old friends lay spread across my office floor, while I tried to select among them the stories for this section. Now that I've made a choice, limited by available pages, I'm bugged by the worry that scores of more interesting jobs in Maine are back in boxes instead of being included here.

Watch out for the government statistics about work in Maine. Problem is not only that statistics lie; but also that Maine people lie to the statisticians. When snoopers ask Mainers how much they make, they get lied to, often. This is the Mainer's polite way of saying: 'It's none of your business; and I'll fix your wagon for asking.'

So average incomes in Maine are, according to statistics, close to the bottom, in national comparisons. But I recall a barber who used to cut my hair. He had a little house in town; summer camp on the lake; a boat with a 50 h.p. motor, so his daughter could water ski behind it when she came home from college; and every November he went deer hunting from another camp in Washington County, jointly owned by himself and three friends. The government statisticians had that barber making $200 a week. What is true for barbers is true for lobster catchers, loggers, people who sell appliances and fix the plumbing. Lawyers and doctors in Maine do well enough here to turn down offers from the cities.

Granite quarry worker, Deer Isle.

Sure, there is too much poverty in Maine; too many Maine people are forever on the brink of physical distress from hunger and cold. But the worst situation in Maine is probably better than the worst in Detroit or Newark, if only because you can get out of it in five minutes.

Salaries and wages are lower in Maine than in most states. And the cost of living is higher. Food, gas, property taxes, needed heating oil and heavy clothes for winter all are high priced here.

Maine may not make economic sense measured by gross dollars made.

If the yardstick is quality of life, then I choose Maine.

Maybe that is why people seem happier in Maine than elsewhere. They are here because mostly they want to be here.

About 35,000 new people move here each year. Mostly they are young, between 20 and 35. Mostly they are high earners, with college education, mostly married with young kids. They come because they seek the quality of life they think Maine offers.

Here are stories of a few people working in Maine, happily.

Captain of O'Hara fishing boat

ROCKLAND — I've spent the day with the Frank J. O'Hara fishing fleet and fish processing plant on the Rockland waterfront. And the first words I want to write are: clean, spanking-clean, prosperous and happy.

O'Hara has six steel-hulled trawlers, each about 125 feet long, fishing out of Rockland, handsome vessels, all freshly painted in O'Hara blue and white.

Family pride may be the best ship-cleaner. Four of the ships are named for the family, the Bradley O'Hara, the Francis O'Hara, the Dorothy O'Hara and the Robert O'Hara, and a new million-dollar stern trawler being built at the Harvey Gamage yard in South Bristol is called the Araho, O'Hara spelled backwards.

One skipper tells me why the boats are spanking clean.

"Frankie O'Hara requires it — that's why. We can muck the boat up while we are at sea 10 to 16 days. But by the time we get dockside and before we go ashore for four days, the skipper is responsible for leaving a spotless bridge; the engineer, for a clean engine room; the cook, for a clean galley; and the two crewmen, for a clean fo'csle. We hear about it if any one leaves part of the boat in a mess."

Prosperity seems to go hand-in-glove with cleanliness. Captain Timmy Asbury, 51 who usually skippers the Massachusetts, says most O'Hara crew members earned $30,000 or more last year — a good fishing year for this fleet.

Skippers made more — probably between $45,000 and $60,000.

The skipper and crew divide equally 60 percent of the value of the catch after deductions for fuel and food and for ice to keep the fish refrigerated. On a 12 day trip the boat might use 4,000 gallons of diesel fuel at a cost of $3,000; food, for five men who eat well, runs over $500; and they'd buy up to 60 tons of ice.

The owner of the vessel gets 40 percent of the value of the catch, and pays back 10 percent of that as a bonus to the skipper.

Sounds good. But the workweek can be 100 hours, in foul and dangerous weather with no guarantee of a good catch.

There is no pay while they are on shore, seeing their families for three or four days, before they go off to sea for another two weeks.

Redfish, called ocean perch, are caught 140 miles offshore, by dragging nets along the ocean floor. A good catch of redfish, after 12 days at sea, is about 120,000 pounds, plus an incidental catch of 20,000 pounds of groundfish such as sole, haddock, pollock. The nets aboard an O'Hara vessel cost about $16,000.

It is often hard to buy fresh fish in Maine, despite all the fish caught by Maine boats. The market is Boston; and that is where Maine fish go. Price paid to fishermen seems very low to retail customers. A fishing boat may get 18 cents or less for a pound of ocean perch which retails at 90 cents; or 50 cents a pound for cusk in midwinter; or 80 cents for haddock which retails at $2.00 or more. Fish dealers say that one reason is they must trim away over half the weight of the fish before it gets to a retail customer.

Capt. Asbury says his richest catch was of swordfish, a couple of years back in 1975-76, "We got 96,000 pounds of swordfish when the price was $1.65 a pound. That catch was worth about $153,000. Each crewman got about $14,000 for that 17 day trip."

Swordfish are caught on a trawl or line that may stretch out 20 miles, carry 1500 hooks about 100 feet apart, each baited with a big mackerel.

The summer of the big catch out on Georges Bank, the swordfish averaged 137 pounds each, with big ones topping 700 pounds. "We live on memories like that and in hopes it will happen again. We need to, when we are wet, seasick, cold and catching nothing in a storm and know we won't head home for two more weeks," says a swordfisherman.

It takes a special madness to be a Maine fisherman in winter. Some of the finest are aboard the O'Hara fleet; and others wish they were.

Maine's gaming girls go to sea

ABOARD CARIBE — Four girl croupiers aboard this cruise ship - ferry between Portland and Yarmouth, Nova Scotia, deal the cards, spin the roulette wheels, take in the long green and pay off the bets in the gaming room.

The pay is good ($12,000 to $17,000 a year, plus air fares to and from England). The hours are long — from 9 p.m. till 4 a.m., and sometimes longer; plus an afternoon shift from 3 p.m. till 7 p.m. The training is intense, taken at special schools run by the gambling clubs of London.

"And it is hell on your back — standing and leaning over the tables hours on end," say the girls.

Since thousands of Maine people gamble on Portland's mini-cruise ships, the gaming girls are a sliver of Maine life.

The girl croupiers who told me about the life and earnings and training are Lynne Bulloch, a pert brunette from Sydney, Australia, and the senior croupier aboard; twin sisters Linda Lindquist and Dawn Danisi, who used to work in London's Playboy and Penthouse clubs ("In the Playboy, we girls wear bunny tails; in the Penthouse we are dressed up in frilly lace pants to look like French maids"); and Lynne Parker, a long-haired, almost platinum blonde with green eyeshadow and a figure which must have caused consternation in Blackpool and Manchester, where she used to work.

Miss Bulloch left Sydney for London 10 years ago. As a highly trained radiographer she spent five years doing diagnostic X-ray work in London hospitals.

"I got sick of socialized medicine and the life and money of a hospital technician. So I answered a Club Mecca ad and learned to become a croupier." Out of the 200 girls who answer such ads, 40 finish training and obtain a license from the British government, Lynne guesses. She estimates a dozen are still wheeling and dealing two years later. The training takes two months.

"At first, your hands and arms ache enough to make you weep until you develop the muscles needed to pick up chips, lean over tables, sweep up and deal out cards for hours on end. We learn to count chips instantly by touch. We are taught all the ins and outs of at least one game — 21 or roulette, usually. Then we must learn our numbers."

This means the girls must be able to multiply instantly the complicated odds of any combinations bet in roulette. Dawn Danisi told me her father had hopes that she would become a chartered accountant. But she turned her bent for math into the gambling business and at 17 became the youngest croupier in England, a better paying job. She is now married to a chef aboard Caribe.

The girls in the London clubs get about $1,000 a year extra for makeup and hairdressing; they are kept supplied with fine looking evening dresses; they get limousine service home at 4 a.m. It is considered a glamorous, high-paying job. But many of the top clubs start the girls at 18 and put them out to pasture at 24.

As for men, a croupier girl's life is filled with them — on the other side of the table.

"The table is a physical barrier and a mental gulf. We are taught to keep it that way. Charming and efficient with the punters — and no more."

The girls say they enjoy shipboard life, mostly in the Caribbean on weekly cruises.

"It is an unreal world. But we are in the work to make money and save it. That is easier at sea. All of us seem to be saving for a root — a home and family and an ordinary quiet life. This is a good way to get it," says Lynne Bulloch. And she steps back, cool, efficient and pretty to deal an hour of blackjack.

roupier, far left, at sea off Maine.

Yvonne, lady of the traps

ISLES OF SHOALS — Yes, that is a lady going single-handed in her 22-foot lobster boat, setting out traps by Appledore Island, several miles out from Kittery.

She is Yvonne Sullivan, a brown-eyed blonde.

"Lobstering is a great job for a girl," she told me. "I paid for my new 22-foot lobster boat last year thanks to my lobstering. I wish I had started fishing a long while ago. I've been married to Rodney Sullivan 15 years and helped him go lobstering often. But I didn't start going myself till three years ago. Began small, in a skiff with just a few traps and gradually added more. Then last year I got my own 22-foot fiberglass boat and I'm setting out 250 traps this year. Hauling 100 traps a day."

A number of women go lobstering along the Maine coast. Most go with their husbands, as helpers on fine days. Others have a skiff and an outboard, and fish a few traps close to shore. Very few have their own lobster boat, their own traps and go single-handed several miles off the mainland as Yvonne Sullivan does.

"She is a darn good, serious lobsterman," I was told by her neighbor, J. Russell Smith, who retired recently after 36 years building submarines in the Kittery Navy Yard. "There are not many as good as her along the coast. Maybe she'll talk to you about her lobstering."

With that, Russell Smith drove me to the Sullivan home and Yvonne talked to me in her finely equipped mainland kitchen about lobstering from the Sullivan cottage out on Appledore Island in the Isles of Shoals.

When it comes to lobstering, the Isles of Shoals are a bit like Monhegan farther down the coast. By tradition, the islands are soverign territory. "A fellow doesn't set traps close in to the Isles unless his family comes from one of those islands. He doesn't fuss around, if he's smart, unless he belongs there," said Russell Smith.

The Sullivan family does indeed belong on Appledore Island. "Rodney's father fished from there. And his father before him. And back through generations, Sullivans have fished from Appledore. Now

Rodney David and I live there and lobster out of there May till November," said Yvonne Sullivan. Rodney goes in a bigger 37-foot boat, fishes more traps farther out.

"I only lobster in summer, from Appledore, and my traps are within two miles of the island. But I make all my own traps. Built 50 new ones this winter. Rodney hires men to build his for him. But I can't knit the heads."

America's roots run deep into these Isles of Shoals. Early in the 1600s Captain John Smith charted these islands and called them the Smith islands. Fishing was so good that 500 people lived here by 1670, although all seven islands total lses than 300 acres. Yvonne Sullivan is out there now, lobstering in Sullivan waters from May till November. Once women were barred from setting foot on the Isles of Shoals.

Sudsy, trainer of the Mariners

PORTLAND — What can a new fan write about the Maine Mariners when experts fill the sports pages? So I asked Ed Anderson, who was a reporter on the Portland Press Herald and is now president of the ice hockey team, for a look backstage.

"Let me talk to the guy who sharpens the skates," I said. And that's how I met Dave (Sudsy) Settlemyre and went backstage to find the story on 50,000 pucks and 125 dozen sticks and why one player gets his blades sharpened flat and why another wants his blades "rockered" so he can "deke" better.

Sudsy himself took me by surprise. He's not just the expert skate sharpener; he's the trainer. Meet Sudsy in a Portland bistro and he's the last man you'd guess to be the trainer of the 22 Maine Mariner players.

Sudsy, 27, and bearded, is soft-spoken, with a gentle southern drawl; and he's little. My guess is that he stands 5-foot-five and weighs about 125 pounds.

"I'm small because I stopped growing when I was 13," says Sudsy. "And I talk soft and southern because I was raised in Greensboro, North Carolina. And I'm a trainer because I'm hockey-crazy and too darned small to play professional."

But today the tiny Sudsy is trainer of the 22 Maine Mariners who together weigh 4,400 pounds and end to end stretch 135 feet — without the skates and the equipment which Sudsy oversees.

In 45 minutes Sudsy can expertly sharpen 22 pairs of skates and do each pair exactly the way each player specifies.

"Different edges for different players," explains Sudsy.

"Take our fast skater Delparte — he wants a flat blade touching the ice all the way and very sharp so he can get speed. But Blake Dunlop "dekes" on the ice. That means he stops, twists, turns a lot. So Blake wants his blades rockered. This means I sharpen his skates

so he can dig in with heel and toe — and less flat surface. Six players must have new sharp edges every day. Sixteen players can go a couple of days happily on the same edges."

Skates cost about $115 a pair. Mariners use up to two or three pairs per player in a season.

Players are as fussy about their sticks as major league hitters are about baseball bats, Sudsy explains.

"Special for each player. Some want handles longer; some want different curves in the blades; some have different size blades. When a man gets the stick the way he likes it most, I send it to the factory and the factory makes up five or six dozen to the player's specifications and stamps his name into the handle.

"All told the Mariners use up to 125 to 150 dozen sticks a season — price wholesale about six bucks each . . . And when it comes to pucks, we'll use up 50,000 pucks in a season. The crowd gets thousands; others get banged up and busted. Practice is tough on pucks. In a single practice session we will shoot 400 to 500 pucks at a goal tender. In a game he might get the puck fired at him 30 times."

Sudsy (the nickname for Dave has nothing to do with beer — a drink Sudsy does not favor) is the man who takes the ache out of bad backs and bruised muscles. He works wonders with whirlpool baths, diathermy and ultrasound, plus some secret linaments.

I ask where he learned all the special tricks of the varied trades that go with being a trainer.

"Look, I have been around players since I was 10 years old. That day in 1959 when they opened an ice arena in my home town of Greensboro, I was there. Every time our home town team — Greensboro Generals — practiced or played I was there. I played my heart out in high school teams, won an ice hockey scholarship to the University of Tennessee and then they dropped ice hockey and dropped me.

"I'd been stick boy for the Greensboro team since I was 13 years old and hoped to play for them. But I never grew any more so I was too small to play professionally. They made me assistant trainer.

"Then in 1971 I went as head trainer to the Roanoke Rebels and, in 1974, came north as head trainer for the Philadelphia Firebirds. And when they formed the Maine Mariners, I came here in August 1977.

"And here I am — training the winning team in the league."

A final secret from the dressing room is that most of the tough Mariners wear garter belts and panty hose under their uniforms.

Bobby Ives, minister with a difference

NEW HARBOR — In Maine, we even grow our church ministers with a difference.

Take Bobby Ives, 31, and his Maine-grown wife Ruth, and their Maine-grown infant Hilda. You'll find them all in the Methodist Parsonage at New Harbor. This is the first time since their marriage that Bobby and Ruth Ives have lived on the mainland, or in a house with oil heat, electric light, running water and a telephone.

"We are a throw-back," says Bobby. "The old-style worker-preacher couple. We'd rather earn cash by cutting wood, painting houses, building peapods, and then do our ministry for free. Here in New Harbor, and with our church in Round Pond, we are full-time, salaried ministers for the first time; and it's a bit strange to us."

Strange because until this year Bobby and Ruth Ives were island people. "First on Monhegan Island, nine miles out to sea. We went there as school teachers in the one room schoolhouse. We got one salary. They got two teachers for the 13 pupils. Bobby taught the prekindergarten and the eighth grade. I got all the murky middle," says wide-eyed, blue-eyed Ruth Ives. "We had one classroom. And when the islanders found out Bobby was an ordained minister as well as a teacher, he became the year-round pastor. For the first time in 10 years, Monhegan's church was open year round, complete with Sunday school for the kids."

The young Ives — he was 26 then — loved the life and the work and the islanders on Monhegan. "But in summer, the population climbed from a few dozen to over 700. So in July and August, we left for a quieter island," Ruth says. They found it on Loud's Island, also called Muscongus Island, just offshore from Round Pond and New Harbor. After two years on Monhegan, the Ives moved to Loud's Island. Here they practiced what so many others preach — an alternate life style, with a vengeance.

"We lived in the church. Our bedroom was in the belfry. The rope for ringing the bells came right down by my pillow," says Bobby. "The kitchen was downstairs, behind the sacristy. In summertime the little island church was often filled. But by the end of October, nearly everybody had left Loud's Island."

From November until May, Ruth and Bobby Ives lived alone on the island, where Indian chief Samoset had once lived before white men settled in New England. "We hoped that by living year round on the island where 50 years ago over 100 people lived year round, we might tempt new young families back to island living. But nobody came."

Ruth and Bobby Ives lived two winters alone on Loud's Island. "I miss that life terribly now," says Ruth. "I miss bringing in the water from the well, trimming the kerosene wicks and chopping the firewood. I miss having to do everything together. Out alone on the island, we did all of our chores together for safety's sake. When Bobby went lobstering, I'd go and handle the oars while he pulled the traps. When the tide was low, we'd go clamming together — in case one got hurt. We chopped firewood together. Together we rowed ashore in the peapod not wanting to leave one totally alone on the island."

Those island days were disciplined in a way no mainland life is disciplined. "We had to get in the wood and the water and the fish, or go hungry, thirsty and cold. We did four to six hours hard physical work each day and felt fine for it. At night, while Bobby knitted heads for his lobster traps, I'd read aloud by candlelight or kerosene. We had time enough to spend four hours a day in prayer together, and meditation. That kind of time vanishes when you live on the mainland. We miss it, badly."

During the summer on Loud's Island, groups of students would come out to visit the Ives. "They came to see an alternate way of living. To see how life could be cut back to the simplest basics and yet be filled with pleasure. Some kids had never seen a kerosene lamp. They had never read a book by candlelight. City kids just refused to believe there was no TV. They were convinced we had a set hidden somewhere. They spent days looking for it. They couldn't imagine life without TV or radio or phone or electricity."

Ruth Ives rocks her infant daughter. "She is christened Hilda, to

honor Bobby's grandmother, Hilda Ives. That Hilda was a remarkable pioneer in her way. She brought up Bobby in Portland and Cape
Elizabeth after his parents died very young. Hilda Ives lost her husband too when she was barely 30. She went to theological seminary
while she was the mother of five young children. Hilda Ives was one
of the first women ordained in Maine's Congregational churches.
That was in 1926 — or 54 years ago. She ministered in the rural
churches of Albany and Casco and Raymond, where her memory is
still loved today. As a lady past 60, Hilda Ives was still swimming
two miles across Casco Bay waters from Cape Elizabeth to Cushing
Island. At age 83 she died in her car, on her way to a church meeting — on December 2, 1969. And that is the remarkable lady for
whom our infant Hilda is named."

I had first seen Bobby Ives on the water. He was rowing his beautiful hand-made peapod, off Loud's Island, and I was headed out to
sea. I did not know he was a minister. He was hauling lobster traps

that day. A year later, I went to interview him and Ruth in their first home on the mainland — the parsonage at New Harbor. Last Sunday I went to New Harbor Methodist church to see the Reverend Robert Ives in action. The wooden church, painted grey and white, sits on high ground, facing east, to the harbor and Muscongus Bay, and across the sea to Monhegan Island. The pews fill with people I know from the village stores and garages and from the fisherman's co-op down on the harbor. But in church they look like strangers.

Bobby Ives looks different too. Until now I have seen him only in work clothes or oilskins. Now he stands behind the altar rail wearing a worn grey suit, with a white button-down shirt and a narrow striped tie. A parishioner leans to me and whispers proudly, "It is the only suit he owns. He puts small stock in possessions. Won't wear a choir robe even." But in his worn suit, the young Reverend Ives speaks out loud and clear, smiling with happy conviction. His dark hair, youthfully long over his ears and collar, contrast with his expert oratory. Without a note in his hand, he delivers one of the most fluent and moving sermons heard in Maine. The young man whose hands built the peapod and hauled his lobster traps now administers Holy Communion.

After the service Bobby Ives stands in the church vestibule, shaking hands and swapping news with his congregation — most of whom are twice his age. "We love him," many of them tell me. I hear him ask each one to come by the parsonage for open house between two and four o'clock to see the new baby, Hilda, and to see the improvements he and Ruth have made in the kitchen.

Topless barmaids and Supreme Court justices

OLD ORCHARD BEACH — Linda, 29, is wearing a tiny bra as she pours a beer for a customer in the Bikini Tavern. And that's new.

The chief justice and the Supreme Court judges of the state of Maine, no less, have decreed that Linda and Cindy and the other girls tending bar at the Bikini Tavern should no longer work topless when serving drinks.

So Linda was wearing skimpy cutoffs and a top that is intended to conform with the dress code issued by the Maine Supreme Court.

I asked Linda if the Supreme Court had affected her life.

"Sure," she answered, "those judges cut my pay 50 cents an hour. Topless, I made $3.50. Now with this cover-up, I make only $3 an hour . . ."

A customer observed that extra pay of 50 cents for 60 minutes of topless was too modest an appreciation by far. Linda thanked the gentleman.

Most entertainment in Old Orchard is boarded up, closed, empty, gone for the winter, dead.

But there is plenty of life in the Bikini Tavern these winter weekends.

The tavern is staying open all winter every day from 11 a.m. for 13 hours of business. "We'll get 200 people in Friday or Saturday night," says Linda.

What draws them is not entirely the newly topped waitresses but the slot machines, the pinball games, the go-go girls (topless still) and above all the legal gambling.

Linda shows me the dice table, the table where five-card stud is played, the slot machines where quarters either multiply into $20 or (more often) disappear. Close to every gambling game is an official license, signed by the chief of Maine State Police.

"The profits all go to charity. That makes it legal," explains Linda. The charity in this case is the Old Orchard Beach Athletic Boosters Association, sponsors of the 'games of chance' at the Bikini Tavern.

I sipped my cola, filled with a kind of admiration of owner Richard Gabriel. Town fathers have often tried to close this tavern unsuccessfully. Now imagine the outcry if the source of money to buy uniforms and athletic gear for Little League to varsity football were cut off by closure of the Bikini!

Linda opens my eyes to the niceties of Maine law. She explains that the Supreme Court ruling requiring tops on topless waitresses does not cover, so to speak, topless dancers.

"I wear a bit of a top serving drinks. But I can take off the top as soon as I get up and perform as a go-go dancer on stage. Different law. My pay goes up then, too."

Linda is a good conversationalist and hides little when interviewed. She has three children and is proud of them and carries their pictures.

"I used to be the best girl rider at Scarborough Downs. For 20 years, I worked and groomed horses. I rode the ponies which led the flighty horses. I exercised the flat racers when I was stronger — galloped 30 horses a day. Started at dawn and often slept in the stable after finishing feeding and bedding down horses at midnight." Linda rides frequently now. "My 10-year-old daughter is a great rider already."

As to the Bikini Tavern, Linda says she likes the customers better, is treated better than at all the "posh hotels and fancy restaurants in Maine where I worked before. The crowd is always full of real gentlemen here. And when we have 650 customers and 30 topless waitresses in summer, we have no trouble. No bouncers. No fights. Any girl who hustles or uses drugs is fired on the spot.

"I like it. But I wonder if those Supreme Court judges know about that 50 cents an hour they cut off my pay?"

Update: Local groups are still trying to close the Bikini Tavern.

Skipper of a party boat

BOOTHBAY HARBOR — Gail is a ladies' Hairdresser in Lewiston and she is crazy about deepsea fishing.

"Gail is on our fishing boat, regular as a clock, every two weeks from June to September. She just loves to fish. She's good. She catches a lot. But the only time she actually touches a fish is when it is iced, filleted and in a plastic bag and she carries it off the boat."

That is Captain Barry Smith talking. He is skipper of the "Mystery," a 55-foot party boat built in 1961 for deepsea fishing by the famed Lash Brothers of Friendship.

I went out on "Mystery" because my own boat is on charter and I hated being land-bound.

Going on a "party boat" was a new experience. I found you can have a terrific amount of good fishing and good cruising for $15.

The fishermen know this in the Bronx better than they know it in Boothbay.

In the Bronx at midnight, charter buses load up with eager fishermen. They drive through the night; arrive at Boothbay before the 8:30 fishing boats depart; fish off the coast of Maine all day; then carry their catch home to New York that night.

"We catch 1,500 to 2,000 pounds of fish a day in the good fishing season of mid-June till late July," says Capt. Smith.

"Once we get over a school of fish, our decks are lined with 40 fishermen, jigging for cod, pollock, cusk and occasional haddock. The two mates and I work flat out — helping land the fish, taking them off the hooks for those who want help. On the way in, we clean the fish so all except the biggest are filleted and bagged for the folks to take ashore. The big cod that weigh up to 60 pounds we keep intact. They use up lots of film, getting pictures standing by their catch."

Smith grew up around Boothbay Harbor. He was mate on a fishing boat for nine years and has been captain for the past five years.

"I love fishing. I go fishing on my day off. In winter I lobstered. But not this year. I'm a bachelor and girls are scarce in Boothbay in January. So this winter, I will be running fishing parties out of Florida."

Barry Smith, a neatly bearded, easy-going extrovert, says that 80 per cent of the thousands he takes out have never been deepsea fishing before and that 30 per cent have never been on a boat before. "But they catch on quickly and most get to love it."

In bad weather, though, there can be a lot of seasickness. "I hand out only sympathy to cure it," says Barry. The thought of liability prevents the party boat captains from doling out any pills.

Only once in his 14 years on party boats has Barry had a bad scare.

"One stormy, rough day, the harpoon got to rolling around the bow. I went forward to secure it. A big wave swept me overboard. The boat ran over me, hurting the discs in my back. But they fished me out and I learned my lesson."

Capt. Smith says he takes a week in June, when the season begins, to find the year's best fishing spots. A good one this year has been in 30 to 43 fathoms of water about six miles southeast of Pumpkin Rock. His passengers fish with rod and reel, 40 pound test line and an 8 ounce silver colored jig.

"My fish finder helps locate schools. But some days, even though the fish are there, they are not feeding. We can tell that quickly because we 'foul-hook' them." This means that the jig hooks the fish in the tail or cheeks.

I watched the fishermen going ashore. One lady of undetermined years glowed like a bride, burbled like a proud young mother. "Look at my fish — a 52 pounder!" she cried at the end of a day she will never forget.

But among the happy crowd in August only a few were from Maine.

"The smart Mainers come in mid-June and take home 75 pounds of fish for the freezer," smiles Capt. Barry Smith.

"They know it will taste wonderful in December. And bring back memories, too."

*How're you gonna keep'em down on Wall St.,
once they've seen Maine?*

CHRISTMAS COVE — The question sounds like a plot for soap opera. But the answer is real, and it's being played out in Christmas Cove.

The question is: Can a 36 year old Wall Street insurance broker give up his job in New York City, uproot his wife and three children from suburbia and find happiness and satisfaction in a small Maine coastal village?

Michael D. Mitchell and family did just this. Have they made it in Maine?

Mitchell himself tells the story, sitting on the dock of his marina-restaurant-motel, dressed in his working clothes of shorts, open-necked shirt and sneakers.

"I guess I was infected with moneyitis, like everyone else in Wall Street, until one day I woke up, knew I was sick and was ready to get out.

"Don't get the idea I was suddenly unhappy selling insurance. I liked it. I miss the excitement even now. I was pleased with my share of success and money. I was a vice-president of the third largest insurance brokers in the nation and I travelled to customers in Liberia and Nigeria and many parts of West Africa and Europe, expense account living.

"Now when the plumbing breaks and I'm on my knees fixing it, I think about those days. But the desire for them goes away as soon as I walk out and look at the harbor. I wouldn't switch back."

A sailing friend told Mitchell the Christmas Cove place was for sale. "I'm a sailing nut. I crewed the transAtlantic race once and the Bermuda race nine times. But one day I realized I was selling insurance even when I was out sailing. I was turning crewmates into customers. When my friend said a marina in Maine was for sale, my wife Barbara and I drove up to see it . . .

"That was the day after New Years, a bad time to look at a summer hotel and marina. Then we drove home to Rowayton, Conn., poured a drink and started talking. Twenty minutes later I was on the phone to Maine making an offer to buy, at 10 per cent under the asking price. The owners took it, $90,000."

The Mitchells, who came back to Maine to borrow the purchase money from the bank until they could convert their house in Connecticut into cash, knew nothing about running a hotel or a restaurant but soon found out. The package was 10 motel units, eight rooms in the hotel, two houses, a gift shop, plus a restaurant and marina and another 18 acres of land out back.

When Mitchell quit his New York job, "My friends thought I was crazy. They wanted me to take a rest, maybe see a psychiatrist. But Barbara and I took the kids right out of school in Connecticut and next day they enrolled here in South Bristol Grammar School." At the time, they were 12, 8 and 6.

"Let me tell you, it was no paradise. Each one of us was working at things we knew nothing about. Day after day I would put in 14 or 16 hours and get nowhere. But we learned how to cope. One night recently, a pipe burst in the third floor of the Inn and knocked out two ceilings. Years ago that would have seemed a catastrophe. Now I've learned to go to work and do what needs doing. Someone here will help you, so long as you help yourself. But sit back and call for a plumber — nobody comes."

Barbara, a Mt. Holyoke graduate, who used to be a happy suburban housewife and mother in Fairfield County, now puts in 16 hours a day sometimes running the hotel side of the business, plus the gift shop, plus being a mother.

A big publicity break helped the Mitchells. The year after he left Wall Street for Christmas Cove, Life magazine did a story about the family and their plunge into running the hotel and marina. After that came NBC's Today show and a flock of newspaper items.

"We were deluged with mail. People all over wanted to chuck their city jobs and move to a situation like this. Some wanted to know how to do it, others wanted to work here, some wanted to invest, buy shares of what we had or expand it."

People still ask his advice about switching to small town livelihood.

"I tell them that far from escaping, they come face to face with reality. You are going to sink or swim. There's no boss, no corporation, no secretaries or computers to back you.

"I tell them to throw away all their old values. That's hardest of all. Believe me, it is hard on a man's ego to wake up at age 40, making less money than in the first year out of college. That's the real yardstick to a lot of people. We get so accustomed to measuring success by dollars that we can't switch values. People are taught to measure themselves by how big a salary they make, if they make vice-president, whether they have a big corner office with two secretaries.

"You kiss goodbye to all that and the cocktail party friends and dances and golf games at the country club. You may say you will never miss that nonsense. But there are nights when you are low and depressed and you do miss them.

"The third thing I say is that you have got to give up the search for financial security. There is no more 'sick leave with pay,' no more having someone else fill your shoes if you are out. There's no pension plan and no more Christmas bonus. This is hard on ingrained habits and it can be especially tough on a wife used to knowing that the grocer and the cleaner and the yard boy can be paid, and that there will be theater tickets next week, and the kids can go off to the dentist to get their teeth straightened without worrying about the bill.

"My kids, though, never have a doubt anymore. The oldest boy runs the docks and gets boats onto their guest moorings, gases them up, and he is good. My middle child is 13, a fine girl who helps with the painting and catering and fixing up. And the youngest, he's 11, makes garbage runs and ice runs out to the boats moored in the Cove. When his tips weren't big enough, he made that sign for his skiff, 'Your tips are my wages,' and he does OK."

Mike Mitchell is glad he had the courage to up stakes and quit his Wall Street job and move his family to Maine.

"I like them better, they like me better, I like me better," he says. "Sure, there are still days when I get depressed and long for some of the comforts, but not often. And as for money I may be better off here in the long run. When I was making big money back then, it sounded great. But it went out as fast as it came. Now here, we cleared $6,000 at the end of our fourth year. That sounds like chicken feed to my friends. But I've got what few of them have — equity. We've put all our sweat and all our earnings right back into this place.

"We put new heating into two houses, redid the hotel, improved the restaurant and kitchen, expanded the marina, we've got 18 moorings out in the harbor, we are handling 350 guests. Over 60 per cent of our business is repeat business. And we've got 27 acres of fine coastal property. That really is something to show for it all, something to leave the kids that you don't find on Wall Street."

Update: Storms devastated the Mitchell's marina in their 10th year. They rebuilt and Coveside is in full swing again.

Two salty authors on Gay island

PLEASANT POINT GUT — More than two million best-selling words about Maine came putt-putting across the Gut in a workboat, and we threw out a bumper and caught up a line as they came alongside at 8 a.m. Sunday.

Amidship is Elisabeth Ogilvie; running the outboard in the stern is Dorothy Simpson; and they are in a scruffy working skiff in which they run back and forth across the Gut at Pleasant Point to their island farmhouse.

Elisabeth Ogilvie has written and published 26 novels, mostly set here in the Maine islands; plus 11 "juveniles"; plus poetry and articles and essays.

Dorothy Simpson, an island girl, wrote that essential book, "The Maine Islands"; plus a series of juveniles featuring Janie Marshall, another island girl.

"Thanks, but can't come aboard," says Elisabeth Ogilvie. "We've got chores to finish by 9 a.m." She tosses me a line and we tie up and do our visiting from boat to skiff.

Barbara has Elisabeth Ogilvie's book, "An Answer in the Tide," in her hands as the Ogilvie-Simpson skiff comes alongside.

She brought the book aboard Steer Clear two days ago and can't stop reading it. "Because of you," I complain to Elisabeth Ogilvie, "I've had to do sanding, painting and half the galley work single-handed. Barbara won't put down that book of yours."

Barbara passes "An Answer in the Tide" to Elisabeth Ogilvie in the skiff. She autographs it, half in ink, half in salt water; the right mixture for the author of so many books set in Maine islands.

Several times every summer we come in our boat to Pleasant Point Gut and pay a call on these two wonderful ladies. They are a grand pair, independent, sweetly gruff and very hard working — at the typewriters, the garden, the fish house, the wharf and the skiff. I go away feeling like a lazy bum.

Elisabeth passes the autographed copy of her book back up to our boat. "Guess you've got another book getting born?" I ask, hoping she'll say no. "Yep," she answers. "My new one is all done. Wrote it this winter. Finished, except for the last four chapters. By the time Dot here types the rest, I'll have finished the final four."

Leaning over the rail, I ask Elisabeth when she writes. "Early," she answers. "Can't sleep after four o'clock in the morning. So I get up and write. By ten I can go pick berries or catch mackerel if I want; and feel smug that I've got a full day's writing down on paper."

In work shirt, pants and boots for mudflats, Elisabeth Ogilvie sits in the skiff and looks slim, elegant, feminine and too darn at home in the Gut to be a lady author turning out novels every year, which are snapped up by scores of thousands of ardent fans across America. She went to school in Quincy but has spent 40 years among these islands off the coast.

Dorothy Simpson was born 25 miles to sea, on Criehaven. Her brothers are lobstermen there and she was married to a lobsterman. "Never lived anywhere but on islands — Criehaven, Wooden Ball, Matinicus, now Gay."

Elisabeth and Dorothy share a 105-year-old white frame farmhouse sitting on 33 acres, with views out to the Caldwell Islands and the Atlantic on one side and the Pleasant Point Gut on the other. Elisabeth is a detective story addict, devouring a book a day. Dot spends evenings knitting bait bags and trap heads for her lobstermen. Sometimes she'll play an accordion.

"Time to push off." says Dot. "We got chores waiting on the island. That winter storm pushed our fish house around, and broke up some of the wharf." She tugs the starter rope. The outboard coughs to life. End of a pleasant encounter with two good Maine writers.

The man in the swallow tail coat

AUGUSTA — One of the classiest, nicest men in Maine is Joe Sewall, president of the Maine Senate. He is the only politician with class enough to stride around the Senate president's panelled office in his undershorts at 10 in the morning, talking to a reporter about school budgets and the state taxes.

Joe Sewall is in his undershorts because he is changing out of a business suit into his work clothes.

Joe's work clothes are the fanciest togs in Maine. They cost $400 from Brooks Bros., courtesy of the Maine taxpayers. 'I will pass them on to the next Senate president. He better be size 42 long."

Sewall wears a swallowtailed clerical grey morning coat of the finest wool, striped pants, a pearl grey vest and a silk cravat or tie.

Those are the work clothes of the president of the Maine Senate when he is wielding his gavel and presiding over the Senate chamber.

Another legislator in a $400 fancy suit is John Martin, an Aroostook boy from Eagle Lake (population 908). Martin is Speaker of the House, and that job requires him to be decked out in tailcoat, striped pants, silk vest and french cuffs.

President Sewall and Speaker Martin, despite their striped pants, are the fastest men in Maine at swinging a mean gavel. In fact, when Sewall presided nervously over his first joint session of the legislature, he swung the opening gavel so hard he smashed it. The wooden head went flying off among ducking lawmakers in the front row.

"This $250 coat is so good that it's too hot in summer," complained Sewall as he slid one long leg into his striped pants. "I had to go out and buy a lightweight imitation for $35 . . . I've got two pairs of striped pants now. That makes a president feel more secure. Former Senate President Ken MacLeod willed me his striped pants, now that he is only a lobbyist . . . And I will pass my $400 suit to my successor. It belongs to the people of Maine, who paid for it. But when they pick the next Senate president, he ought to be a size 42 long."

Now Sewall holds out four silk cravats or ties. "The chief justice comes to speak today, so I will wear the richest, most formal one. This is what I wear on crucial debate days, when as presiding officer I must look pompous, impressive and uncontradictable."

Close observers can predict Senate weather by Sewall's neckwear. If he sports that informal glen plaid, there will be no floor fights requiring a referee.

Sewall, 56, is a licensed multiengined pilot, a famous salmon fisherman, a good martini-mixer, an expert on state finances, a very successful businessman, and the scion of an old and famous Maine family.

"My branch of the Sewall clan left Bath and shipbuilding in 1810, headed to Farmington and the Sandy River, then moved to Old Town in 1830. My greatgrandfather was speaker of the House in 1851. He built the house in Old Town which I live in now."

Knotting his serious tie for the chief justice's arrival, Sewall says that he has served 12 years in the legislature, three of them as Senate president. "I enjoy the job. I like presiding. I like listening to debates. We get some good debaters here." He mentions Floyd Harding, Harry Richardson, Sam Collins, Bennett Katz and Phil Merrill as among the best.

"Ouch!" cries Sewall as he puts on the tailcoat. "My right elbow hurts more than any tennis elbow ever did!" He shows a swollen elbow joint. "Gavel elbow. An occupational disease. Can't bend my elbow now. Must swing the gavel straight-armed. Tonight I will write to all Senate presidents in all state legislatures, asking if they have a remedy."

At day's end, out of his $400 tailcoat and striped pants, Sewall drives a sporty two seater Mercedes Benz. But he switches to a pickup truck to conquer the winter streets of Augusta. "I keep a tow bar, jumper cables and shovel handy," says the rich but practical Senate president.

The Wildes men of Cape Porpoise

CAPE PORPOISE — Sam Wildes is a well-liked fixture on the Cape Porpoise fish pier, one of the prettiest and busiest along the Maine coast.

As the lobster boats come alongside, Sam Wildes is the burly man who rigs the barrels of bait (often at $27 a barrel), and winches them down onto the deck of the waiting boat. Sam is the man who passes down the long snake of the gas hose and flicks on the pump so fishermen can top their tanks at 68 cents a gallon or more.

"I began on the Cape Porpoise pier way back — when Capt. Frank Nunan, and then his widow, ran the fish dock. Put in a 70-hour week and got paid $15. Capt. Nunan, died in 1945. His widow sold the store to me. My wife and I ran it for 25 years. Called it The Shack. Pumped gas. Sold lobster retail to the summerfolk. Well, after my wife took sickly, I came to work here for Hale Whitehouse."

Sam slings two barrels of bait and pumps a tank of gas to a boat. Then he comes back to talk some more.

"My father was harpooner on the fishing boat 'Richard J. Nunan,' a 92-footer . . . My father was a top man with the harpoon, when they went ironing swordfish in the summer. He ironed 99 fish in a row, and just missed the 100th out of 100 throws. They sold swordfish then at 4 cents a pound to the Boston Fish Pier. Some days they'd get 14 to 16 big swordfish, back in the 1920s. And in winters they'd go trawling out to George's Bank."

The Wildes Family have been working and living around this handsome harbor for 200 years. Take the story of an earlier Sam Wildes, in 1782.

On a hot August day during the War of Independence, an English brig of 18 guns and an English schooner of 10 guns came plundering into Arundel, as Kennebunkport was called then. The hated British seized an American schooner and sloop as prizes of war. Wildes, standing on the shore, watched the invasion and blew his stack. He jumped into a canoe, paddled out to the side of the British brig, and

demanded that the English captain surrender the captured vessels and get the hell out of his harbor.

Wildes may have been out of his mind making this kind of demand — one man in a little canoe trying to take on two ships with a total of 28 guns. But Sam Wildes had lost his only brother fighting the British. And Sam Wildes had lost his son — who'd been taken prisoner by the British.

When the British mocked the wild man in his canoe and ordered him to climb aboard, Wildes cursed the British and their cause, and paddled away. The British shot him in the back as he went. He made it to shore, but his wounds lamed him for life.

Yet, Wildes had saved the day for his fellow citizens. While Sam had been out in his canoe, giving the English hell, other Arundel men had sneaked weapons out to Goat Island, which put them in range of the British. The angry British sent a 17-man landing party to capture the rebels and the island. The Arundel men let go with a barrage of musket fire, killing 16 of the 17 Britons. They then brought up two cannons, firing on the British ships about 70 yards away.

The British fled.

So that victory was the result of another Sam Wildes at work 196 years ago.

The Wildes have been part of Maine and Cape Porpoise ever since. A section of town is called the Wildes Section even today.

Every lobster boat that heads out to haul traps from Cape Porpoise goes with bait and gas loaded by Sam Wildes, today's version.

Come down one clear day and stand on the Cape Porpoise fish pier. You'll see one of Maine's prettiest harbors and how the gillnetters and trawlers and lobster boats work. You'll see where the British men of war, with heavy guns, were run out of the harbor by a group of local fishermen. You'll see the plaque in the rock, telling the story of that day 196 years ago. And you'll see Sam Wildes' descendant, out there on the pier working with today's fishing fleet.

In Cape Porpoise you can stand and see the continuity of Maine.

The Leslie twins and the FBI

FREEPORT — Truck drivers were giving directions over the CB: "Go past the FBI at Freeport, for 12 miles, then take the first right . . . "

Julian Leslie, also tuned to channel 19, frowned. "I'd never heard of the FBI in Freeport," he said. "And I've run a retail business here for 30 years. So I broke in and asked. They told me FBI is a landmark in Maine. It stands for 'Freeport Big Indian.' It really stunned me because I own the FBI."

Freeport's big Indian, 40 feet tall, stands outside the Casco Bay Trading Post on Route 95, Freeport. Julian and his twin brother, Bill Leslie, bought it for $10,000 in 1969 "and I bet 10,000 kids have had their pictures taken beside it since then," says Julian. "The Indian attracted so much attention, he jumped our business 25 per cent in the first year alone. He was made in Strasburg, Pa., especially for us. They had to close the New Jersey Turnpike when he was being trucked here, he stopped so much traffic."

Julian and Bill Leslie began their Casco Bay Trading Post in 1947 selling duck decoys which they made. "We built our first log cabin showroom and factory ourselves — just 32 by 45 feet, but nobody wanted to buy duck decoys. That first year we only did $1,477 worth of business. Everybody seemed to want Indian moccasins. So I learned how to make moccasins from Harold Turner of Freeport. I worked for a year as his unpaid apprentice, 6 p.m. until midnight. Then we went into the moccasin business. And that was the turning point."

Today the Leslie twins stock 62 different kinds of moccasins, supplied by seven factories. Their moccasin business alone tops half a million dollars. The original store has been enlarged many times to contain not only moccasins but all kinds of hunting, camping, backpacking and leather goods.

"I still make special order moccasins," said Julian last week as he consulted his order book. "We've made special moccasins for President Harry Truman, for the Rockefellers, for the Sergeant Preston TV show, for John Wayne, Amy Vanderbilt and Robert Montgomery. But bandleader Guy Lombardo has been our biggest customer. He's been getting shoes from us for more than 30 years."

This now-famous Maine business, the second biggest moccasin seller in the world, almost folded several times.

"First we almost went under making the decoys. Then, when we got into moccasins and business was growing fast, we suffered our second calamity. They built the turnpike from Portland to Augusta and after that hardly anyone drove by our store. Business dropped 42 per cent that year.

"In desperation, the Canal Bank told us to try increasing our catalogue and mail order business. So I got my wife, TaTa, to do mail order fashions for women to wear outdoors and she did so well we weathered that storm."

Julian met and married TaTa in Calcutta. Her parents had been murdered during the Russian Revolution. She had first fled from Russia to China with her aunt and uncle, then escaped to India after the Japanese overran China. There Julian happened to be stationed as an American liaison officer in World War II.

She and Julian, together with Bill Leslie and his wife, Gail, all moved to Maine from Massachusetts and in 1947 the twin brothers opened the store in Freeport.

Julian and Bill Leslie say a Connecticut restaurant owner stopped soon after they opened and gave them the advice they needed. "Put some old cars in the parking lot," he said. "Nobody stops unless they see other people already there."

So back in 1947 the Leslies spent their precious few remaining dollars to buy car bodies. "They had no engines, we just painted them, and parked them," recalls Julian Leslie. "Finally we had to relicense them, or we would have been classified as a junkyard. But it worked. When you go duck hunting, you take decoys. In this business we used nine old cars to tempt in the customers. After a couple of years, it wasn't necessary. Real cars filled the parking lot."

Just as one road took away business, when the Augusta-Portland 'pike was opened, another hugely increased the Leslies' business. When Route 95 opened right by their front door, business zoomed 100 per cent.

From $1,477 in 1947, the first year, business grew to $45,000 by 1957, to $400,000 by 1967, and in the 30th year it topped the million dollar mark — about $600,000 through mail order, and $400,000 retail store.

Besides the big Indian, another crowd-catcher outside the Trading Post is a locomotive.

"We got it from Crotch Island," says Julian. "Bill and I were cruising off Deer Isle and we'd anchored at Stonington and rowed to Crotch Island where the old granite quarries are. On the wharf we found men with blowtorches cutting up this little railroad engine. We got them to stop and called their boss in Massachusetts, who agreed to sell us the locomotive for $4,500 — what he would have gotten for it as scrap. It cost us another $2,000 to get it onto a barge to

Rockland and trucked to Freeport, but it's paid for itself many times over."

The locomotive, built in 1913, worked for 30 years in the Boston Navy Yard, then went to the granite quarries on Crotch Island, where it hauled stone for many great public buildings, and finally, the granite for the gravesite of President Kennedy.

The Leslie twins and their younger brother, Jack, used to come to Wiscasset for their summer holidays from Massachusetts when they were children. Jack who married a Wiscasset girl, Joan Warland, now runs the Casco Bay Country Stores in Boothbay Harbor and Brunswick. So all the Leslie brothers have made business successes out of coming back to work and live in Maine.

High fashion in second hand books

CAMDEN — Never be surprised at who is doing what in Maine. I know a dignified bishop who points his seat to heaven and regularly digs a bushel or two of clams on a low tide.

And a former top researcher in psychiatric disorders quit his big city hospital, came to Maine and now finds happiness in making beautiful stained glass.

Strange? Not a bit. Such wonderful transformations abound in Maine and one of the nicest and most successful is on Bay View Street in Camden.

Go to the sign "A B C D Et." Books, enter the store where up to 30,000 precious volumes are stocked — and there you can find a highly successful jewelry and handbag buyer for Saks Fifth Avenue and Bergdorf Goodman, the lady who was one of Manhattan's top fashion buyers in many top stores.

Now in Maine, Lillian Berliawsky is a seller of second hand books. She is a delightful magnet to collectors from around the nation and across the ocean. To the fashion merchants of Fifth Avenue she was the bright and beautiful young Lillian Mildwoff, who was married to Nathan Berliawsky of Rockland in a ceremony performed in 1948 by the chief naval chaplain and followed by a Manhattan reception at the Pierre Hotel.

"If you can buy jewelry, you can buy books. If you are a good buyer, then you are a good buyer — of anything," smiles Lillian Berliawsky. She stands barely five feet tall, brown eyes brilliant when the talk turns to books or painting.

"Once my office was on the 74th floor of the Empire State Building," she says, "on that summer day when a plane crashed through the 76th floor. Camden is better."

Her husband, owner of Rockland's Thorndike Hotel and other real estate and brother of Louise Nevelson, one of the dozen most famous artists in America, brought Lillian to Maine in 1948.

"I was into books by 1962. Then in 1967 I lost the lease in Rockland and moved into these two adjoining stores here in Camden."

Books are everywhere. Labyrinthine paths run between shelves piled with books higher than a man. Book browsers wander to their favorite pastures. A baffled newcomer is lost — but ask Lillian for a title and her smile lights up the room. She marches you unerringly to the very spot where your heart's desire is waiting for you to buy it and take it home to live.

The passing parade of tastes is fascinating. While I was in the store, one lady bought a choice copy of the Chinese Tales of Genji; a man from Boston came in searching for rare monographs by Bernard Berenson; a student bought a paperback on economics; another man came in to buy guide books to Africa; a professor came to find Clarkson's History of Russia and Raiasonovsky's History of Russia; another buyer found a first edition of a Gladys Hasty Carroll and another got a first edition of a children's book by Nathaniel Hawthorne.

Then I saw the most touching buy of the day . . . a choirmaster came back, money in hand and a lot of it, to buy a very early edition of Handel's Mesiah with Handel's alterations in his own hand. He left happy, clutching his cherished prize.

"Now Handel has the home he deserves. It makes me happy, too," says Lillian. There is emotion in this trade — the long, hard search;

the unexpected find; then the sale to just the right buyer. Some fetch many thousands of dollars.

"Of course, a good sale is a joy. But the right buyer, the happiness — all this is as important as the money."

Lillian showed me through her special world. I ask her why the odd name of "The A B C D Et." And she tells me. "Those letters are the beginning of all knowledge, all literature, all the books — and a tremendous amount of happiness."

In Maine, there are 28 antiquarian booksellers listed. Among the best is Lillian Berliawsky, the high-fashion buyer with flair, who has found — and is giving — a new kind of life to old books.

Marvel of Wells Beach: Vander Forbes

WELLS BEACH — Through a reporter's luck I came out of the storm and chose to go into the Driftwinds Motel to make a routine phone call to the office and ran into Marguerite Forbes and one of Maine's most heartwarming stories of husband-and-wife business success.

Marguerite Forbes is 81. Her husband, Vander, is almost 82. When I first saw Marguerite she was going like a whirlwind, arms filled with linens, bossing the back-stage linen-closet operation known only to hotel keepers. Her gleaming white hair was fashionably piled above her vivacious face. She wore a vivid coral dress, I guessed her to be about 60 and was floored when Helen Garnsey at the front desk told me Marguerite Forbes is 81. "Talk to my son about the business. We've turned it over to him now," said Marguerite, and vanished smiling behind an armload of pillowcases.

No sooner had I begun talking with her son than he sent word for his father to join us. In from the rain and the gale came Vander Forbes, erect, wiry, laughing at 82.

Wells Beach is Vander and Marguerite Forbes country. They are its children, its parents and grandparents.

Today the Forbes family runs five beachfront motels with 68 rooms and the big Forbes restaurant. The Forbes are the dominant and longest established business on Wells Beach. In all, they have some 700 feet of oceanfront — which officials now want to value at $600 a foot and up.

Vander and Marguerite Forbes began small, very small, 64 years ago on the same Wells Beach where they flourish today.

"I began in 1913 with a horse and cart, selling fruit and vegetables to the huge wooden oceanfront hotels here," says Vander Forbes, Bananas, 18 for 25 cents; oranges, 15 cents a dozen; fresh corn, 10 cents for a dozen ears; native strawberries 10 cents a quart. I got my produce from Weinstein's in Kennebunkport, drove my horse and cart here two days a week and two days to Ogunquit, two days around Kennebunk. Long days they were. I'd fall asleep at the reins. The horse would find his way in the dark of night from Wells to Kennebunkport and it would be 11 p.m. before I unhitched him."

Standing in the great picture window overlooking a stormy sea. Vander remembers the day he quit working for Weinstein and struck out on his own. "In 1920, I began with a 9 x 12 foot hot dog stand near the beach. Then Marguerite and I began another one. These eventually led to Forbes Restaurant where hundreds eat every summer day today.

"In 1938 I bought the old Oceanview Hotel, a four-story, wooden structure with big porches right on the ocean. It was Depression. I bought it on condition that Ruth Turner, my wife's sister, would manage it. And she's been running all our motels for 40 years now. She's loved by customers from 40 states. We renamed that wooden hotel "The Marguerite" in honor of my wife. Now it is gone. And bit by bit we built four motels we have now."

Vander's son, Vander Jr., runs most of the family business from his big, comfortable oceanfront home. Vander Jr. is still part Maine fisherman as well as hotel keeper. He hauls his lobster traps and tells glowing stories of catching halibut weighing 218 pounds. "I was born here on Wells Beach, went to school from here, went to Maine Maritime Academy and into the Navy during the 1950's, was engineer on a 133-foot ocean tug operating out of Japan. When I got home in

1957 father and I kept enlarging and modernizing and adding new units."

Vander Sr., at 82, is alert, wiry, strong and brim full of energy. He and his wife Marguerite still put in a full day's work daily. "My father shipped before the mast," he says. "His brothers and his father were ship captains. They fished the Georges Bank in the hard days of tub trawls and dories. My father went to California in 1890 to build seawalls and lighthouses. I was born there. We came back to Sanford and then Wells by 1900. We grew up knowing more about work than anything else. Schooling stopped when I got long pants . . . I've loved this beach for 65 years."

Vander shows me pictures of Wells Beach as he first knew it about 1913. He points to the great hotels with 350 rooms, to the bathing beauties who wore more clothes to go swimming than today's girls wear to go to church.

I say goodbye and go out again into the storm. Through the torrents I can see most of the Forbes hotels and the Forbes Restaurant. The streets are empty. I cross the causeway road through the gale and rain. And all the way I see a horse and wagon, a load of strawberries at 10 cents a quart and a young man in 1913 clothes, asleep on the driver's seat, heading for the stable.

Ames': Ice cream in the parlor

THOMASTON — The giant ice cream cone stands at the entrance to the driveway, soon after you cross the bridge on Route 1, driving south from Thomaston.

"Ames Ice Cream" is the kind of ice cream parlor you may never find anywhere else.

You turn into a cool, tree shaded drive to an old white frame farmhouse — "the first farm built hereabouts," says Edgar Ames. "Built in 1790. We've got floorboards 27 inches wide in the upstairs rooms. It was a criminal offense to have boards that wide then. Because, to get 'em that wide, the man would have had to cut down a tree so big and tall it was marked and kept for the king's masts. The King of England claimed all the tallest trees for making the masts in his navy."

The ice cream parlor is in the cool room between the kitchen and the parlor. Three local girls dip the ice cream in 18 flavors, made in the kitchen daily by Edgar and Louise Ames. "We've been at it 33 years now, working as a team, Edgar and me. We start freezing by eight each morning and keep going until two in the afternoon. Make four flavors a day. Here — look at the people who signed this guest book. Thousands and thousands; from all 50 states and 44 foreign nations at last count."

Edgar, still a big man in the Masons, fields my question, "Why did you first get into the ice cream business?" He replies, "Because I wasn't too bright . . . We'd been married two years, Louise and I, and lived in a little apartment in Thomaston. We remembered the Depression. And both of us liked the idea of a farm to keep food in our bellies, if need be. And after supper each night, we'd eat ice cream. And say we could make it better. So in 1945 we found this farm and tried making ice cream better."

Louise frankly says she has no secret that makes her ice cream better. "I use the best milk and cream and sugar and fresh fruit or the best flavoring and first grade nuts. Then I take all the time needed. And, remember, Edgar and I have been doing it 33 years.

A few baskets of fresh raspberries are close to the ice cream. "We got 800 pints from our own raspberry patch last year."

Eating Ames' best at tables in the old family dining room are groups from California, Iowa and Pennsylvania. Five Maine kids from nearby come in for theirs. This is surely the only ice cream parlor in the world where a huge model of a Thomaston sailing ship is part of the decoration; where the paintings on the wall are done by Mrs. Ames' mother — a wedding present 35 years ago; and where pet fish swim in circles as you try the chocolate mint chip. Over a mirror hangs a New York Yankee baseball cap. "I love 'em so much, you'd think I owned the team," says Edgar.

Louise takes me on a tour, showing how she and Edgar make all the ice cream and sauces. "We mix up 10 quarts of eggs, milk, sugar, fruit or flavoring right here. Then put it into this freezer. See, it operates on just the same principal as this little one my grandmother had; only this is a lot quicker. Makes five gallons in 15 minutes. Then we put it into these two gallon stainless steel cans, made special for us here. Stays 24 hours, freezing hard. Then 24 hours more in this other freezer, where it is not so cold — so we get it to a scoopable consistency. Vanilla is still the top seller. I guess because it doesn't take much thinking, choosing out of all those 18 flavors. Easier to say 'make mine vanilla' and then concentrate on the fruit or nuts on it."

Cutting fish keeps 'em Young in Rockland

ROCKLAND — Meet Colin Tinker, spry as a March hare and well past 72.

Then meet Maynard Smith, fish cutter supreme, and a top bowler — and 82 years old.

Finally, meet Mildred Thompson, whom you'd think is too pretty and too sassy to be 75. She's one of the fastest workers on the packing line.

To see Maine men and women in their 70s and 80s doing a fine day's work and having a fine time doing it, visit the F. J. O'Hara and Sons fish processing plant on Rockland's waterfront. If anybody could bottle the Maine secret of their bounce, he'd outsell Geritol.

Colin Tinker is the lively fellow who supervises close to 100 people slicing, candling and packing 100,000 pounds of fish a day at the O'Hara plant. Age 72.

Maynard Smith is the first man you see on the fish-cutting line. You can't miss him. His crushed hat perches rakishly on his gray head and a long knife flashes in his skilled hand. Flash, flash, flash — another fish expertly filleted. Does he tire? After eight hours on his feet at work, Maynard Smith goes bowling at age 82.

Mildred Thompson, 75, is working on the packing line today. Sometimes the workers change jobs. Slicing one day, packing another, candling another.

Slicing and packing is "piecework" and the pay is geared to the amount of fish sliced or pounds packed. Candling pays a $3.40 hourly wage. Candling means inspecting fillets by shining lights through them and cutting out blight— "buggers and boners."

Joseph Campbell, 60, a young, grinning gray-haired Irishman, says, "My job is to keep the girls on the line happy. We work 7 a.m. till 5 p.m.; take a coffee break at 9 a.m. and 3 p.m., plus time out for lunch. This is a family plant. No union. Nobody got fired here, ever."

The plant has three major production lines with people working on each side of each line. In the center of each line, the fish come along on a conveyor belt. On the first line men and women do the slicing. Two quick cuts on each side of the redfish (ocean perch) and the fillets go into one plastic box, and spine, head and tail into another. A top cutter earns $400. Packers and cutters make an average $200 to $250 a week.

"In a week, we process half a million pounds of whole fish through here," says Paul MacFarland, 33. MacFarland is the tallest man in the plant — maybe 6 feet, 5 inches. He will succeed Colin Tinker when Colin retires.

MacFarland says that 31 percent of each ocean perch becomes fillets and the rest lobster bait. These fish skeletons used as bait fetch a high price, $27.50 a barrel, from the lobstermen, who may take two barrels to bait their traps in a day.

MacFarland watches a truckload of lobster bait pull out, then shows me the entire process. It starts when the O'Hara boat comes dockside after two weeks at sea. A huge vacuum pump siphons 125,000 pounds of ocean perch out of the hold. On conveyor belts, the fish are washed, de-iced and scaled by machine.

Now they are sorted into 70-pound baskets, which go by conveyor belt to the cutting and filleting line. A good cutter gets 21 pounds of fillets out of 70 pounds of fish — and a bonus if he or she can get more than 21 pounds.

Thence to the candling line, where the bone or blight is cut out, and finally to packing, five and 10 pounds to cellophane bags. The bags are iced and put into 60-pound boxes — and thence by the truckload to faraway places.

Millions of pounds of fish and millions of dollars move off this O'Hara wharf. It is a fine family business. And I walk away thinking back to that 14-year-old boy who arrived from Ireland without a dollar, took a man's place in the Army and fought in the Civil War for the fee paid him, and then began the first Francis J. O'Hara fishing venture. He'd like what his grandsons are doing in Rockland today.

Maine apples and the New York Daily News

WALPOLE — The last of Maine's wonderful apples are being picked this second week in October. When the crop is in, about 300 million Maine apples will have been picked.

There's a marvellous poetry — and history — in the names of apples. Golden Delicious; Astrachan; Red Duchess; Ben Davis, those hard, inedible apples they stored in schooners, and sent around the world to England, where they arrived ripe and fetched premium prices; Courtlands; Northern Spy.

Have you ever picked apples? Most orchards will let you pick your own at a bargain price. Local folk come year after year to pick apples in local orchards — and make money for Christmas. It is hard on the arms and back, standing on a ladder, reaching out and up steadily for hours on end. A good amateur picker may manage 60 bushels or so in a day. But the professional pickers, often brought in from Canada or Jamaica or Puerto Rico will pick well over 110 bushels a day. Pay is by the bushel.

October is apple picking time. I went to see the Maine Coast Orchard in Walpole, owned by Vincent Koch, a blue-eyed, white-haired, lean man who is a bit handsomer than Anthony Eden used to be.

Vincent has 700 apple trees. And to see a look of total happiness on a man's face, look at Vincent Koch's face surveying his orchard, his wood lots and his waterfront as an October sunset blesses his handsome land in a golden glow.

"Before this, I worked for 20 years as a linotype operator on the New York Daily News. Right on 42nd street, setting type for over 7,000 editions. We lived at Flatbush, in Brooklyn . . . And all that seems like the other side of another world from this orchard, here in Walpole, Maine."

Vincent says he and his late wife Natalie came here for a vacation

in 1942, loved it, and bought at a low, low price, 100 acres and a farmhouse that had no electric light, no running water, no heat beyond a wood stove in the kitchen.

"I went back to the Daily News and 42nd street and worked all the overtime I could get. Then at the end of a month, I'd have vacation time enough to let me come here for three weeks. We slaved, fixing over the house. When we had money, we'd buy 50 or 100 trees a year and plant 'em. Then in 1952, I had 20 years in at the Daily News, and retired from that to work 20 more years setting type at the Bangor Daily News and coming to the farm weekends."

At day's end, Vincent fondles and sniffs the apples packed and picked this day. "Quantity down a bit from last year. But quality is up. Good big apples. Fine color. Sweet and juicy. And we are pressing all the cider we can make from now till Thanskgiving."

Vince knows every one of his 700 trees by first name. He planted each one. "A batch of fog and rainy days in the middle of the 'set' hurt this year's crop. That was in mid-May. Right at the height of the bloom. And the foggy rain kept the bees hiding in their hives, when they should have been out pollinating. But the MacIntosh and Red Duchess and Courtlands are fine. This week, we'll harvest the last of the Golden Delicious."

In the sunset, I bite into a fine smelling, juicy Mac, as good as only a Maine apple can be. We watch the sun go down, glowing over the reds and golds of Vincent's woodlot, kissing the river beyond. All the while, we smell the harvest smell of fresh picked apples, and to slake a dry throat there stands a keg of fresh pressed cider.

Vincent Koch looks out over the land. Happiness lights his eyes. "Sure is a long, long way from the New York Daily News on 42nd street," he smiles. "And I'll tell you a secret. I don't miss Flatbush one darn bit."

VI
PIPER'S BEND,
DAMARISCOTTA

HAVOC IN THE ASPARAGUS BED

MAINE BREAKFAST AND ROBERTS KETCHUP

WHEN EAGLES SOAR, HEARTS FLY

OUR FOURTH OF JULY

DALLYING DALMATIAN'S LIPSTICK ORGY

BITTER NIGHT, ICE-OUT DAY

DICKENS THE COON CAT COMES HOME

MEMORIAL DAY IN A SMALL TOWN

CHRISTMAS IN THE NEW WORLD BEGAN IN MAINE

OUR CHRISTMAS TREE MADE OF MEMORIES

PIPER'S BEND is the first and only house that we have designed and built. We harbored no desire to build a house. Rather we hoped (like everyone else) when we came to Maine to find a perfect old ship captain's house with a wonderful water view at a bargain price.

They don't exist.

So we found land we loved; and designed the house to suit us. Barbara and I put two ping pong tables into a big unused room in a rented house; we filled one table with clippings and pictures of homes we admired. On the other table we drew plans of our own. This went on for four winter months. When the eighth house we designed matched our first house, we decided we had come full cycle and settled on this design.

Next an artist friend, Laurence Sisson of Boothbay Harbor then, rendered exciting drawings of how a finished house would look. With that as courage and our amateur plans we went to builders. Finally we found one who would give us both a firm price and a firm date for completion. And in eight months the house was built. We moved in on Ground Hog's Day 12 years ago.

Chiloe.

Piper's Bend has been and is a never ending joy to us and to our children. We've lived in and owned many houses in a lifetime of domestic and foreign assignments. But no home anywhere has given us the pride and pleasure of Piper's Bend — so named because the land we bought belonged to Alvin Piper, and it is on a bend in the Damariscotta river.

The weather, the animals, the river, the town, all these play a big role in our lives at Piper's Bend. And to give a report on living at home in Maine, here are a few snapshots from one family album.

Havoc in the asparagus bed

DAMARISCOTTA — My wife is a person with a sweet temper and unflappable devotion to her seedlings, compost heaps, pea poles, cucumber frames, broccoli stalks, beds of lettuce and furrows of corn. Working in her vegetable garden, Barbara is a picture of happy and soothing productivity.

But last evening, Barbara rent the pastoral peace with shouts of fury. A cannonade of cacophony exploded as this normally blissful gardener came pounding out of her vegetable patch waving her hoe like an avenging sword.

Shouting imprecations to heaven, she sprinted past the cucumber frames in hot pursuit of a spotted dog. The dog, tail tucked between its hind legs, looked backward over its shoulder astonished at the danger gaining from behind. It wavered, torn between making a fast dash for safety in the woods or dropping to the ground and begging for mercy.

Piper is a smart dog. She dropped, rolled on her back and surrendered, begging for mercy. Barbara pulled up sharp, stood momentarily over the crouching dog as if about to wreak fearsome vengeance — then threw down her hoe, and collapsed laughing: "What do you do with a Dalmatian that eats the asparagus?"

Piper, our Dalmatian, likes to go gardening with Barbara. While Barbara works hard, the dogs sits haughtily, looking on giving encouraging barks. Last season Piper began to take a more active interest. When we were harvesting peas, she would sneak up on the pea-basket and help herself. It was amusing to see her sneak a treat, then tiptoe off to the side grasses, there to lie down and bite open the pod and munch approvingly on a few fresh peas. Or sometimes she would unearth a ripe carrot and chew with relish on its root.

That was fun to see. The harvest of peas and of carrots was rich: We could well spare a few. And Barbara enjoyed the dog's tribute to the good taste of the fresh vegetables she had raised. The thump of

Piper's wagging tail, the crunch of her long, white teeth biting into fresh carrots or toying with a rolling pea sounded a bit like applause.

But asparagus — that's different.

Asparagus is not to be shared with a dog. The first sweet stalks of asparagus in May are not for sharing. Every gardener who nurses an asparagus bed from infancy to maturity knows why only the closest of blood relatives, only the oldest of dear friends, are allowed a taste of those early benefits of spring.

Hell hath no fury like a gardener whose asparagus bed is raided. So when Barbara looked up from her hoeing and saw Piper standing among the new asparagus, nibbling at the purpling heads like some canine gourmet, she just exploded.

"She's your dog," I tell my wife. "You should be proud she is so discriminating that she enjoys a little fresh asparagus along with her bone from the butcher."

Tomorrow is my birthday. And this May, at last, I am learning that when someone keeps both a boat and a garden, he is headed for trouble just as surely as the person who keeps a wife and a mistress. When you pay attention to one, you are automatically in hot water with the other.

I sneak off to my boat early in the morning, before Barbara is awake enough to say the word "garden." But all day while I am at the boat I feel guilty.

So I return home, get out the lawnmower and decapitate thousands of innocent yellow dandelions, which Barbara despises.

"Think of them as first cousins to daffodils," I suggest.

"I say they're weeds," she replies.

Bill Fagan, my son-in-law, is fibreglassing the roof on the cabin of my boat. Being a yacht-builder by trade, he will settle for nothing less than perfection.

That cabin roof was sanded and filled, sanded and filled, until it became as smooth as a proverbial baby's bottom. Then, with the neatness of a maiden-aunt seamstress, Bill pieced out the fibreglass and finally swoshed it on with carefully prepared resin.

Now he has spent hours sanding that layer of resin down to total smoothness. On goes another layer of resin today. Then more sand-

ing. A third layer of resin. And final sanding. Then will come the gleaming paint job. At last, "Steer Clear" will be in the water again.

I watch and help a little and do the boat painting jobs which are better suited to my meagre talents.

We are a weary group at day's end. After her labor in the asparagus beds and other parts of her too-large garden, Barbara has also prepared the dinner. She showers and changes while I make a drink for her to enjoy on the porch as the sun goes down.

It is a happy moment. But after many years of marriage I can read the unspoken message: "If men spent as much time weeding their gardens and painting their homes as they do scraping and painting their boats, this house and this garden would be immaculate showplaces. Which they are not."

Maine breakfast and Roberts ketchup

PIPER'S BEND — Is there a better meal in the world than a Maine breakfast, homemade, self-served?

I've just made one, and eaten a better meal than all the chefs in all the Ritz hotels will prepare today.

And all it took was Maine-smoked ham, from Waldoboro Lockers; Maine brown eggs, from a farm across the Damariscotta River; crusty sourdough bread, made at Slate's in Hallowell, and a heaping plate of cold, Maine, home-baked beans enlivened by (and here is the secret weapon) a big dollop of Kenneth Roberts' ketchup made in our own kitchen, true to his grandmother's recipe.

I'll give the recipe later, and you are in for good news if the ketchup you know is that, store-bought disguiser of bad food. A new world of ketchups will soon open. But beware! This recipe, courtesy of the late, great Maine writer, may make you a ketchup drunkard.

Secret of a really good breakfast is this: Do not eat right after you get out of bed. Work for two hours, preferably outdoors and preferably early. To deserve and enjoy a good breakfast, get up at 5:15 a.m. in winter and an hour earlier in summer.

Next, get up alone. This is important, although it is never stated in cook books. It is important because walking or working outside, alone, at 5:30 a.m. on a cold, black winter morning works miracles on the tastebuds. And other parts of the anatomy.

Shiver a little as you gulp in the night air, so pure and cold it hurts going down. Look, and marvel, at the night sky; at 5:30 a.m., you feel a close companionship with those stars and that moon, still hanging in there, shining for you while most of Maine sleeps.

Take another deep gulp of that winey, icy air; take one more look at those scintillating stars — and then run inside for the strong coffee on the stove. It smells better, tastes better, even than the best coffee brewed in the French Quarter of New Orleans.

To make it still better, munch on a Maine apple, chilled and kept carefully from November. Then do two hours' work out doors.

Now, at 7:15 a.m., you are ready for the best meal of the week — the big Maine breakfast you make for yourself.

I start with a huge lump of whipped butter, dropped into a hot skillet; the smell of it browning makes the dog drool. Now I crack two outsize, speckle-brown eggs on the rim of the iron spider and listen to 'em hiss as they hit the bubbling brown butter.

Now I take the longest, sharpest knife in the kitchen and slice five thin strips of home-smoked ham. As each piece falls off, I can smell that pungent, nostril-tingling smell of wood smoke in the smokehouse where this ham was cured.

I dish up a heap of cold, home-baked beans. It's not quite imposing enough, so I treat myself to two more tablespoons full of those reddish delights. The crusty sourdough toast is ready. Whipped butter melts into every open pore of that rich crust.

My table is set. My dog's eyes brim with desire and hope. From the refrigerator I bring out that dreary-looking soda bottle, now filled with the precious magic of Kenneth Roberts' grandmother's tomato ketchup recipe. In color, it is dark mahogany, instead of commercial red; in smell it is salty and tangy, instead of sweet. I pour a generous dollop as a crown atop my baked beans.

As I pour and sniff, summer memories flood back. From our garden, we carried in baskets upon baskets of tomatoes, then spent long nights cooking them. With wooden spoons, we pushed the cooked tomatoes through a sieve, removing skins and seeds; one peck of tomatoes made one gallon of tomato liquid.

Following Kenneth Roberts' recipe, we brought each gallon of liquid almost to a boil, slowly. While that was going on, we worked other magic in another wooden bowl. In a pint of sharp vinegar we dissolved 6 tablespoons of salt, 4 of allspice, 2 of mustard and 1 of powdered cloves.

Then came the inevitable "pinches" — two of black pepper, and one tiny one of red-hot pepper.

We stirred and then poured all this lovely brew into the almost-boiling tomato liquid, stirring over a slow heat till it thickened. This is a time for conversation because it takes 90 minutes of standing there and stirring.

Let it sit and cool — maybe on a windowsill overnight so a sliver of moonlight can shine on the brew.

Next morning, stir and decant into small bottles. Top each neck of each bottle with a half inch of good olive oil. Store in a cool and secret place. And then serve — on cold beans, on hash, on fish cakes.

And if you are alone, take a heel of fresh crusty bread, and lace it heavily with Kenneth Roberts' tomato ketchup. Then go and conquer the world.

When eagles soar, hearts fly

DAMARISCOTTA — "Look, he's there flying just by the far tree — the eagle!" My wife spoke and pointed spluttering with excitement as one of our Damariscotta eagles soared over our land.

Seeing an American eagle is a special event in anybody's life. Seeing it close, in flight, is like a thunderclap.

The size is exciting. You are awed by a giant bird with a seven foot wingspan. It symbolizes our nation. That is a thrill — seeing the symbol alive and flying.

And then there is the terrifying power of the bird — the fierceness of the curved beak, the menace of the talons, the hunter's deadly look in the cock of the head and the staring eye.

The other evening we saw the Damariscotta eagles in flight for the first time. We had seen the pair more often on their big, straggly nest.

A Maine photographer and filmmaker is responsible. He is Paul Fournier of Hallowell, who has made remarkable films on Maine eagles.

"I have been filming the Maine eagle project for three years, and have been watching eagles for 12 years," says Fournier.

He has made more than 5,000 feet of color film of Maine eagles, especially the Damariscotta pair.

"I have filmed them from blinds with very powerful lenses, so we seem to be in the nest. I've filmed them catching food and feeding the young. I have even filmed them in the act of mating," says Fournier.

The Damariscotta eagles, says Fournier, changed nests.

"I think they failed to raise their young. The egg broke. Or the baby died. Anyway, they left that nest three years ago because of tragedy. And built a new one nearby. I photographed them building it. They carry in a tiny twig one moment. And then they bring along an eight foot branch."

In this new nest — in order to protect the eagles, I won't reveal its exact location — the Damariscotta pair of eagles raised young from eggs last year, and Fournier says they are on the nest again this year. But if the eggs have already hatched, the young are still too small to be spotted.

"Those young are fed so well, they grow fat and big very fast. Last year we banded a baby eagle near Bangor in May and by October that baby was as big as its parents, weighing 14 pounds with a seven foot wingspan," Fournier says.

He used the new carcass of a beaver as bait to bring the eagles within close range of his cameras and has studied and filmed Maine eagles wintering in the tidal reaches of the Penobscot River.

"Eagles feed on eels. They often will seize an eel that a merganser duck has caught. Sometimes the eagle may take the duck too. And both eels and ducks are high in DDT counts, from the stuff they eat. It may not hurt them. It may not directly hurt the eagle who eats the eel or the merganser. But it can cause havoc with the eagle's eggs later on."

The Damariscotta eagles envy the fish catching ability of gulls and ospreys. Those birds dive under water to get their fish.

"I have filmed the eagles attacking a gull and an osprey and forcing them to drop the fish, and then the eagle will swoop down so fast that he can catch the falling fish in mid-air," says Fournier.

Fournier does some of his spotting on eagle nests from his own light plane which he flies over locations thought to contain eagle nests.

"We have pinpointed 38 nests in Maine now. But we know of only 30 pairs of eagles. Of course, eagles will abandon a nest where they have had a stillbirth or broken eggs and build another nest nearby, hoping for better luck."

The Damariscotta eagles are on their nest now. The incubation time is usually six weeks. Maybe more eagle young will be hatched this year.

Update: Maine's eagle population in 1977, 1978 and now in 1979 seems to be staying at about 150. In 1978, 35 bald eagles were born in Maine. Nine of these were born in Cobscook Bay, down east in the Lubec-Eastport-Calais area; and the other 26 eagle births were scattered from Damariscotta north to Moosehead Lake.

Our Fourth of July

DAMARISCOTTA — Anyone who thinks life is restricted in small-town Maine, just hasn't lived in a small Maine town. You can find just about everything. Especially on a holiday.

On this July Fourth I saw the joyful sight on Muscongus Bay of lobster boats crammed to the gunwales with families headed for island picnics.

Every other day of the year, those lobster boats have one lonely man aboard and sometimes a helper. But on the Fourth of July infants, teen-agers, grandmothers, mothers, aunts, uncles, and visiting cousins pile aboard. In the corner where the bait barrel usually stands, 2-year-olds suck on a bottle of milk. The only milk aboard is in that bottle with a nipple on top.

Families and fixin's go ashore. It takes a pile of trips in the skiff to get all those people and all that food and drink onto the beach.

Island beaches, deserted most Mondays on these remoter, smaller islands, are filled. Yet there are enough islands and beaches and coves off midcoast Maine to permit most family expeditions to have one to themselves.

Standing on a rock at our island spot, I looked around and counted 27 islands, some tiny and others big. Standing off most every beach or cove was a lobster boat.

Below the high tide mark, sweet-smelling white smoke curled into the clear air. Driftwood, salted and dried white, was burning, to make a fire for boiling the lobsters taken from the father's traps. This day the family eats lobsters. And corn. And digs clams. The great day goes slowly, wonderfully, deliciously by. Only tiny kids, impervious to cold, swim. Grownups walk, snooze, play ball on the beach, sit on a rock, watch the tide run and drink beer. They are kings of all they survey.

On television that night I saw another island beach. Coney Island. The report said 1.4 million people were on Coney Island Beach on

July 4. That one beach was crowded with more people than live in the entire state of Maine.

Back on shore early, we stood on the bridge between Newcastle and Damariscotta and watched the Crazy Raft Race come downstream. A hundred young people riding 25, homemade rafts compete in this annual crazy-raft race. I've seen bikes strapped atop rafts, propelled by homemade paddle wheels rigged to the bike pedals. It is a funny sight to see a guy pedaling his way down the middle of the Damariscotta River on a bicycle.

This year Barbara Simonds, 19, her friend Amanda Russell, also 19, and another friend Beth entered the race as a last-minute lark.

"We got a big long table with six legs," reports Barbara. "We begged three old truck inner tubes. Roped each tube around each pair of legs. Then Amanda and Beth nailed plastic snowsliders onto the other side of the table. Amanda's theory is that if you can slide on snow, you can slide on water; so she strapped those snowsliders on for speed. Then each of us clung to the legs and inner tubes and floated downriver, round bends, over rocks. Got drenched. But had a glorious, hairy, funny half-hour ride." Barbara came to the good Maine life from Southern California two years ago.

Oddest entry this year was the floating shell of a Volkswagen bus. Strapped to a raft buoyant with inner tubes, five or six brave young men and women tried "driving" the VW bus down river. But the body turned turtle, and sank till recovered.

At trip's end nobody knew who had won. Nobody cared. Drenching wet after a hilarious river ride, young people gather on The Pier restaurant which juts out over the river; and there they drink a cool one, and tell each other tall tales of wild rides on the Damariscotta river.

Up Academy Hill, half a mile away, an auction is under way in the gym at Lincoln Academy, where many of the crazy rafters went to school.

This is a country auction with a difference. Inside the first hour, auctioneers Bob Foster and Robert Hall had taken in $112,000. By lunch, sales totaled more than a quarter million dollars. By day's end, the total was more than $440,000. And the sale went on for

two days after that. Prices were high, and action was fast. I saw 186 guns and swords sold separately in 119 minutes.

Ten years ago, at this same Foster-Hall country auction, I was top bidder on a Franklin stove at $5. Then, the auction was on the front lawn of Bob Foster's home in Round Pond. By selling from breakfast till dark he'd make $1,000. Now he did a quarter million before stopping for lunch.

And that's the Fourth in this small Maine town.

Dallying Dalmatian's lipstick orgy

PIPER'S BEND — I walked in on my dog unexpectedly and found the animal in what human beings call "a compromising situation."

There was lipstick smeared across Piper's mouth. Lipstick traces on the cushions of her bed. Lipstick even on her paws.

I stared hard and accusingly into my Dalmatian's pale blue eyes. They blinked.

I stared at her white muzzle with one black spot, now foolishly smeared red with telltale lipstick.

I swear the dog blushed.

Down between her paws went her head. Thump, thump, slowly banged her tail in a kind of unspoken apology. Up came those downcast blue eyes, asking forgiveness: "Lost my head. It meant nothing," the dog seemed to be saying.

As a man, I was ready to forgive a few smears of lipstick, especially in this season of holiday parties. But the lady of our household has a harder heart.

"Piper!" she shouted. "You ATE my lipstick! Bad, bad, bad dog!"

Barbara held up her empty lipstick container in dismay.

"Gone. All of it gone. Brand new $6 lipstick in my sexiest shade. And my dog eats it!"

The Dalmatian, lipstick smeared across her jowls, crept on her belly across the floor to Barbara's feet, begging forgiveness.

And of course, the dog wasn't disappointed.

Barbara's flash of anger turned into a gale of laughter at the close-up sight of the lipstick-smeared dog.

"You sweet, foolish, idiotic animal" she murmured, fondling Piper's ears, "eating my newest, best lipstick!"

Playing detective, I examined the evidence: one empty lipstick case embossed with fake jewels and real teethmarks. The smears of lipstick on Piper's paws and on the pillows in her bed indicated to my detective's eye that the dog carried the lipstick to bed, held it in its paws, bit it out of the case and ate it bite by bite.

"Perhaps, Barbara, you could write up the whole incident, shoot a few documentary pictures of the lipsticked dog and sell the package to the manufacturer," I suggested.

"What a commercial: 'This purebred Dalmatian adores Estee Lauder's Heather Mist Rose . . . if it's good enough for a dog to eat a whole lipstick, the mere taste of a smidgeon will drive men wild!' "

Christmas and New Year's have taken their toll on the dog in our house.

It's not just the lipstick-eating, it's the change in sleeping habits and beds, plus a new technique of howling to the TV set, that has me worried about Piper.

Now a dog's bed is, I reckon, about equivalent to a man's castle. It is the dog's house, sanctuary, special place.

So with loving hands I built a huge, luxury bed for Piper, made from the best scrap lumber I could pinch, stained it mahogany and lined it with a baby-blue blanket.

Once my handiwork was done, I placed this dog's equivalent of a king-size water bed into a window seat with a commanding view of the great outdoors.

Piper loved it. And I was proud of having built the dog so grand a bed.

Then, just before Christmas, Piper quit the bed and began sleeping in a kind of basket-weave laundry basket — something we'd used as a car bassinet for a baby grandchild.

The problem there is that the dog is much too big for the basket. Her head droops over one end. Her tail hangs out over the other. And her body is cramped.

Piper loves to sleep. She spends not eight but close to 18 hours a day thinking and sleeping in that tiny basket. When she gets out, she has charley horses in her legs and must perform stretching exercises.

Sirens are Piper's latest heaven — or is it hell? Her ears are capable of hearing sirens from the police cars or fire stations miles away.

Maybe it is the fire engine tradition among Dalmatians.

But when the siren blows, up from the bed she springs, back goes her head and out comes the longest, eeriest wailing and howling.

It is funny to watch. But it qualifies as exercise for a dog addicted to hour after hour crunched up in the basket.

So now, when we are out of the house, we leave on the TV tuned to "Emergency" or "Hawaii Five-O" or any police drama in which squad cars keep sounding their sirens.

Every time a siren wails on the screen, Piper leaps up from sleep, throws back her head and howls and wails like a wilderness wolf.

There it is. Lipsticks. Bassinet. Sirens. What a trio!

Tell me, dog lovers, is there something queer going on with my Dalmatian?

Bitter night, ice-out day

It is midnight: Dead of winter.

The bitter cold hurts.

Ears hurt. Nose hurts. Lungs hurt with each intake of icy air. Eyes sting and weep with the cold. The wind is a knife twisting in your side.

Underfoot, even the snow squeals and squeaks, protesting the painful cold.

Overhead, branches of great trees 100 years old moan and groan like babies from the cold, aching behind their bark.

I stand huddling for shelter next to a giant tree trunk The ancient tree, a veteran of a hundred Maine winters, shrieks. A weird cry of pain sounds from within the frozen trunk.

The faraway moon, bigger, whiter, clearer than on an ordinary winter night, hangs in icy, disdainful beauty.

The pale light she throws down to Earth tonight is a white, sterile light — no gold, no warmth, no love in the moon this night. Even the moonlight glints and cuts like chilled steel tonight.

Snow is no blanket over the earth. Tonight the frozen snow is a hostile hard sheet, so hard it rejects and bounces back moonbeams like a cruel mirror.

Nearby, the river and ponds are brutal tonight. Tonight the friendly river and the timid pond will kill you. If tonight you should stumble into their wet embrace, you'd be dead within a few minutes.

The world outside tonight is a freezebox of silent, cold death.

Where do the birds keep warm tonight? How deep can mice and blind moles dig down to avoid death? Will hunger drive some night prowler out in desperate search for food? What besides frozen moonbeams could even a coyote find to eat this bitter night?

All Maine aches, enduring the beautiful killer cold.

In bright morning, the world is new and warm.

This is an 'ice-out' day of blue, cloudless skies, hot, bright sunshine and only the gentlest kiss of a breeze stirring the pine branches. This is a day to work at home and glory in Maine weather.

Down river, to the south from where I am writing, I see open water for the first time in many weeks. To the west, by ledges where baby seals soon will frolic again, the ice is breaking into floes.

This day is an outrunner for spring.

But the snow-covered ice still stretches deep and far into the river. Blue water is an occasional island surrounded by snow-covered ice.

I think there is no beauty to match a winter day in Maine like this one.

Pristine meadows of white snow are marked only by a few tracks of the animals who have been out scouting for food since the light snowfall at midnight. The green boughs of the pines are dusted white with powder snow. The willows in early morning are sheathed in a skin of ice.

Night wind has blown patterns in the new snow on the ice in the river. The snow pattern is the same ripple pattern as the wind forms in sand, so the snowfields, over water, look like a white sand desert.

Crimson red are the branches of the dogwood bushes planted beside the drive. As soon as the sun climbs higher, the brilliant redness will vanish.

Shadows change their color as well as their shade with the climb of the sun. By afternoon, when the sun shines from the westerly shore, there will be giant trees etched in shadow on the white snow.

The nights have been cold. So there is a crust on the snow. The corn snow shines, each kernel winking in the bright light of the sun. And the sun, changing position in the heavens, changes its colors on the snow. There is pink and gray and mauve and soon, at evening, there will be a blue hue to parts of the snow.

Sea gulls play high in the sky. The birds seem to be out joy riding. For so long, sleet and half gales and slashing rains have made a misery of the air and of a bird's life. So now they cavort in the clear bright air, the blue sky, the warm sun.

Five gulls sweep and soar, dive and turn, climb and roll in happy acrobatics. The bright sun scintillates on the leading edges of their white wings and, as they roll and turn, the sun bathes their white underpinnings and bellies with a blaze of light.

I call up my Dalmatian and we take a walk across virgin snowfields, leaving our mark on the world for a fleeting hour or two. We walk beside a stream, covered now by ice and snow. But if we stop and listen in the woods, we can hear rivulets of water dripping and running beneath the ice. The sun warms even the hidden icy water as it trickles down to join the river. Near the mouth of the tiny stream, I stop to gauge the spots where we will dip smelt on the night tide come spring. Even now life is stirring to new beginnings under our feet.

By afternoon, when school breaks out, the boys will be sorely tempted. By 3 p.m., upstream in Great Salt Bay, or even around the rapids at Johnny Orr's Rocks, the ice floes will look mighty tempting. By then the tide will be running downstream, too.

And can there be more thrilling sport than jumping from ice floe to ice floe, and poling along with an 8-foot stick? Some kids will arrive home cold and soaking wet today.

Now, at the river's edge, where the smelt stream meets the river, my dog and I slither and slide on the salt ice. Strange, funny stuff, this salt ice. It builds into weird shapes, pushed by tides and rocks.

And there is a mysterious smell of salt and seaweed and the beginnings of creation locked faintly into these weird layers of salt ice.

And beneath the salt ice groans, there is a soft melody — the chanting of the tide moving out to sea.

Dickens the coon cat comes home

PIPER'S BEND — Dickens, our tiny coon cat, who lives only upstairs, is back — thank heaven.

She vanished for a week. No amount of calling, of searching the woods and meadows nearby, of putting out food could tempt her back.

Then, while I was on the phone last evening, Dickens was suddenly there, arching her back, purring, behaving exactly as she always behaved. Automatically, I was scratching her behind the ears — and then with a shock of joy, realized I was petting the missing Dickens. The tiny wanderer was back home, after we had given her up for lost or even dead.

Joy brimmed to the top. I quickly hung up on my call, cradled the prodigal Dickens in my arms and went in search of Barbara, who was busy in a different part of the house. Without a word, I walked in, saying nothing. She spoke, without looking up from her sculpting — then turned, saw Dickens, did a triple take, and came rushing over to hold and pet Dickens and rejoice over her reappearance.

The cat, of course, looked bored. 'She purred. Seemed happy to be back. But clearly thought so much fussing over her was unseemly. With some persuasion, she nibbled at a meal, swished her bushy tail, and streaked to seclusion in her sanctuary upstairs.

I tell the story, because I would never have believed how deeply the disappearance of that tiny coon cat dented this household.

Dickens lived the last few years upstairs (an explanation is forthcoming in a moment). Her outdoor domain was the porch on the east side of the house upstairs. Fifty times in the last week, while Dickens was missing, I'd step out onto that porch and call, "Here, Dickens. Come home, Tom Dickens! Wherever you are, come home, Dickens!" And then I'd make idiotic kitty - kitty - kitty sounds to tempt her home.

The cat, of course, was out of earshot, turning a deaf ear, or had something better to do than come home. I knew all this. In that small, rational corner of my mind I knew that Dickens would come home, if she could, when she was good and ready. Or else she'd never come. But still, I'd go out and call from that porch early in the morning, late at night — whenever I was near it. And Barbara would do the same. Her cat-calling is much more enticing than mine.

In the evenings, after we got home from work, on weekends, and first thing each morning, we'd walk in the nearby woods, calling Dickens in vain among the trees and underbrush where she used to go mousing and mole-ing. We called animal shelters in all towns nearby. We placed a "lost" ad in the Lincoln County News; we phoned and alerted all neighbors.

I suppose everybody who has a pet missing does all this and more

and probably everybody is more shook up by that animal's unex-
plained absence than we like to admit. I suppose everybody else in
the same situation gets those dreadful pictures in their mind — of
their cuddlesome kitten mauled by a fisher, or with a leg broken, or
crying, lost and terrified and bone tired from futile attempts to find
the way home. Those wild and horrible imaginings drive you outdoors in the wee hours to stand in the night and idiotically call
your cat.

Now, like a cat, Dickens stalked home, without a hint of apology,
a word of explanation. Far from being starved or hurt, she looks
absolutely fine. It was only we who suffered while she was gone.
And she doesn't give a darn about that. She's just a doggone coon
cat. But this is a better, happier household now that prodigal cat
is back.

Memorial Day in a small town

DAMARISCOTTA — This is Memorial Day.

This morning there will be special parades, but they will be most special in the small towns of Maine. That is where parades — and memories — mean most.

In my town of Damariscotta, and our twin village across the river, Newcastle, signs of the parade begin about 10 a.m. Then the first fathers arrive, with the big kid held by one hand and the tiny kid riding on their shoulders, up high where the view is best. One father with two children also qualifies for a dog in tow.

Memorial Day parades are great reunions for dogs. Dogs which haven't been downtown all year come down for the parade.

Our twin-village parade is small, a few floats from the same local businesses, although this year the Lincoln County News reports there will be floats from as far away as Boothbay, Wiscasset and Waldoboro.

There is usually a fine turnout of the youngest Cub Scouts. Their bikes are jaunty with red, white and blue bunting. Some years we have a fine band from a distant school.

But small-town parades can carry a big load of meaning. The most moving moment in our parade is when our small platoon of marching veterans halts at the center of the Damariscotta-Newcastle bridge. The bridge is not wide and it is not long. But the river which it spans is beautiful and the water runs swiftly below.

In a short, simple and moving ceremony, a wreath is thrown off the bridge into the river. It is a wreath in memory of the men from these two small Maine towns who have died in battle — especially those whose graves are the oceans.

Wind often blows away the words of the ceremony. But we can always hear the crack of the rifles, fired in salute, and those spine-tingling, tear-provoking notes of Taps, blown on an old bugle by an old bugler or, in some years, by a young Boy Scout.

But the saddest, most tender sight is the wreath. When it hits the Damariscotta River, it swirls in the fast current. It sinks, rises again to the surface, sinks, and comes back again.

Then, mastered by the tide, it is pulled away from us. Many of us watch it. Then we watch where we lost sight of it, and we keep watching. But like the lost men it symbolizes, the wreath vanishes to places that we cannot see.

The little platoon shoulders arms again and continues the march down Main Street.

The first parade I watched here had a lot of high brass. Admiral Wray Fitch, who went down aboard the aircraft carrier Lexington in the battle of the Coral Sea and survived to fight again, was in those early parades.

Wray Fitch died at the age of 94, the oldest four-star admiral in the Navy. He was a much-loved man in these parts, a short, jaunty figure with a huge heart and bearing the very aura of the sea. His memory will live even longer than he did.

General Bill Wyman, commander of the 1st Division, marched in those parades with Admiral Fitch. And the long thin frame of Admiral Fred Richards, down from his historic house on the hill, Kavanagh. Fred Richards marched and watched the wreath drown in the river.

Those big brass are gone now. But other veterans of Marines, Navy, Air Force and Army are on the bridge today.

The Veterans Administration says that in Maine we have 40,000 veterans of the Vietnam War, 26,000 from the Korean War, 67,000 from World War II and 5,000 from the Great War.

Maine veterans occupy 661 beds at the Togus Veterans Facility. In the nursing home there I visited Arthur Merigold, 101, a veteran of the Spanish-American War. He charged up San Juan Hill with Teddy Roosevelt 80 years ago.

Togus itself is the oldest old-soldiers facility in our nation.

Across Maine there are 140,000 veterans alive today. And in graves from here to China lie many thousands more who never came home again. At Veterans Memorial Cemetery on a hillside beyond Augusta another 1,680 Maine veterans have been buried since 1970.

For a few minutes they live again, while that wreath spins in the current. Among the onlookers too, these are moments laden with memories which may lie buried; but today come briefly, piercingly to life.

The parade is over. The picnics, garden-plantings and softball games will soon begin.

Christmas in the New World began in Maine

BRISTOL MILLS — Last night, on Christmas Eve, we drove to a bell-ringing and carol-singing service in a country church — the Congregational Church in Bristol Mills, rooted in Maine history.

In February 1839, 12 men and their friends joined "to build a suitable house for the public worship of God, 43 feet by 53 feet by 18 feet."

This Christmas Eve, descendants of those very men gathered in the church 140 years later, and their voices filled the night with songs of praise and gratitude.

The church seemed filled far beyond the numbers of people present.

The spirits of thousands who had worshipped here, fished from these harbors, who had been baptized, married and buried in and from this church — all these seemed to assemble in happiness where they, too, had once celebrated Christmas Eve.

And there was great warmth in this continuity that reaches back across generations and nations, across seas and continents to a stable in Nazareth nearly 2,000 years ago.

Were those wise men and shepherds who came to the stable, guided by the star, wise enough to foresee that two millenia later bells would be ringing, carols would be rollicking on the night air, celebrating the birth they celebrated in that stable?

The night was bright and joyful with Christmas lights in almost every home, as we drove back from the bell-ringing and caroling, remembering that the first Christmas in the New World was celebrated here in Maine.

It happened 374 years ago, in bitter, lonely cold on a tiny island in the St. Croix River. There, on a few acres of land on Christmas Day 1605 amid the ice packs, 79 Frenchmen kneeled to celebrate the birth of the Christ child.

The Frenchmen were from two ships under the command of Sieur de Monts. His navigator, 37-year-old Samuel de Champlain, wrote an account of that first Christmas celebration in North America.

By springtime, 35 of that company of 79 were dead from unrelenting cold, sickness and starvation.

But the close ties between Christmas and Maine circle on.

Ten years after that first celebration on St. Croix Island, Captain John Smith dropped anchor in a cove at the mouth of the Damaris-

cotta River, close by the present site of the Bristol Mills church, and in 1615 celebrated the birth of Christ.

After the services, he marked the uncharted cove on his chart and named it Christmas Cove, the happy name it carries still.

But when Oliver Cromwell ruled England, the Puritans outlawed celebrations of Christmas, Easter and Whitsuntide, by act of the English parliament in June 1647. This dourness infected the Massachusetts Bay Colony, and the General Court in 1659 enacted a law which said: "Anybody who is found observing by abstinence from labor or by feasting any such day as Christmas, shall pay for every offense five shillings."

That's Massachusetts for you, taxing even Christmas.

But in Maine, the carols rang out, the venison roasted, the wine ran strong, the bells chimed and every man and woman and child here shouted "Merry Christmas to the world."

So on Christmas Day, here is a toast:

"Joy to all in Maine — first in the celebration of Christmas in the New World!"

Our Christmas tree made of memories

PIPER'S BEND — It is Christmas eve. Most Maine families are probably enjoying some special family ceremony that, more than anything else, spells Christmas to them. Usually it's something small, something strange to outsiders — but special to the family.

In our house it is hanging the last box of special ornaments, some moth-eaten, some tattered, some outlandish, some strangely beautiful, but each rich in memories.

These are the oldest ornaments left — pass-alongs from generations ago, survivors for up to 150 years. Or they are primitive ornaments, made in remote villages of distant countries and carried home to the States to brighten up our tree; sweet alien notes signifying ties to a village in Cambodia, a temple in Siam, a minaret in Constantinople, the Wailing Wall in Israel.

We hang these ornaments last, partly to save them from the perils of Piper, the dalmatian with the side-swiping tail; Dickens, the lightning-fast undersized coon cat; and Ski, the haughty elder-statesman of a cat, bossy in his marmalade coat. This trio erupts into wild steeplechases around and through every Christmas tree, causing havoc in two seconds.

The reason we hang this special box of ornaments last is because they are memories more than they are ornaments. To hang memories requires time that moves slowly, as on Christmas Eve, and gentle, unrushed hands. It also requires a very tolerant audience of one — to wit, my two-year-old granddaughter, Chloe, who has charm, interest, patience and laughing, loving eyes.

She unwraps the crinkled newspaper, slowly pulls away the soft tissue paper — and there is the tiger, and the elephant, and the lions, and the zebra, and the giraffe with the endless neck.

Chloe squeals happily at each. And in a flash my mind leaps from Maine to a village in Bengal, and I can feel the heat and sniff the strong smells of the tent where these wooden animals were carved. While Chloe hangs her tiger and elephants and lions and zebras, that Indian hamlet and this Maine village are blended on the eve of Christmas.

Next, out of a tiny box, come milkweed pods, sliced in halves, inside each half a tiny angel. And I tell Chloe about the little church in Bristol Mills which lost its belfry and where the ladies made quilts and toys and milkweed angels to raise the money for a new steeple. I promise to take her to that church for the bell ringing and the carol singing.

Tiny hands, remarkably gentle, unwrap a miniature Chinese dancer's hat: tall, white, conical, with scarlet sides. Next come papier-mache grasshoppers and brilliant-hued jungle birds from Thailand. And fat carp, fish for holiness and fertility and luck. And Chloe hangs these Buddhist symbols amid her angels and her Santa Claus.

Now her little hands unwrap minature temple hats, then rice baskets and tiny bamboo balls. And memories flood into this Maine house.

These ornaments were a present from a rice-planting lady and her four children in the Delta of Vietnam. They survived the war itself, but I have since heard that the mother died and two children — now about 16 years old — were among the "boat people" to escape Vietnam without, however, finding a haven that would allow them ashore from their leaking craft.

Chiloe hangs the rice basket and tosses the balls in happy laughter for Dickens, the miniature coon cat. I tell her no history here. Her father fought there and he has told her none.

A happy, gurgling shout of soprano pleasure and Chiloe pulls out fish dolls and cow dolls and turtle dolls from Guatemala — brilliant oranges and purples and yellows and reds, sent to us by friends.

She scoffs at the next dull Christmas ornaments. But I fondle these old, sacred, cheap-stuff friends. These are the survivors of the ornaments Barbara and I bought together for our first Christmas of marriage, in New York City in 1944.

Ours was a wartime marriage. I was back from Guadalcanal, not long out of military hospitals. Storekeepers would tell me, "No ornaments for Christmas trees — no material to make them. Don't you know there's a war on?" We made do with shoddy plastics whose thin, cheap paint has chipped away. I hang them with joy now.

Next come some heavy ornaments. The good old, solid mirror glass of grandmother's time and earlier. The tree boughs bend under these century-old ornaments that put to shame what we make today.

Now, wooden cutouts of toy soldiers, their fixed grins and colorful uniforms brilliantly painted. And again memories flood in. My daughter Susan made these for the tree when we were running a newspaper in London and she was attending an English boarding school. I see her bringing home these toys — a tiny blonde in gray flannel coat and hat, the uniform of English schoolgirls.

We hang them next to a partridge in a pear tree.

Chiloe shrieks with laughter as she pulls out the long-tailed Christmas mice. I had forgotten them until this moment: goodluck mice made of red flannel, with long, long tails. And I remember now the very pretty debutante (they had such creatures in London in 1960) next door who made these little mice for her Irish Guard escorts, who wore them at parties, hung by a paper clip to the epaulettes of their splendid uniforms. And what a way for them to end up — here in a Maine winter.

The next package is another sad one: camels, Wise Men, shepherds tending their flock — all handsomely carved and bought from a shop in the old city of Jerusalem, within earshot of the wailing wall. I arrange them tenderly at the foot of the tree and feel a surge of love for that magic city and hope that peace may soon envelop her.

Chiloe leaps up, dancing. She is holding some tiny brass temple bells from India and Siam whose lovely, pure liquid sound brings back the sounds of bells being rung by saffron-robed, shaven-headed monks in gaudy, Buddhist temple courtyards. Chiloe dances to their sound today in Maine.

From a special box we unwrap the old wooded angel choir and orchestra, carved long ago in the Black Forest of Germany by a Bavarian wood cutter. With these jewel-like figures are some heavy, waxed German Christmas tree balls, embossed with gold and blue and red crosses and crowns.

Finally, the creche figures, made for Chiloe's great-great grandfather, made in Vermont. Survivors of 150 Christmases and as many children Chiloe's age. We place them around the tree.

The special box is empty now. And you would have to look carefully to find most of these last ornaments we have hung, because so many other lights and brilliant pretties are also on the tree.

But I know, you know, and now Chiloe knows about the most important part of the Christmas tree — the memories and joys and hopes that lie in every branch, hard to see, but filling to the heart.

Merry, happy Christmas.

Had Your Bottom Coppered Lately?

DAMARISCOTTA — In writing columns, I have touched on some pretty personal topics.

But today is the first time I have ever gone so far as to discuss in the public prints the whys and wherefores of getting my bottom coppered.

This is no solitary problem. Now the weather is warming up, maybe 100,000 Maine men are worrying about getting their bottoms coppered, too.

This is an important and expensive masculine business, which preys on a man's mind about this time of year.

When you see a man looking as poor as if he had just paid off the national debt, and with his hands and forehead seemingly streaked with bloodstains, sympathize, ladies! That man is probably on his way home from getting his bottom coppered.

He needs love. He needs a stiff drink. He needs a bit of careless rapture. Give him what he needs, ladies, for a man gets his bottom coppered only once — possibly twice — a year.

And it hurts. It hurts his pocketbook; it puts kinks into his spine; it tears flesh off his knees and elbows; it strains the sockets in his eyeballs; it leaves bloody looking stains on his hands. If he wears a beard, he may look as if he had slashed his throat with a rusty razor. One glance at his pants and shirt might make you think he was Jack The Ripper.

Love him, ladies. That man has not only got his bottom coppered; he has also gone overboard. He is launched!

A man with a freshly coppered bottom may look like a murderer; but there is a song of love in his heart. For his boat is in the water again. He is free at last from land-locked winter.

Love him, ladies . . . but never, never ask "How much did it cost you to copper your bottom?"

VII
PORTLAND, A CITY GROWING YOUNGER

Portland City Hall Tower

PORTLAND *is an old city, suddenly getting younger.*

'I came, expecting a dull, prim, city. But after 48 hours here, I found Portland is the unknown gem of America's small cities.' Sounds like a chamber of commerce blurb? Actually that's a quote from a visiting official from another city.

A Delta airline pilot, who flies everywhere and could live anywhere, said 'A year ago I chose Portland over any city anywhere on our routes.'

I like quoting these people. Because after working in Portland about 15 years, I too discovered the city only recently. Really it is a new city, in its prime again. In recent years an influx of young people has imbued Portland with new vigor. They have brought old buildings back to fashion; have brought music, theater, restaurants, shops into stylish bloom; have filled concert halls and hockey arenas.

Sure, the Establishment and the big banks decided to swim with the tide started by the young people. And when they did, credit and investment funds loosened up. Portland is a transformed city, visibly, conspicuously exciting; whereas a few years ago, Portland was fading, boring, without verve.

Portland Symphony, Portland theater groups, Portland School of Art, the University of Southern Maine, the Law School, the

Maine Medical Center, the big banks, the burgeoning law firms, the insurance companies, the investors and dreamers are together now, fused into a fine force for a better, cheaper city.

Soon the Portland waterfront will catch the fine infection and this, the heart of the city, will beat again strongly.

Now, instead of a buck-up trip in mid-winter to New York or Boston, more and more Maine people head for a few days in Portland. 'It's all here; on a smaller scale; friendlier, safer, easier — and at half the price,' they say.

Here are a few glimpses on the light side, at the good life of Portland. Find the rest firsthand.

The Loft: Home of Rock in Portland

PORTLAND — Lights flashed. Rock music blared. The building seemed to heave and shake and tremble with the explosive combination of sound, light, and 300 dancing kids. It was The Loft.

And it was great.

I stood in the doorway of The Loft with my eyes half-blinded and my ears half-deafened, and I let the rain pour off me. Outside it was 11 p.m. and Portland was being drowned. Around town barely a car was stirring through the torrential rain.

But at The Loft, down on Boyd Street between Bayside and Marginal Way, the parking lot was jammed. New arrivals searched, then found, parking spots. Shapes wrapped in raincoats would leap out of the cars and dash through and around puddles, racing for the entrance. The door would open; out would pour noise and light; in would go still another batch of youngsters, out for a piece of fun.

A bunch of us new arrivals stood dripping by the entrance, getting used to the noise and the dryness, the wildly spinning lights and the rock dancing.

I was the only gray-haired, gray-bearded guy in the place, and felt as conspicuous as a nude. Everybody else seemed to be 20 to 23. I had been out earlier in the night, making a speech to a large meeting in a church. I therefore had on shirt, tie, coat — all the trappings of ancient age.

That's when the kids drifted up. First a bearded guy in jeans. "Aren't you the writer in the Press Herald?"

We talked, shouting over the uncountable decibles of Beaver Brown's drummer in hell-bent pursuit of the world's last great bang. Then a girl with the bright dew of lovely youth came over. She introduced herself.

We had met up at The Country Club Inn at Rangeley, where she had helped out by waitressing. I went back to her table, and soon a dozen kids were around drinking beer, telling me what they did, why they were here in the Loft, and how the band ranked with them.

My friend, the girl from Rangeley, is an English student at University of Southern Maine. "I worked till 10:30 tonight and needed a break. Tonight is Ladies Night here. My girl friends and I drove over to get our heads out of the books for a while. But at 2 a.m. I'll be back at the books again. Exams soon."

The guy across the table, a good-looking, quiet fellow said he was a microbiologist. He recently graduated from University of Maine at Orono and was "shaking down" before getting into a career.

On stage, Beaver Brown was putting on the hardest working show I've seen a band do. They played for 50 minutes flat-out: loud, energetic, frantic — and good. The leader, in brown topper, brown silk clothes and white clown face, sang, danced, pranced and kept the rock group together. On the floor more and more kids danced. Between the lot, they generated enough energy to warm half the city during the coldest week of winter.

The girls got up and went to the bar. "Half price for us on Ladies Night. So we are treating you."

I yelled questions over the blare of the band and strained to hear the kids yell back their answers. We got the messages back and forth to each other all right for a few fascinating hours. I liked the kids. I liked the lights. Liked the music.

Bill Dowd, the 29-year-old owner of The Loft, came over. He says he's put over $250,000 into The Loft, a site which once housed Capitol Motors. (It still has the concrete floor, loading doors and platforms for trucks.)

He spends around $2,000 a week on music. "But the ban on selling beer to 18 and 19 year olds is killing a lot of nightclubs. The 20 year drinking age has put some spots out of business. That means bands, waiters, bartenders — lots of lost jobs.

"It's a domino effect. Drive the 18- and 19-year-olds out, and the crowd gets small, the dance floor gets dull, and pretty soon you are shut. . .

"Tell me, where are those 18 and 19 year olds that can't get served here? Are they home in bed? Not likely. They are maybe raising hell. Better they were in here dancing, having fun."

The Loft is the biggest, noisiest, supervised playpen in town.

Gutsy ladies turned 65

PORTLAND — Old ladies who've had it tough have more guts and courage and mule determination than General George Patton, or Sergeant York, or any bemedalled war hero you care to name.

I passed two of these ladies on the street in Portland. One was walking toward me, tapping her way with a white cane, signaling blindness. She came along sure-footed, despite slush and snow underfoot. She came along straight-backed, erect, proud.

She was immaculately groomed. Her white hair was fluffy and wavy and pretty. She wore a beige coat, a matching kind of oatmeal-colored dress and shoes with highish heels. And she wore thick, rim-less glasses.

She went sailing by, headed up Congress street, alone, undaunted by sightless eyes. She was a pretty looking woman of close to 80. But what I admired was her guts.

For seconds I watched her go, wondering how long it had taken her to get dressed to go out. Does she live alone? How hard is it for her to do the ordinary things? What kind of determination does it take to decide to get up, get dressed, get the white cane and go walking up Congress Street on a cold windy day with slippery slush underfoot?

As she turned the corner, I wished we had more like her — about 60 years younger.

Just moments later came another gutsy lady. She, too, seemed between 70 and 80 years old. But her sight seemed fine. She was built more slightly — frail might be the word, except her spirit was so strong. She had been shopping.

In each hand she was carrying a big cloth bag; one filled with groceries for the table and the other with books — food for her mind on a lonely night.

I watched her go. Slowly she went. The load was heavy, but well balanced. And I wondered how far she had to walk, how many steps she had to climb to her room. But, by the look of her walk and the expression of her eyes, there would never be the sound of a whimper or the whine of a complaint from her.

The third lady whose guts I greatly admire I met in a supermarket in my hometown. She is a lot younger than my Portland ladies. She is, I think she said, going on 63. She is lithe, bouncy, vigorous.

And she is the paper-lady.

She delivers the Portland Press Herald.

She brought up six sons. Today she holds down other daily jobs after she delivers her 60 papers each morning.

One of her sons is a long-distance runner at the University of Maine in Orono. It fits.

"I set out on my paper rounds at 2:30 a.m.," she told me. "I have a little cart I pull along. Sure, it's a weird hour. But at 2:30 in the winter morning, there are no cars around to bother or splash me."

She described the route she walks in the wee hours. I had never walked so far in my town. I never will. But she does it, rain, sleet, snow, dark of the moon or brilliant, star-lit night.

"My friends told me to give up the paper route this winter. But I said no. It makes me feel good to get that walking every day."

She says she finishes her rounds about 4:30 a.m. "Then I have time to climb back into bed and get two hours of sleep before I start my next job."

Her name is Lois Holmes of Damariscotta. She is small and she has more guts and gumption and mule determination than most men I've met.

Around Maine, there are scores of wonderful ladies like these. God knows how deep they dig for their endless reserves of spirit and stamina and courage. Gods knows what sorrows they have seen to build up such strength.

What a nation of giants America would be if we were all like them.

Art gem; Payson gallery

PORTLAND — Treat yourself well and go to the Joan Whitney Payson Gallery of Art on the Westbrook College campus. It is open to the public, free.

Note the words — "Gallery of Art." This is not a museum. It is small. It is intimate. It is simple. It is elegant. If you have never before been to an art gallery, go to this one. Maine has never had such a collection of gorgeous and easy-to-enjoy paintings by so many of the world's great contemporary painters.

Some of the great artists whose works are now here in Portland are: Marc Chagall, with a brilliant joyous burst of flowers; Degas, with that famous painting of the ballet lessons; Gaugin, the French impressionist with a landscape, and Maine's Winslow Homer, with one of his great seascapes.

Also, Pablo Picasso is at Westbrook College with three small, exquisite and charming pieces. You'll love the big Renoir with that wonderful way he makes light shine on and reflect from a girl's white dress and the way he can create a scene of physical love by painting a man and girl just sitting in a park reading a newspaper together.

Sir Joshua Reynolds is here with two lovely aristocratic portraits. There are two early Andrew Wyeths, filled with more color than he puts in most of his work, and two paintings by John Singer Sargent. (By the way, Wyeth and Sargent are the only two Americans ever elected to the Academie des Beaux Arts in France.)

Then there is the smasher that will blow your mind. It is the first painting you see as you enter — smack in front of your eyes — Vincent Van Gogh's painting of iris, flowers painted in a shade of blue that will live on, indelible in your mind's eye.

And more, much more. Probably more than $3 million worth of beautiful masterpieces are gathered at the Payson Gallery for your pleasure.

John and Nancy Payson gave this gem to Maine in memory of his mother, Joan Whitney Payson of Falmouth. This remarkable lady — a unique, unabashed lover of life and beauty — was a Renaissance woman. She collected great art, owned magnificent races horses and was such a baseball fan that she wound up as president and owner of the New York Mets.

When you come to see the paintings be sure to take a special look at the building. In size it is modest — a cube 32 feet in all directions. Thanks to a pyramidal skylight and an atrium, natural daylight floods the building. Note how all the beams and ducts are exposed, yet do not intrude.

Designed by Thomas Larson of the Architects Collaborative, the total plan calls for up to six more similar modules to be added by future benefactors to Westbrook College and Maine.

The Payson Gallery of Art is a new pearl in Maine's crown. Go to see it and be enchanted by the treasures it holds.

The Phoenix; church turned disco

PORTLAND — They told me the "gay" bar in Portland was the Phoenix on Oak Street. So I went there at 11 p.m. one Thursday night to see if it lived up to its racy reputation.

It did not.

Sure there is half-truth to it. Some gay boys were there; and a few were on the dance floor together. A pair of striking looking girls were also dancing together; although in disco-dancing no couple is together much. But the majority of the people on the dance floor were straight male/female couples having a darned good time.

The Phoenix was the first to open in Portland with the real disco-sound and disco-lights and disco-photo murals in slow dissolves. Now there are many.

The Phoenix is the only disco to rise from what was an old church.

The wide red-carpeted entrance hall, complete with uniformed security guard, is where the minister used to greet the congregation. Down a few steps to a pleasant looking restaurant. Upstairs to a long bar which is separated from the dance floor and the 50 or so tables. The high ceiling is appropriately — a cathedral ceiling. The disc jockey and his sound machines are in a kind of loft high above the dance floor — which is just under where the great arched church window used to fill most of one wall. The window is covered now; and serves as a screen for the revolving photo murals projected on it as an extra dimension of the disco-beat.

Disco music in the Phoenix has a special sound tailored by d.j. Timmy Cyr, 26, to suit this room. Disco beat is magnified by the light show. Strobe lights and spinners, reflectors and dimmers and the silver globe in perpetual motion, add another dimension to the disco music. The lights are hooked into the woofers and tweeters of the sound system. The beat and blare of the music are magnified by the synchronized beat and rhythm of the ever changing lights; and all this is linked to the visual wallop of photo murals dancing on the window wall. The pictures are slides of Maine scenes mixed with pop art and a weird effect is achieved by wrapping the slides around a revolving drum in the projector. Result is murals which pulsate and alter shapes in conjunction with the sound and light. Total effect — a kind of happy hypnotic blending of dancers with sound light and pictures.

Randy Toothacher, 24, manages The Phoenix for owner Roland Labbe. Toothacher says the renovation of the old church into a modern disco cost over $200,000; and that the sound-light systems are a $30,000 investment.

Toothacher comes from the Rangeley region, went to Mt. Abraham High School there and studied political science at the University of Southern Maine. Asked about the reputation as a gay bar Toothacher said "Our policy is to run a liberal and cosmopolitan establishment appealing to a high cross section of all life styles . . . If we have a code, it is decent behaviour and good taste and thoughtfulness for the way others feel."

He says the job of the uniformed security guard on duty everynight is to keep out anyone offending these codes. "Also all coats must be checked at the cloak room before going up to the bar and dance floor. This way nobody will lose a lovely leather coat slung over the chair while dancing; and nobody can conceal a big knife or other weapon under a coat."

"This is a world more and more people are enjoying" says Toothacher who often welcomes 200 to 300 people a night in the Phoenix."

As I opened the old church doors to leave the music amplifiers and the light spinners fused in a multi-decible multi-watt crescendo of "What's Your Name? What's Your Number?"

And I wondered if the Quakers who once held services here would understand.

Old Port reborn, style setter for the city

PORTLAND — At the top of a steep flight of narrow stairs in a six-story building on Exchange Street, I found Frank Akers, the man who has had more impact on the revitalization of Portland's Old Port Exchange area than anybody, including banks, city, state and federal governments.

Akers has bought, remodeled and sold 14 buildings in the Old Port area in eight years, 1970-78, and is holding on to two more. One day, he realized he had 130 tenants in 14 buildings inside four blocks.

Portland's Old Port section has become one of the most notable success stories in the rejuvenation of inner city neighborhoods in New England. When people in other cities want to know how to restore their heritage to new prosperity, this is where they come to find the answers.

Frank Akers, who spearheaded the transformation, points out that he and others who helped had to fight Portland's City Hall almost every step of the way.

And even now, he says, he's not liked by a lot of people, "because I bought half-derelict buildings for $5,000 and $10,000 right under their noses and sold them for $150,000 a couple of years later." The bankers and city councilors who scoffed at the idea of turning these once rundown streets into sought-after property didn't like the way he operated, says Akers.

Swiveling in his old fashioned office chair in front of an old fashioned roll top desk rescued from some half-abandoned building, he looks out over this now-prospering area of Victorian real estate and says, "And you know, we did it without a nickel of federal money — well, until 1973, when the feds kicked in $7,500 to help put the sidewalks into walking condition."

The sidewalks were relaid so people could walk on them safely, recalls Akers. "Then two days later the city assessors came down and upped the valuation and taxes on all the buildings."

Frank Akers, 49, came to Portland from Cleveland when he was 31. He'd married a Maine girl, Nancy Brewster, and she wanted to come back here. So he quit his job with an Ohio steel company and bought into O. P. Peterson, an old Portland company respected all along the coast for the brass propellers, ship's bells and other brasswork it produced.

Business was pretty good, with a foundry on Union Street and a retail store on High Street across from the Sheraton-Eastland, says Akers. "Then in 1968 city hall told us we'd have to move: They wanted to tear down our building on Union so they could drive through a road."

City planners, recalls Akers, suggested he relocate in places unsuitable or too expensive. "And that's what forced my attention onto the Old Port."

Buildings that now fetch $100,000 or more could be had for $5,000, but city officials and local bankers and merchants warned him against investing in them, says Akers. They told him there'd never be any foot traffic, not to risk locating there.

So in 1969, forced to move by the city, Akers bought the building on Fore Street, near Exchange, where Joseph's, the fashionable clothing store now operates. Although the purchase price was only $4,500, no bank would make a mortgage on it.

After moving in he found it was too small, so in 1970 he bought the building a few yards further along the street that he's in today. He paid $10,000 for this prime corner block, in excellent structural condition, and still couldn't get a dime out of the banks toward a mortgage.

Akers is very proud of this old building where his offices now are and where he lives in a penthouse he created to overlook the harbor.

"I've dug back into history," he says. "Phineas Fox had a building on this site in 1770 when this was called Falmouth. In 1828 his sons operated clipper ships and stored axes and shovels here, shipped them to the Caribbean and brought back molasses for rum. This building went up in 1828 and then was extended in 1854.

Akers says that soon after he moved his Peterson Brass Co. into the building the city warned him not to get too settled because they

were planning to extend Exchange Street right through to the water-front and would demolish his building.

"This time I decided to fight," says Akers. "They'd gotten me out of one building and then had never demolished it, and I wasn't about to let it happen again."

Akers says he got together with Henry Willette, another man who started buying buildings in the area when the prices were as low as $2,000, and with Curran Electric and Kenniston Linoleum, two local firms, to form the Old Port Exchange Association.

"Henry was a powerhouse," says Akers. "He'd worked in the city planning office and he knew the ropes. But we knew that if we were going to carry any political clout we had to have more people in-volved. If we were to survive, we had to get other buildings with retail stores to attract traffic. How was the big question.

"About this time, customers coming into the brass store would rave about the historic buildings all around. Honestly, I'd had no aware-ness of them. They were rundown warehouses. But these people opened my eyes.

"Then one day Henry Robinson stopped me in the street and said: 'Frank, why don't you buy the C. H. Robinson block?' I said I didn't have that kind of money. He said, 'Make me an offer.' "

The Robinson block is actually four city blocks: Moulton, plus the pieces of the three other streets it fronts on: Commercial, Market and Fore. It comprises five substantial buildings including one of Maine's most notable architectural structures, the Mariners' Chapel, and Akers got the lot — which he now thinks is worth around $1 million — for $75,000.

This time he found one banker willing to take a mortgage: Bill Graham at Portland Savings.

"Bill had been a loan officer in Hartford and knew what city res-toration could do. But he got into a lot of criticism for making me that loan."

By spring, Akers had 38 tenants running small shops facing onto four streets.

One of the earliest of the businesses to open was the Old Port Tavern. 'But we got no services from the city. Even the streets here weren't on the list to be cleared of snow by the Department of Public Works. Some days city plows would throw snow so high in front of the tavern you couldn't even see the restaurant, let alone get to it.

"So we bought our own snowblowers and cleared our own side-walks and the city manager, John Menario who'd helped us with other things, ordered the public works equipment to help out."

City hall was so cheap, says Akers, that he even had to buy street signs and pedestrian crossing signs out of his own pocket.

In 1973, Akers bought three more buildings on Fore Street, close to Exchange, renovated them for stores and rented them at 75 cents a square foot to bring more life and business to the area.

"All told, I've bought and sold 14 buildings and I still own two and may buy more," he says. And he still holds mortgages on build-ings he sold, so that he can control what kind of business goes into them.

Even with prices and taxes climbing, Akers says he tries to keep rents down to $1.50 a square foot so businesses can start, grow and prosper.

But one cause of higher rents, complains Akers, is the way the city keeps jumping the property taxes. "When I bought the Robinson block it was on the city books at $18,000. Two years later, it was $138,000. And all I'd done was put in windows and electricity and rent out the store fronts. This is a fine city. But we've got to en-courage young people to come in and take risks to make it better."

In eight years of transformation in the Old Port, Akers has become a wealthy man. He has made far more money than he ever dreamed of making with Peterson Brass — which he sold five years ago. Now his real estate operations spread far beyond the Old Port area and he has seven brokers and several companies.

"Maine is filled with opportunity if you'll just take a risk and work hard," he says. "I made mistakes. I missed the chance to buy Long Wharf and Pocohontas Wharf and the building where Canal has a branch bank on Commercial Street. I could have bought it all for $75,000. Today the price would probably be over a quarter million."

Wet T shirt night

PORTLAND — Seeking a taste of the action-after-dark in Portland on a Wednesday night, I walked out of the Holiday Inn Downtown about 9:15 p.m. and saw that the Rook and Pawn was a lively magnet — pulling in customers from all directions.

I joined a line at the entrance, where an amiable chap in a heavy, open-necked plaid shirt took a dollar from all comers.

It was my first visit. Plainly, this was a place ready for action of some kind. It was jammed to the rafters. I managed to finagle a spot midway along the bar.

A burly bartender with graying hair and a fine grin put out his hand. "Tony Cremo," he said. "What'll you have?"

I got a giant ginger ale over ice (big deal) and asked my neighbor what the drawing card was, why the place was jumping with flesh — 90 percent masculine and under 30.

"Man, this is T-shirt night, wet T-shirt night. That accounts for the crowd."

People were three deep at the bar. Every table was jammed. The so-called corridor was jammed. Tiny waitresses balanced huge jugs of beer on trays over their heads and cut a dangerous path through throngs of happy, anticipatory males.

Tony Cremo's candid color photos now started showing on an overhead screen. His pictorial records of last Wednesday's wet T-shirt performance gave me the drift of what was to come. Tony and his brothers were building suspense higher among an eager crowd.

Cash registers never stopped ringing. Beer never stopped flowing. I got talking with guys to the left, to the right and behind. From Peaks Island, Yarmouth, Gorham they had come for the wet T-shirt gala. The South Portland Fire Department had a goodly turnout at the nearest table.

People told me the Rook and Pawn was a tough spot. Maybe it is. But it was not during the 90 minutes I was there. Boisterous, crowded, noisy, loud-mouthed, beered up a bit in places. But not mean and not tough.

I noticed a few signs warning that no motorcycle club colors could be worn inside. That was the clue. If rival motorcycle clubs, juiced up on a few beers, got into a dispute, the argument could turn into a gangfight quicker than in any Dublin waterfront pub.

But now the wet T-shirt preliminaries occupied all eyes. First, judges were chosen amid whoops and hollers from those wanting the job. Then up went the cries of encouragement for contestants.

Competing girls were given T-shirts. Once they were on stage, some macho man was given a giant pitcher of water by Cremo. He doused the girl. Another pitcher of water, and he doused her again — over the head, over the chest, inside the shirt.

Cheers rang. The girl who got the loudest cheers won $50. Second prize $20. Third prize $10.

I stayed only for the first three contestants and then gave up my ringside vantage point to eager spectators.

Now, a lot of readers will think this wet T-shirt nonsense is degrading. To lots of girls it certainly would be. But not to all. These contestants threw out their chests in prideful rivalry. They reacted happily to the applause.

Outside, the cold February air tasted sweet and clean. My lungs, eyes, ears, nose smarted from the dense smoke and madhouse sounds inside.

To me the wet T-shirt deal was new. Yet it was the sort of thing that was all the rage at fraternity parties, about the same time college boys proved their manhood by swallowing goldfish.

But today's point is that the Rook and Pawn was busting at the seams; the cash registers were ringing higher and faster than most customers could count; and all thanks to the wet T-shirt show on Wednesday nights.

It's about the cleanest, coolest, silliest and wettest game in town between 9:30 and 10:30 on a Wednesday night.

C. Q. Clapp's legacy of buildings

PORTLAND — This is a column of thanks to Charles Q. Clapp of Portland. Never heard of him? Nor had I until I enjoyed a day of looking at handsome buildings in downtown Portland. Then I learned about Charles Q. Clapp.

As soon as I walked out of the Holiday Inn Downtown, where I had spent the night, I was face-to-face with a big, handsome, white-pillared unforgettable house, next to the YWCA on Spring Street. Charles Q. Clapp built it as his own home in 1832. Now it is the Portland School of Art. And it's a beauty still, Mr. Clapp.

I walked up the Spring Street hill to the handsomest street of row houses in Portland — Park Place. C. Q. Clapp had a hand in building these, too, in 1848. In fact, Clapp had a hand in more than 600 real estate transactions in old Portland, and the mark he left is still a lovely imprint on our city.

KCM   1832 CLAPP HOUSE

Down to Fore Street in the Old Port for lunch at the Seaman's Club. I stood across the street to admire its magnificent, huge, arched second story window. Went inside for a splendid lunch and discovered that friend Charles Q. Clapp had built this handsome building, too, right after the great Portland fire of 1866.

That's when I began to feel sad and guilty about having worked in Portland for so long — and seen so little of its beauty. To see it, you must walk. So I took a book called "Portland," a handsome and excellent guide to Portland's loveliness, issued by Greater Portland Landmarks Inc., and walked.

First stop — Portland City Hall.

I'd been in city hall scores of times. But this day I spent 20 minutes outside, really enjoying its elegant beauty. A cop on foot patrol eyed me carefully. City halls in Portland meet violent ends. Maybe he figured I was an irate taxpayer with a bit of demolition or arson in mind. This is the third city hall built on this same site since 1862. The others went down in flames, in 1866 and again in 1908. This one is a gem among all city halls.

Our city council of 1909 went out of state to hire Carrere and Hastings, the fashionable New York City architects, who had just designed the House and Senate office buildings in Washington and the New York Public Library. I think Portland City Hall is the best of all their work.

My next stop along Congress Street, just beyond Monument Square, the Wadsworth-Longfellow House.

When General Peleg Wadsworth built this in 1785, it was the first brick house on the peninsula. Two ships brought the bricks from Philadelphia.

Going up Congress Street, I pass the handsome new Maine Savings Bank and plaza, then stop at a landmark I never really knew before. . . . The Maine Charitable Mechanics Hall.

Sure, at street level I have shopped Carter Bros. jewelry store and the photo store. But until this afternoon, I'd never looked up to see and admire those three, huge, arched windows on the second floor. They seem almost three stories high. Stop and look for yourself and enjoy the busts. Archimedes, the greek mathematician and mechanic, is above one window; Vulcan, the Roman god of fire and metal-working, is above the next; and over the third is the muscular arm of Labor, wielding a sledgehammer.

At the top of Congress Street is another wonderful heritage from Charles Q. Clapp . . . the flatiron building called Hay's Drug Store, at the corner of Congress Square and Free Street. This was designed and built by Clapp in 1826, early in his career. Maine has only one other flatiron building. Look at the second floor and enjoy the fine round windows, lovely mark of late Federal architecture. The top floor was added almost 100 years later, in 1922, by Portland's most famous architect, John Calvin Stevens.

Landmarks, the citizen group doing such a fine job of preserving and restoring Portland beauty, hopes to make restoration of this flatiron building a cornerstone for the restoration of other buildings along Congress Street. Soon the city will rejuvenate Congress Square, the way it did Monument Square. Soon a great new gallery of fine art may be here.

All through Portland miracles of restoration and rejuvenation are happening. But to see them you need to walk slowly and look.

Try it. Take a city walk soon — and enjoy seeing Portland.

Peddler to millionaire; Portland's John Martin

The hot beat of disco music pours out on the snowy streets from John Martin's Play Room in Portland.

The sound works like a magnet, pulling in the crowd exiting from the Mariners ice hockey game at the Civic Center across the street. Despite two feet of snow, Portland wants to disco tonight.

Inside the Play Room is a good moving portrait of the new Portland.

First, the dancers: More than 300 of them, mostly between 25 and 35 years old, all stylishly dressed, all spending freely, and most dancing well to the latest disco steps. Where were such Portland crowds a few years ago?

Where, indeed, was the Civic Center? Or the Maine Mariners Hockey Team? Where were the restaurants such as Marcel's and Parker Reidy's and Gardner's and the Baker's Table and the Old Port and the Seaman's Club and the Hollow Reed and many others like them — which today are packed at noon and night.

John Martin tells me, half in sign language over the thumping disco beat, that he dropped a bundle on the room that predated the Play Room.

"We got the best designers and decorators and good bands; but that room never took. Too cold. So I took my loss and closed it. Traveled the country and looked in every city for the kind of place I thought Portland would like, and we got this. Portland loves it.

"Sure, $175,000 worth of decor helps; and the DJ, Paul LaRoche, came in from Phoenix. He's a crowd-pleaser. The crowd we want is the 25-year-old and up. So we do soft, not hard, disco. Our $15,000 lighting system won't blind you; and our sound system won't make you deaf. Paul runs the gamut with the music. But dancing, dancing is the heart of the matter."

Martin, now 61, got his start in business with a vegetable pushcart, working Portland streets with his father, who came from Armenia. "We did $100 a week in sales, tops."

Thirty-five years later John Martin sold his nine huge supermarkets. He was doing a million dollars a week instead of $100, just 35 years after his days on the pushcart.

"When this poor boy sold out and became rich in money, I thought I'd sit back and enjoy it. Drove me nuts, sitting. So four years ago I bought The Art Gallery. Turned a loser into a winner. Two years ago, we bought cheaply what is now the Merry Manor in South Portland and now its lounge does the biggest volume north of Boston.

"Just a year ago, we got another low-price buy, the old Jefferson in Waterville, and we've turned that around. The next spot for another Martin restaurant and disco is Bangor."

John gets up and does some disco himself. His son Peter, who works here, comes off the floor to talk. Martin's wife Sybil does much of the decor and promotes the sale of Maine artists whose paintings she hangs everywhere. Daughters Andrea and Marcia are in TV; Andrea, a top comedienne on ABC-TV's Second City, and Marcia, as a TV producer in Toronto.

John Martin comes back to the table, beaming after his disco dancing. "What a city? Who'd guess a pushcart peddler would end up owning a spot like this? And dancing to Boogie Shoes and Freak Out? Portland can't be beat — anywhere!"

Island ghosts of Casco Bay

CASCO BAY — There are ghosts among the islands of Casco Bay. On stormy nights in October, close to Halloween, they prowl the rocky shores. Any night now, you may hear ghostly cries, or see ghostly lights, coming from the Casco islands. So here are a few of the many ghosts who may be prowling, waving lanterns or wailing on the night.

On Thanksgiving a fisherman-farmer by the name of Wilson, took down his gun and went hunting on Orrs Island. His wife worried when many hours after she had heard his shots, her husband still had not returned. So, good wife that she was, she took down her own gun and went out to Orrs Island to look for him.

Neither returned that long night. Nor the next morning. Whereupon their friends and neighbors got up an expedition to search for them on Orrs. They rowed out to the Island. There they found, by a giant rock, two skeletons — one of a man, the other of a woman. Their bones were picked clean. Close by they found the skeletons of twelve wolves, picked clean.

What happened? And is that howling sound you hear at night the wail of the Wilsons? Or the wail of the wolves?

The ghost of a part-Indian lady has already done her supernatural work on Great Island, known also by the Indian name of Sebasco-degan.

In the early 1800's there lived an old, part-Indian lady, a strange and lonely woman who stood far apart from her neighbors. They spoke of her in whispers behind the palms of their hands, muttering that she had witches' powers. But the old woman most disliked a man who lived next door. He mocked her. And she swore that she would come back to torment him after death, if she were buried near his body.

In due course, she died and was laid into her grave in the island cemetery, like all other dead islanders. Her threat had been long forgotten, until the night was rent with wails and weeping, and weird witch-like incantations. Then the folk of the island recalled her vow.

They realized that the body of the neighbor she disliked so much now lay in the same cemetery. What to do? Meetings were held by the frightened and disturbed islanders who had heard the wailings and incantations. They voted to dig up the part-Indian, part-witch lady and move her to a new grave far distant from the neighbor she disliked in her earthly days. This they did. And the ghostly sounds and sights ended. 'But who can tell whether they might begin again on this Halloween?

On Pond Island, there is a strange ghost story concerning a hermit and his dog. On stormy nights some have said they see the ghostly figure of a man walking the beach with a dog at his heels. Others say they hear the ghost calling to his dog. Still others say they hear the long, sad howls of the dog baying to heaven.

The macabre story behind this is that the hermit and his dog lived alone, but together, on Pond. They were seen almost daily from other islands or from passing boats. Then they were seen no more. And some concerned neighbors came ashore to look for them. There on the beach, hidden by a rock, they found the skeleton of a dog.

And five feet distant they found the skeleton of the hermit. And the question asked, but never answered, to this day is; Did the starving man eat his dog? Or vice-versa?

Captain Keiff of Cliff Island may have been the most miserable villain in Casco Bay. On stormy nights he'd tie a lantern around the neck of his horse and ride up and down the shore to mislead ships at sea onto the deadly ledges. As the ships hit and broke up, Capt. Keiff would murder any survivors who struggled ashore and bury them in a meadow still known as Keiff's Garden. Then the evil man would salvage the ship's cargo and sell it. On stormy nights, sad cries still rise from Keiff's Garden — the cries of drowning sailors begging not to be shot by Keiff.

In the great storm of 1869, the schooner Helen Eliza was wrecked on Peaks Island. Portland's famous poet, Henry Wadsworth Longfellow, immortalized that wreck in his epic poem, "The Wreck of The Hesperus."

But one member of the crew survived. The same young man had also been the sole survivor from a ship which was wrecked just previously in a hurricane in the West Indies. To make sure he was not caught in a third wreck, this sailor bought a farm, far inland, in New Hampshire. There he fell into a brook and drowned. But some say he comes back once a year to the rocks on Peaks Island, where his fellow sailors met their watery deaths.

There is a different kind of strange story from Haskell Island, off of Harpswell. Almost 100 years ago an old hermit-lobsterman named Humphrey died on Haskell, and huge rats picked his bones clean. Rats took over the island and no man dared set foot on Haskell, until two young Mills brothers brought a tribe of savage cats ashore with them and settled in. The savage cats multiplied, and finally killed off the rats. But the multitude of savage cats now drove off the rightful owner and anyone else who tried to land. The irate owner set out poison on the beaches, and killed all the cats. To this day they say no cat and no rat has ever set paw on Haskell Island.

VIII
MAINE NOSTALGIA

WHO IS MAINE'S GREATEST MAN?

MOXIE: IT BEGAN IN MAINE

TOAST TO PURITANS

PATTANGALL: MAINE'S GREAT HATCHET MAN

TOWN BULL: INDISPENSABLE CRITTER

WHO DISCOVERED AMERICA? NOT COLUMBUS!

MAINE INVENTED EARMUFFS: CHESTER GREENWOOD

ROOTING FOR THE DEER

INDIANS AND MAINE: THREE VIEWS

DRINK TO PORTLAND GLASS

CAMDEN, COASTAL JEWEL

PULLING HORSES OF MAINE

THE DRINKING DAYS OF OLD PORTLAND

THE DEFENCE: DIVING ON HISTORY

CONFLICTS, CONFLICTS

WHERE MAINE MAGIC BEGAN

Kavanaugh House, Damariscotta Mills

The past in Maine is not forgotten. It is treasured.

Go to almost any town or city library, and you'll find a good town history written or being revised. They are expensive books to publish, and often Maine towns finance them the old fashioned way. They sell the copies in advance, for about $20 each, collect the money and take the cash to the printer. In the small towns, people who have not bought a book in years seem ready to put down $20 for a local history of their family, their roots, their town.

A fine crop of small museums gives a wonderful picture of the local area. Bath, one of the richest cities in shipbuilding history in all the United States, has a big, fascinating, lively Maritime Museum. At Searsport, you'll find another fine local museum, featuring the ships and ship captains who made this harbor world-famous a hundred years ago. To see a splendid museum of Maine's greatest days of lumbering, visit the local Lumberman's museum in Patten, Maine, in the North Country.

The State Museum in Augusta has fine dioramas of Maine's working history — agriculture, lumbering, ice cutting, fishing, the making of pottery and barrels and ships. At Pemaquid Light is a special local fisherman's museum, furnished from the fish houses and attics of local fishermen and local boatyards. The list of such treasures of small museums is very long, because more towns are gathering together under one roof the local history of which they are proud.

Maine is where our nation began. Five hundred years before Columbus, Vikings explored the Maine coast. European fishermen used the Maine islands year round long before there was a settlement at Jamestown. Travel the coast today and look in awe at the great rocks and ledges, and you are looking at the handiwork of the last ice age, the last glaciers which 10,000 years ago cut Maine's coves, bays, inlets and made the 2,000 islands along our coast.

The first deed and the first sale of land recorded in this nation can be found in Wiscasset. It records the land sold by Samoset, the Indian chief from Loud's Island to a purchaser named John Brown. The first good charts of the mid coast were made in 1603 during the voyages of Martin Pring. The first settlement of English colonists in the New World was at Popham. Some of this history is mentioned in the story 'Who discovered America? Not Columbus!' in this section.

But the stories chosen here are light pieces, of a more recent Maine history. History that is often still in the fields and the barns, in the country fairs and the old logging camps.

This too is part of the Maine magic . . . this sense of roots, of continuity, of good traditions kept fresh, alive and loved. One result of this sense is that in a quiet, effective way, Maine is in the forefront of the nation in protecting its environment, through strong state laws. Maine people largely love and greatly respect their land; and thousands whose forefathers settled here hundreds of years ago, regard themselves as caretakers, entrusted for a lifetime, with the privilege of enjoying Maine and the duty of passing Maine on for their grandchildren to enjoy and safeguard.

Who is Maine's greatest man?

AUGUSTA — Who is the greatest man in Maine's history?

Joshua Lawrence Chamberlain would have been the instant answer of most Maine residents just a lifetime ago; today, few even recognize the name.

When Chamberlain died in February, 1914, more than 2,000 people jammed Portland City Hall for the funeral services and thousands more lined the streets to pay homage to his cortege on its way to the railway station. A special train carried the casket slowly to Brunswick where 300 Bowdoin students escorted the great man's body to its final resting place.

Newspapers ran huge portraits of Chamberlain bordered in black, with headlines such as "Brave Soldier Crosses River to Pitch His Tent for All Time with the Great Commander." The Portland Daily Press devoted five front page columns to his funeral.

As I write this column, my desk and a big table adjoining it overflow with yellowed news clippings of Chamberlain's spectacular career; as the hero of Gettysburg and Little Round Top; as the governor of Maine, elected four times by record majorities; as the president of Bowdoin College for 10 years; and, finally, as the surveyor of Portland, appointed and reappointed by three presidents — McKinley, Roosevelt and Taft.

Laden with honors and suffering still from the wounds caused by a shot which went through his body while leading the charge at Petersburg, Chamberlain died at age 86, just six months before the outbreak of the Great War.

That and the Second World War, Korea, Vietnam, a Great Depression, a dozen presidents and nearly a score of Maine governors have erased popular knowledge of Joshua L. Chamberlain. But not all knowledge.

Just 93 days ago a former airline stewardess paid $1.95 for a paperback version of a Pulitzer Prize-winning novel by Michael Shaara, "The Killer Angels." It is a fine story about the battle of Gettysburg and Joshua Chamberlain. On the flyleaf of the book, she wrote, "To my Husband Mark, with Love — Sherrel, April 5, 1977."

Sherrel gave it to her husband, Mark, a former Navy pilot, Maine born and raised, for their second wedding anniversary. He'd never heard of Chamberlain before; he quickly became fascinated.

As a result, Mark Gartley, then secretary of state for Maine, transformed a corner of his office into a living memorial to this Civil War hero.

Gartley resurrected Chamberlain's desk and chair, used while he was governor of Maine, framed large facsimiles of Chamberlain's handwritten letters sent from the battlefield of Gettysburg and supplemented the decor with maps of Little Round Top and a photograph of Chamberlain astride his war horse, Charlemagne.

Joshua Chamberlain at 34, commanded the 20th Maine Volunteers at the battle of Gettysburg, where he led the famous bloody bayonet charge on Little Round Top. Some historians claim that Chamberlain and the 20th Maine turned the tide of the war at Gettysburg, that without their bayonet charge the Confederates might have won and the Civil War ended differently.

Gen. Ulysses S. Grant, commander of the Union Army, so admired the bravery of the 20th Maine that he chose Chamberlain to accept the surrender of Robert E. Lee and the Confederate Army at Appomattox. Years later, in the old Portland Hotel, Chamberlain told a reporter his memories of that day of surrender.

"I was on my war horse, Charlemagne, when General Lee handed me his sword, as his lines passed by laying down their arms and giving up their colors.

"I offered the sword to General Grant; but he refused it, and said graciously, 'Return it to General Lee. They are to keep their side-arms.'"

But Chamberlain was an unlikely soldier, even though he seemed to relish close combat and bayonet assaults.

After studying at Bangor Theological Seminary, he was ordained as a preacher in 1854, then accepted an appointment at his college, Bowdoin, as professor of "Natural and Revealed Religion," a position he took over from Calvin E. Stowe, husband of Harriet Beecher, author of Uncle Tom's Cabin.

Chamberlain, a tall and handsome Phi Beta Kappa scholar, spoke seven languages, but yearned to be a soldier. The college, however, would not free him for military service. So, in 1862, he applied for a year's sabbatical leave to study in Europe, then enlisted instead with the 20th Maine Volunteers.

The war over, Chamberlain returned to Bowdoin College. But he was so popular that he was prevailed upon to run for governor on the Republican ticket and was elected by the greatest majority in history.

After four terms in the state's highest elective office, he went back to academic life, this time as president of Bowdoin. In 1900 President McKinley named him surveyor of Portland — a political patronage post he held till his death in 1914.

Fifty years later, Democratic Gov. Kenneth Curtis became an ardent admirer of Chamberlain, and asked James Mundy, then director of Maine Historic Preservation Commission, to find some Chamberlain memorabilia for his office.

Mundy traced Chamberlain's desk and official chair to the University of Maine at Orono, where the chair, especially carved with Chamberlain's war eagle and general's star, was being used as a throne for the homecoming queen each year. The desk was found in the library. After Mundy got them documented, Curtis no longer thought them right for his office. So they went down into the cellar of the State Museum along with 8,000 other historic items.

There they stayed until Mark Gartley read, "The Killer Angels," and got bitten by the Joshua Chamberlain bug.

After the desk and chair, Gartley recovered more period furniture from the now closed Stevens School in Hallowell.

From the former girls reformatory, he rescued a sofa and some chairs, which he had refinished and then reupholstered in red velvet at the Maine State Prison, to fit the descriptions from Chamberlain's records and the pictures of how his desk and official chair looked.

Thus, the revival of Chamberlain as a great son of Maine may be underway. One of the former governor's homes in Portland or Brunswick may become a living museum to perhaps the greatest man in Maine history.

Moxie: It began in Maine

UNION — The man who invented Moxie was a Maine native.

And Moxie, as all grandparents, but few grandchildren, know used to be the biggest selling soft drink in these United States. Long before Coca-Cola, Seven-Up, Pepsi were born, Moxie, with its strange bittersweet taste, was the most popular soft drink of the Western Hemisphere.

It was so much a part of American life that it became part of the language. Webster included "moxie" in his dictionary. If you had moxie, you had nerve, courage, energy.

The man from Maine who invented Moxie was Dr. Augustin Thompson, born to a farm family in Union on Nov. 25, 1835. What brings Moxie to mind now is the reappearance in Maine of the life-size Moxie horse mounted on the shining chassis of a 1930 LaSalle.

I saw the Moxie horse stop crowds, amaze kids, make grandparents nostalgic, when it appeared at a recent Rotary auction in Damariscotta. Kids were amazed to see the jockey atop the horse steer and operate the car from the saddle. Old-timers reminisced, dewy-eyed about the days 77 years ago, when they first saw the Moxie horse at Maine fairs. Now the Moxie horse and the Moxie drink are back in Maine.

Robert L. LaBrie of Lewiston is president of Eastern Inc., which is the Maine and New England distributor of Moxie. I met him, acting as the jockey aboard the Moxie horse. "We are bringing the horse and the car and Moxie to Maine summer events," he said.

The Moxie horse, trademark of the drink, was for years an annual visitor to Union, the birthplace of Mister Moxie — Dr. Thompson.

Back in 1902, the stuffed Moxie horse toured the Atlantic Coast atop an early automobile. In nine months, horse and car travelled from Norfolk, Va., to Rockland, Maine. Considering the state of the roads and cars 77 years ago, that was a feat. In the summer of 1917, the Rockland Courier-Gazette reported that the Moxie horse-on-a-car came to town and "attracted as much attention as a circus parade."

Joseph E. King of Bangor was the driver-jockey then, covering 10,000 miles on a two-year promotion trip. On his ride through Maine, thousands of Moxie ash trays, fans and balloons were given away.

"The horse has received more publicity than any advertising feature ever designed," reported the Courier-Gazette. Now, it is happening again.

Old car buffs will delight in the 1930 LaSalle on which the Moxie horse is mounted. Bob LaBrie told me the restoration cost over $25,000. (The current owner of Moxie is the Monarch Nugrape Company of Georgia.)

"The car has a V-8, flat-head engine, updraft carburetors, mechanical brakes and four speed transmission. The jockey riding the horse has all the controls for driving the car, right up there in the saddle," said LaBrie.

I have dug up a few facts about the Union farm boy, Augustin Thompson, who invented Moxie. He quit the farm early and went to Rockland to make barrel staves for the lime plants at Thomaston. When the Civil War broke out, young Thompson enlisted, then mustered a company of volunteers to fight.

He was a go-getter and promoter from the start, evident when he went in as a private and came out as a lieutenant colonel. But he suffered wounds and that gave him a desire to become a doctor. He graduated from the medical school in Philadelphia. But before he left the Army to become a full-fledged doctor, Thompson supervised the building of Fort Popham, which still stands at the mouth of the Kennebec river.

Dr. Augustin Thompson hung out his shingle and began developing a big practice in Lowell, Mass., a booming mill town.

Lowell was also home to such famous and profitable patent medicines as Lydia Pinkham's famous tonic for women. Other Lowell-made patent medicines were sold in huge quantities to Latin America. And young Dr. Thompson from Union apparently decided that he too would launch his own patent medicines.

In 1884, he launched Moxie Nerve Food; Moxie Catarrh Cure; and The New England Cure for Alcoholism. Soon, they were household words.

By 1895, the author of a book called "Union, Past and Present" boasted "Moxie is already a household word in two hemispheres. There scarce exists a city where Moxie is not used."

But Moxie, as Dr. Thompson invented it, was not a soft drink at all. It was a "nerve food." Millions imbibed it in liquid concentrate form by the spoonfull. Advertisements guaranteed that a spoonful of Moxie after meals would make you eat better, sleep better, feel better. This Moxie nerve food was promoted as being "of the greatest value to all persons suffering nervous exhaustion and incipient paralysis."

Some research reveals that its primary ingredient was extracted from the Gentian root, a blue flower named after Gentius, an Illyrian king who was defeated by the Romans in 161 B.C. Apparently King Gentius, hiding in a cave in the Alps, ate the roots of the blue flower at the cave entrance. The food made him well. He recovered from wounds and sickness and returned to his own country, carrying with him the magic root which was named "Gentian" in his honor.

And that is the root which Dr. Thompson made into Moxie, the smash-hit nerve food and catarrh cure.

After Thompson died, the first Pure Food and Drug Act was passed in 1906. That is when Moxie changed from a nerve food elixir to a nickel soft drink. Thereafter, began the mammoth promotion of such Moxie trademarks as the Moxie horsemobile, the Moxie dog, and the Moxie bottlewagon.

Moxie was everywhere. Everyone drank it. There were Moxie

songs. Comedian Ed Wynn said with a grin, "Make mine, Moxie!" Songwriter George M. Cohan sang, "Make Mine Moxie!" Baseball player Babe Ruth hit a home run shouting, "Make mine Moxie." All were featured in Moxie ads.

Americans got their first commercial jingle to become a hit-song. All America was singing, "Just Make it Moxie for mine."

The Maine family of Dr. Thompson finally decided in the bottom of the Depression to sell out.

New stars rose in the soft drink world. Coke, Pepsi, Seven-Up and others leapfrogged over the flagging sales of Moxie. The drink that had been a national symbol, a part of the American language, faded almost to total obscurity. Only a handful of devotees to its special sweet-sour taste kept the name alive.

Then, in 1967 the Monarch Nugrape Co. of Georgia decided to revive the nation's oldest, first, greatest soft drink. Its still-secret formula comes now from Atlanta.

Here in Maine, the Moxie horse is riding again, back where her original master was born.

Toast to Puritans

POPHAM BEACH — New England Puritans started the Thanksgiving tradition . And they may not have been so prissy, drab and dreary as history books say.

Today's women, "liberated" or not, might stop work this Thanksgiving and raise a glass to those old Puritans. Why? Because 359 years ago, the men must have done the cooking.

Some 100 pilgrims landed in November 1620. But only half survived that first hard winter. And of the surviving 50, only five were women.

That first Thanksgiving, those survivors asked Indian chief Massaoit to join the feast. The Indian chief brought along 90 braves with him, thinking Thanksgiving by the white men was probably equivalent to the Indians' green corn dance.

The Indians also brought five deer.

But who did the cooking? Who simmered the clam chowder? Who cooked the venison? Who turned the turkeys and who basted the geese?

I like to think that the five women sat back, taking care of infants and supervising the white men and the Indians, telling them how to pry out the kernels of corn, and roast them on the fire and pour maple syrup over them to make the first popcorn balls for children. I like to think of the men doing dazzling feats of prowess, to impress the five women, and then dancing wildly with them, between turning the turkeys. I like to imagine those Puritan Pilgrim fathers doing all the housework on the first Thanksgiving in America.

Those early Puritans came in droves, like the droves of cut-rate airline passengers today. In the first six months of 1630, 15 ships docked, bringing 1,000 Puritans. In the next 40 months, 10,000 more Puritans landed in New England.

Not so puritanical were they, for these fellows started the rum trade.

When the Cavaliers and Roundheads were fighting each other in Merrie England, all trade with the mother country stopped. So the Puritans, who were canny businessmen, began trading with the West

Indies. They sailed to the islands with puritanical salt pork and dried fish, some chickens and a horse or two. They brought home molasses. And they converted the molasses into unpuritanical rum, getting rich by the trade.

The Puritans had a taste for fast horses, too. They bred racehorses and built racetracks. But they gave more R's to the culture than Rum and Racehorses. The early Puritans made the teaching of "reading, writing and arithmetic" the legal responsibility of parents. They passed such an Act of the Bay Colony in 1642, which might be revived today as kids graduate without the three R's.

And while Maine wrestles with property tax and argues about whether state or town should have most to say about schools, we might remember those old Puritans who started New England education.

By 1647 — 332 years ago — the Puritans required that villages with 50 families had by law to "appoint a schoolteacher to teach all such children as shall resort to him to read and write." Towns of 100 families had to establish a grammar school, to take in boys of six, and for six years teach them reading, writing, arithmetic, Latin and Greek.

Do schools today do as much?

Those Puritans began higher education, too. In 1636 they used 400 pounds to start their first college. It began in a cow yard in the town of Cambridge. That cow yard was renamed Harvard Yard in memory of the Rev. John Harvard, who died at the age of 30 and left 400 books to the infant college. In that Harvard College Yard the Puritans set up the first printing press in the nation in 1639. And as a news-paperman, I, too, owe them a toast on Thanksgiving Eve.

Pattangall: Maine's great hatchet man

WATERVILLE — The real reason so few people vote is because they are bored stiff. Bored with politicians and bored by the way newspapers write about politicians.

But if we can't change the politicians, maybe we can liven up the way we report them.

Maine is the place to start. Because Maine has had some of the nastiest, funniest and wittiest political commentators ever to prick a windbag.

Best of the bunch was William Robinson Pattangall, who died on October 21, 1942.

Today, he might have gone to jail or at the least been swamped with libel suits for his kind of writing. But his stuff ran in two Maine papers, first in a little weekly, the Machias Union, later in a paper called the Maine Democrat.

Here is a sample of Pattangall, writing about U. S. Sen. Eugene Hale, when Hale was 73.

"Eugene Hale has held public office for 51 out of a possible 52 years, which is doing pretty well even for a Maine Republican . . . He has spoken in every campaign in Maine since 1860 and he has never uttered an original word which anybody desired to quote or could remember if they tried . . .

"After a lifetime in Congress, he has been responsible for no single piece of constructive legislation, nor for the repeal of one bad law. He has, however, worked faithfully for himself and his own. His younger brother is a federal judge, one son a diplomat, one in office in Washington, the youngest about to be nominated for Congress by the united influence of his father's political power and his grandfather's money.

"He has been true to the companions and associates of his youth. Not in small part has it been due to his influence that Ellsworth, a city with four thousand people, with no visible industry, excepting politics, has supplied the state during the past decade with two chief justices of the supreme court, an associate justice, and an attorney general and minor officers galore.

"Earning money was too slow a progress to suit Hale, stealing was too risky, circumstances prevented him from inheriting it, so he married it. And as Mr. Hale never does anything by halves, he married a whole lot of it."

Pattangall was, at various times, a state legislator, an attorney general, first president of Depositors Trust, trustee of the University and editor of the Waterville Sentinel, before becoming chief justice of Maine. He was 200 per cent Democrat.

His scathing profiles of Maine's Republican politicians were so barbed and so truthful that the men he profiled often sent out friends to buy up every copy they could lay hands on.

Here is Pattangall, writing about Edwin Chick Burleigh, who at age 66, had been governor, state treasurer and congressman:

"He has lived 66 years and held office 38 of that time and bids fair to continue to draw a public salary for the rest of his life, but he has not been dependent upon an official position for his livelihood.

"Maine once owned large tracts of timberland. Maine does not own any timberland now. He, Burleigh, owns considerable timberland now. Maine sold its timberland at a low price, a very low price, indeed. It has since become very valuable. Those who bought it prospered. It was sold, in part, through the land agent's office. Mr. Burleigh and his father had charge of that office 11 years.

"Politics to Mr. Burleigh has been a means of making money, of advancing his personal fortunes, of helping his personal friends and relatives. That he has done nothing for the voters who have loyally supported him for 40 years, goes without saying. But perhaps this is not his fault, because men bred in the narrow school of Maine Republican politics do not take a very broad view of their public duties. Why should he worry about the people?"

Pattangall mostly burnt the hide off Republicans. Protecting an anonymous Democrat, he wrote: "I wouldn't expose him because he is a Democrat, and a Democrat in Maine, exposed, is lost forever."

Commenting on the Republican Convention in Chicago in 1904

where Teddy Roosevelt was nominated, Pattangall wrote: "Everything was arranged just like a three-day fair at Pembroke. Nothing the first day. Very little the second day. And a horse race the third day that was all fixed up the day before."

Pattangall collected his profiles of Maine politicians in a book called "Maine's Hall of Fame." One man profiled was Byron Boyd, whose picture faced Pattangall's text. "If anyone is curious to see just what a long course in Republican politics will do to a man," wrote Pattangall, "he should gaze upon the innocent, not to say vacuous countenance depicted on this page . . .

"Boyd is a living refutation of the generally accepted theory that there is no money in Maine politics . . . He became Secretary of State when legislators made $150 every two years, when the governor was satisfied with $2,000 as an annual salary, but Byron was getting $10,000 a year as Secretary of State, plus the trimmings."

Pattangall wrote that Byron also held the job as secretary of the Republican State Committee and, in 1908, took charge of the campaign funds.

"There was just one way to carry Maine that year. That was to buy votes . . . Buy them wholesale, retail, in job lots, singly, in carloads, any old way, but buy them. No man in Maine could carry on that kind of campaign as well as could Byron Boyd."

A final Pattangall item, concerning Maine elections in a presidential year. This comment, which ran in the Machias Union, reports a political conversation about the chances of Gov. William T. Cobb to be re-elected in 1904.

"Mr. Cobb is going to be elected governor."

"Honest?"

"Perhaps and perhaps not. We don't usually elect them honest in presidential years."

Town Bull: Indispensable critter

DAMARICOTTA — My town property tax bill came the other day, and it was big enough to make a home owner think about living on a boat. Wet water is cheaper than dry land.

In the old days, town selectmen made good use of the few dollars they collected in town taxes.

For example, they procured a Town Bull.

Each town had a Bull committee and each year, the townspeople voted a sum of money for the Town Bull, along with a salary for the schoolteacher and the minister.

The Bull committee got its funds through a "cow tax." Every person who owned a cow paid a tax to support the Town Bull. And the Bull committee chose the bull and decided where that bull should be kept so that it would be handy to service the town cows, and which farmer should be paid how much to take good care of it.

The town's future supply of milk, butter, cheese, beef and oxen, all depended upon having a good Town Bull.

But in colonial times, bulls were in such short supply that government action was required to make sure that every citizen would get a fair share of the bull available.

"Young bulls either became veal early in life or underwent a change which transformed them into oxen — peaceful, useful, draft animals," reports Massachusetts author-scholar Charles F. Haywood.

"A bull, allowed to reach maturity unaltered, was a difficult character to have in town. He was so ugly he might attack anyone at any time. He was useless about the farm for work because no man could compel him to submit to the yoke. And in old age, he was good only for sausage."

Yet, without the Town Bull to keep the ball rolling, there would be no more calves. And so, the Town Bull Committee came into being in Maine and New England.

And it has never quite died out. Those curious to see it in operation can go down to the firehouse, where, on most Wednesday nights, today's town officials meet in a room behind the hook and ladder.

Schoolrooms and schoolteachers took a good slice of town taxes in the old days, as now. Every community with 50 families or more was by law supposed to have school houses and teachers. The selectmen had the duty of providing the school and hiring the teacher. One selectman was taken to court and fined 27 shillings for failing to provide a town schoolmaster.

Harold Clifford, now retired in East Boothbay, and a former superintendent of schools in that region, writes that by the end of the Revolution, most towns were financing their schoolrooms and schoolteachers by appropriations of taxes at town meetings.

"Costs of building a one-room schoolhouse, fireplace included, were from $150 to $250. In 1793, Parsonfield voted 30 pounds for the school, to be paid to the tax collector in corn, at four shillings, or rye at five shillings a bushel. A town meeting at Waterville passed an ordinance forbidding ball playing or snowballing within 15 feet of the new schoolhouse, on penalty of a fine of not more than $4 or less than 50 cents.

Clifford reports that by 1820 men teachers in Hartland were paid $2.50 to $3.75 a week and women teachers got from 75 cents to $1.50 a week. The town also paid for the teacher's room and board — and they usually moved to a different home each week.

School lasted about 10 weeks a year. Children owned their own textbooks, which were handed down, like clothes, from older to younger children. Pupils often had a small writing slate. But Clifford reports that "if a pupil brought to school a smooth piece of birch bark, he could write with a quill pen, and ink made from maple bark, and then carry his school paper home."

This year, Maine's towns have to raise hundreds of millions of dollars in local town property taxes. "Local" is a misnomer. Most of the amount is dictated by the state, and local voters in town meeting today have little voice in their own financial affairs.

We can't even pick the bull of our own choosing. The bull comes straight from Augusta and Washington.

Who Discovered America? Not Columbus!

PORTLAND — Who really discovered America? Was Columbus the first?

This October 12 is the real Columbus Day anniversary, despite the fact that to get a three-day weekend most of the observance was on Monday, October 10.

Well, a 48-hour error would be nothing to Cristoforo Colombo from Genoa. He may have "discovered" America, according to our history books, but he went to his grave believing he had discovered the eastern regions of China.

The fact is, that at 2 a.m., October 12, 1492, the lookout aboard a ship named Pinta was standing watch in the light of a waning moon. "Tierra!" he cried. And land it was — an island in the Bahamas called San Salvador. Columbus was convinced he had found the short route to the Indies. So when the friendly natives of the Bahamas greeted him on the shore, Columbus named them "Indians."

Columbus, of course, never set his feet on the shores of the United States of America. On his first trip, commemorated today, Columbus found San Salvador; then went on with "Indian" guides to Cuba and Haiti.

He came back again from Spain, with more ships, the next year, and on November 3, 1493, he discovered Hispaniola, then Puerto Rico and Jamaica.

On a third voyage, in 1498, and on a fourth in 1502, Columbus discovered Trinidad and the coast of Central America. And all the while he thought he was discovering China and Indies of the Orient.

So who did discover America?

By "discovery" we seem to mean only discovered by Europeans.

Maine and Newfoundland are the regions where the earliest voyagers probably first set foot. These northern waters were the exploring grounds of the Irish, the Norse, the English, the Portuguese.

Did the Irish discover America first? Did Irishmen first land on the coast we call Maine?

Irishmen swear this is the truth. They were great sailors in tiny boats, built on a wicker frame and covered with ox hides, called "curraghs."

There is strong belief in many quarters that Vikings discovered Maine and North America around the year 1000, about 500 years before Columbus saw the Bahamas and thought he was in China.

Vikings in their beautiful long ships sailed the seas of the known world then — and beyond. Eric the Red was driven out of Iceland, accused of murder. He sailed west and discovered territory he named Greenland, in order to attract settlers. And here we come to a known link to Maine and Newfoundland.

Eric the Red has a son named Leif Ericsson. In 999 A.D., Leif was sent on a voyage to King Olaf of Norway. On his return home he set out on an exploration westward, to look for land where large trees grew, since Greenland had nothing but bushes.

His ship was sturdy. Probably 54 feet long, 15-foot beam, clinker-built and fastened with iron rivets, according to sea historian Samuel Eliot Morison. And Leif Ericsson undoubtedly discovered North America. In the year 1000, his crew was in Newfoundland.

Ericsson sailed through Maine and landed at Mount Desert and other places along our coast. Some experts insist that stones with Viking writing on them have been found and will be found again in Maine. Leif's brother Thorvald is said to have been wounded by native arrows when he sailed the Maine coast.

Surely, Europeans such as these Vikings visited Maine hundreds of years before Christopher Columbus "discovered" America. Now a Viking coin has been found in Maine, vintage 800 A.D., which indicates the Vikings may have landed here almost 700 years before Columbus.

Maine invented earmuffs: Chester Greenwood

FARMINGTON — A nice thing happened to Chester Greenwood, the Farmington boy who invented earmuffs 100 years ago. Chester Greenwood and Queen Elizabeth II, a girl from London, England, went down in a glorious page of history together on Tuesday, June 7, 1977.

The Queen, as everybody knows by now, rode in a golden coach drawn by Windsor greys through the streets of London. Escorted by outriders, postillions, beefeaters, a regiment of cavalry, breast-plated, helmeted and plumed, mounted on prancing black horses, and by foot soldiers in scarlet tunics and bearskin busbies with brass-chain chin straps, the Queen of England was cheered throughout the world as she celebrated her silver jubilee upon the throne.

Well, in Farmington and Augusta, also, June 7th was a day of triumph and honor, and a different kind of pageantry, for Chester Greenwood.

A slip of paper was posted on the wall outside the governor's office in the Statehouse, and Chester Greenwood Day became the law of our land. Forever, December 21, the first day of winter in Maine, shall be Chester Greenwood Day, honoring the Maine genius who, at the age of 15, invented the earmuff.

The law goes into the statute books minus the signature of Gov. Longley. For 10 days and 10 nights the Greenwood bill lay on the governor's desk, while His Excellency mulled over its merits.

"Shall I or shall I not pick up my pen and sign my 'Jim Longley' to this bill?" agonized the governor of Maine. As the final moments of decision ticked by, the governor summoned Rep. Richard G. Morton of Farmington, father of the bill, to his chamber. With due solemnity, the governor explained that he would allow the Greenwood bill to become law of Maine without his "Jim Longley" signed to it.

"Vital to our state and our nation as are earmuffs, I fear that it would appear I am turning a deaf or muffled ear if I sign this bill. So I will allow it to become the law of Maine without my 'Jim Longley' on it," explained Gov. Longley. Rep. Morton murmured "spoken like a true politician," accepted a long letter of explanation from the governor and backed out of the gubernatorial audience, while clamping earmuffs on — out of season.

Chester Greenwood, an outdoor kid when Ulysses Grant was president, loved to skate and go belly-flopping on his sled. But poor Chester's ears darn near froze. They stood boldly out from each side of his head, targets for the biting winter winds.

Chester tried to flap his ears. He tried wiggling his ears. He tried putting his ears to the ground. Nothing would warm them up. In desperation, Chester became an inventor. He got two old socks, rolled them into two balls, hung each on either end of a bit of bent wire and clamped the apparatus on his head. It looked stupid, but it warmed up his freezing ears.

Soon Ma Greenwood got out her needle and sewed some old hunks of beaver fur, and Pa Greenwood came up with a bit of spring steel. And smart 15-year-old Chester Greenwood kept his ears so warm that by the time he got to be 19, he decided to make a million dollars.

So, 19-year-old Chester filed a patent for his earmuffs. In March 1877, patent No. 188,292 was issued for the "Greenwood Champion Ear Protectors." He designed a machine to mass produce 'em. Built a factory and Farmington became the earmuff capital of the world. And Chester got rich.

He died in 1937 at age 79. Now, every December 21 will be his day of honor.

Rooting for the deer

The deer are moving in the last glory of the autumn leaves.

Every day, as I drive midcoast Maine or inland to Oxford County or up the Kennebec Valley, I've been seeing deer. Every time my heart jumps with delight, and then is pinched by a tinge of apprehension for their survival as the November hunting season looms ahead.

Gentle, vulnerable, delicate as our white-tailed deer look, especially when you see them tense up and then race off at a warning sound, our Maine deer are a hardy breed, with a genius for survival. They've survived poachers, legislators, coyotes, wardens, wolves, Indians, dogs, hunters and biologists. Survived too much and too little snow, rain, forest growth. And this fall, the herd as a whole will survive 200,000 modern hunters as well.

But there are always days in November when we doubt it. We watch, with dismay, dozens and then dozens more of out-of-state cars head down the turnpike with dead deer hanging from the roofs or mudguards; and we sometimes wonder if the Maine herd can long survive the onslaughts of invading armies of hunters. But they can.

Long before the white man came, long before today's Indian tribes even came to Maine, the Red Paint People — earliest humans on this land — were using the bones of deer as tools and ate the flesh of deer as food.

Then came the Algonquin Indians. They hunted deer in small armies of 200 to 300 braves. They set fire to the undergrowth and drove the deer herds to cliffs or to rivers or to the sea, where hunters in hiding would kill them.

But as late as the year 1600 the total Indian population here was no more than 3,000, and those Indians also hunted moose, caribou, bear, duck; so it is not likely the mass "deer-drives" made much of a dent on the deer herd 378 years ago.

Timber wolves, roving panthers, bobcats and lynx killed far more deer than the Indian hunters or white settlers combined. So big were the packs of timber wolves roaming the state that towns such as Scarborough and Falmouth were paying bounties of four British pounds per wolf in 1730.

As the human population grew, deer herds vanished from the coast, then from the river banks. As more settlers cleared and farmed more land, the deer moved to the deeper forests.

As the great pines in the forest were felled for the king's masts, and as the smaller trees were cut to make barrels for the growing trade with the West Indies, the deer benefited. New browsing plants grew in the more open forests; deer found more food and for a while multiplied fast.

But the human multiplied faster. At Maine's first census in 1790, the population was 96,540, and by independent statehood in 1820 it had mushroomed to more than 300,000.

One result was that a family could barely find lumber or firewood enough. In the early 1800's it took a man and four oxen two long days of hard work to get a cord of firewood along the coast. This lack of 'cover' pushed the deer inland.

Then came the massive slaughters called "market hunting." Boston warehouses were packed full of deer carcasses from Maine. That resulted in the Deer Law of 1873, setting a three-deer bag limit and limiting the hunting season from October 1 to December 31. Licenses were required. As a measure of inflation, in 1913 residents paid 25 cents for a lifetime license to hunt deer.

This November hunting season more than 200,000 licensed hunters will kill more than 30,000 white-tailed Maine deer. A "big kill," as those figures are called, is sign of a big, healthy, well-managed deer population, say the experts at the State Department of Inland Fish and Game.

These November weeks are the peak of the deer mating season. Now is the peak of 'rutting.' The bucks are running now, chasing does. And I wish them good hunting, too.

The deer experts really don't know why the love-life of deer warms up in November. My theory is that these frosty moon-bright nights are what send the bucks rutting after the does. But some scientists think it is the clock. They say the change in the length of daylight hours stimulates the sex drive in the young bucks.

Bucks wear the antlers. The bigger the antlers, the older the buck and the greater the number of points on his rack. And 'points' are what score big in the deer hunters' world. Greatest number of points (spikes of one inch or longer) was 20, after the experts examined 5,150 sets of antlers. A set of antlers is called a 'rack'; and racks with 10 or more points occur on about one in every 40 antlered deer.

New sets of antlers are grown yearly. They start small in April or May. A soft velvet protects and nourishes the growing antlers. Come September, the velvet vanishes; the soft antlers harden; and become the fighting weapon between rival bucks in the rutting season. When the breeding season is over and the fighting spirit is gone, the bucks turn gentle and shed their antlers.

For the females, pregnancy lasts 199 days, on average. Assuming mid-November is the peak of the breeding season, mid-June will be the birth peak of next year's fawns. About 100,000 may be born next June; and 30,000 of them will not survive long.

Very young does usually have only a single fawn; but when they are two years old or more, they often have twins. One 17 year old doe in Maine produced twins. Another, aged 11 years, gave birth to triplets.

But I make a wish each time I see those ears twitch and bobble in alarm, see those proud antlers toss and those trim, strong — yet delicate — legs bound across the open ground, leap the brook and head for hardwood cover on the high ridge.

I watch its last flick of that white tail and whisper, "Good luck, deer! Stay alive!"

Indians and Maine: Three Views

Indians Got Raw Deal; One View

PLEASANT POINT — Have you ever talked with a Maine Indian?

Not many of us have had a chance. After all, there are now only 1,700 Indians living on three smallish reservations while a million white settlers occupy the rest of Maine.

It used to be the reverse. There used to be 35,000 Indians occupying all of Maine, when the first handful of white settlers came, according to a census of 1615.

The decline since then makes us wince. For the record, in 1976 there were 869 Penobscot Indians at Indian Island in Old Town; 509 Passamaquoddies at Pleasant Point, outside Eastport; and 209 more Passamaquoddies near Princeton.

These are the Indians who had a million white settlers by the short hairs. They sued to get back two-thirds of Maine and more than $20 billion in damages for lands they say were wrongfully taken long ago. The final settlement was much, much less, but the shock waves sent us to the history books.

The first treaty on record in Maine was signed with the Passamaquoddies by Col. John Allan, U. S. commander of the Eastern Indian Outpost. Allan, their friend and admirer, said the Quoddies had fought hard and well against the British and George III. He commended them highly to George Washington and our first Congress. He told of how Francis Neptune, son of an Indian tribal governor, and himself a governor, killed the British captain of a British warship sent to assert English authority. Neptune lived to be 113.

In his treaty with the Passamaquoddies, Col. Allan promised, "they should be forever viewed as brothers and children under the fatherly care and protection of the United States."

But Congress never bothered to ratify Allan's treaty with Indians in Maine. But the U. S. Constitution adopted in 1789 promised that all Indians were the responsibility of the federal government. A year later, in 1790, and again in 1793, two "Non-Intercourse Acts" made it absolutely illegal for anybody except the federal government to negotiate treaties with the Indian tribes for lands or anything else.

Despite this, the Commonwealth of Massachusetts went ahead and signed a treaty with the Passamaquoddy tribe in 1794. Under its terms, Massachusetts took 1.5 million acres of Indian lands located in what is now Maine.

And when Maine got statehood in 1820, the Maine Legislatures kept on authorizing white timber interests to seize and cut Indian lands without any payments. Timber companies built dams and flooded Indian land. One white settler got hold of 15 islands on the St. Croix River belonging to the Indians, and a Maine court upheld him when the tribes protested.

One ironic reason why Maine's Indians have had a raw deal is because they were friendly. They fought with us against the British. They were our allies. The Penobscots and Passamaquoddies were not defeated enemy tribes like the Sioux and Apaches. If they had been our enemies instead of our friends, Maine Indians would have been getting enormous benefits as wards of the federal government. But as friends, they did not get any of the federal aid given former enemies.

Some amends have been made. I remember seeing Pleasant Point 10 years ago — a sorry place compared to today. An Indian leader named Joe Nicholas sent me there. Joe had talked to me in eye-opening fashion about Indians in Maine as he cut my hair in Eastport. He was a barber then. He has since been an Indian representative to the Maine State Legislature. The Indians have two elected representatives out of 186 people in the state legislature.

Knox Oblivious To Indian Land Law: Second View

THOMASTON — Henry Knox may be turning in his grave these days. I wish we could hear him talk about how and why he bought three million acres of land in Maine, but paid no heed to the law he helped get passed, "The Nonintercourse Act of 1790."

Henry Knox was secretary of war under President George Washington for the nine years 1785 to 1794. He built a great mansion for himself in Thomaston. Today, you can see the Knox mansion — called Montpelier — white, columned, elegant, standing high on a hill beside the road to Rockland.

In 1791 and 1792, Knox bought three million acres of Maine land in territory claimed by the Indians in 1977. A year later, in 1793, Knox sold his land to William Bingham.

But what makes Knox's land buying so interesting is that when he bought those three million acres, Knox was secretary of war, and as such he had supervision over Indian affairs; and this includes supervision of any sale of land belonging to the tribes. Knox was largely responsible for the Nonintercourse Act under which no land transaction with Indian tribes could be made without approval of the federal government. Knox did not seek any such approval when he bought his three million acres in Maine. Hence these questions: Did Knox believe his three million acres were not owned by the tribes? Or was he so dishonest a politician that he dared lobby for passage of the Nonintercourse Act, take responsibility for enforcing it — and then violate it to the tune of three million acres?

Digging back into the history books, it is clear that Massachusetts tried to sell off 17 million acres of the District of Maine on the assumption they did not belong to the Indian tribes. Sales did not move fast enough to suit the Massachusetts treasury. To speed up sales, Massachusetts began to sell lottery tickets on the land. Between 1783, when the Massachusetts Legislature created a Committee for the Sale of Eastern Lands, and 1820, when Maine was made a separate state, more than six million acres of public lands in the eastern part of the District of Maine were sold and lotteried off by Massachusetts.

Thus by the time Maine became a state in 1820, only about 10 million acres were left as public lands and ownership of these was divided between Maine and Massachusetts.

To make matters more complicated, the federal government has been buying Maine lands in areas claimed by the Indians — and neither did the federal government pay heed to the Nonintercourse Act.

For example, Uncle Sam bought from whites — not Indians — the Allagash Wilderness Waterway, Acadia National Park, the land for Dow Air Force Base in Bangor, for Presque Isle Air Force Base and for Loring Air Force Base. The Indians claim all this is their property. But their trustee, the Federal government, didn't think so.

The Indians claim that Millinocket is theirs — and Uncle Sam has put millions into schools, airports, courthouses, post offices, not to mention all kinds of farm home loans. Uncle Sam did all this without a word with the Indians who claim it all belongs to them. And the final irony is that Uncle Sam (the Department of Justice and the Department of Interior) must now argue on behalf of the Indian claim, as the protector and trustee of the Indians. Yet Uncle Sam is also the culprit accused of abusing Indian land claims. As trustee and trust officer, Uncle Sam was a double dealer.

Indian Suit Prompts Quick History Lesson: Third View

PORTLAND — There is nothing like a big lawsuit to send people scurrying for the history books.

When 2,500 Indians sued the State of Maine for two-thirds of the state, I was one of thousands of people who boned up on Indian history in Maine.

Maybe we should start with that misnomer — "Indians."

The name is a mistake.

Christopher Columbus was trying to find a passage to India (remember?) when he landed instead in America. So, partly to save face, he called the natives who met him "Indians," even though they did not live in India.

The mistake took root. Eventually, the mistake was modified by calling them "American Indians."

Well, how many American Indians lived in what is now Maine when the first white settlers came here?

The best estimate I can find is that about 35,000 Indians were in Maine in 1615, when there were 100 or so white settlers here.

Two-hundred years later, just before Maine became a state, those 35,000 Indians had dwindled down to a mere 500 or so. But the whites had multiplied to a population of 298,388 by 1820.

As for the land occupied by the native Indians, there was no such thing as "ownership" when the whites first came — if "ownership" means land title, deed and bill of sale.

But after some 200 years of white settlers, land ownership was mostly in black-and-white and on paper. According to the legal paper of 1818, the 500 or so Indians left in Maine then were squeezed into two spots.

The 250 men, women and children left in the Penobscot tribe had sold all their remaining lands to Massachusetts, except for four townships. These appear to include present day Millinocket, Mattawamkeag, Woodville and Indian Purchase, and all the islands in the Penobscot River from Indian Island, Old Town, north.

After Maine became a separate state in 1820, the Penobscots sold even these four townships to Maine, in 1833.

In 1977, the Penobscot tribe, who numbered about 1,000, owned 4,500 acres.

The Passamaquoddy tribe was also down to only about 250 in 1820, and they had sold all their lands except for some 23,000 acres. By 1977, they were down to about 15,000 acres while the tribe numbered 1,500.

In just two centuries, from about 1615 to 1820, the Indian tribes, once powerful, numerous, and the sole possessors of all this country, were reduced to a pitiful remnant of the original tribes and were restricted in land to the islands on the Penobscot and a spot on the banks of the Passamaquoddy.

The 200 years had been marked, on both sides, by savagery and compassion; by brutality and love; by trust and by deceit.

The Indians had been wracked in six Indian wars and their own War of the Tribes, 1615-1617. Each of the wars lasted from three to 10 years, each killing hundreds of Indian braves. Famines and disease killed more. Thousands fled from Maine to Canada and to the west.

Those 200 years, between the first white settlers at Monhegan Island and Popham and the statehood of Maine, saw the end of Red America and the rise of White America. Much of it happened on the soil where a million Maine people live now.

Drink to Portland Glass

PORTLAND — Those most handsome wineglasses on our table at my son's birthday party were made 110 years ago by the original Portland Glass Company. Seeing those Tree of Life goblets sent me digging for more facts about Portland Glass — a short-lived, highly successful Portland company we can remember with pride today.

The glass factory — not to be confused with the current firm — began operations on the Portland waterfront November 11, 1863, and became an overnight success. In two months, 100 workers were turning out 5,000 pieces of glassware each day. Production hit the million pieces mark within two years, and the little company was declaring a 14 per cent dividend and putting additions on its plant. But it made more than money; it made such fine products of such artistry that Portland quickly became a famed center for fine glass.

I walked along Commercial Street (or Canal Street as it was called then) trying to locate the spot where Portland Glass stood at the foot of Emery Street on the waterfront close to railroad line and shipping wharf. The factory was made of brick, stood four stories high, 125 feet long and had chimneys reaching 100 feet high, and a 70-foot-square furnace building belched smoke, according to pictures of Portland painted then.

In my mind's eye, I could see wagons arriving and departing, steam-

boats loading, steam engines panting on the railroad sidings, and the great fires burning in the glass factory.

That lovely glass came in all colors. The clear glass was often embellished with gold bands and gold rims; and the glassmakers offered every shape, size and color. Portland Glass came in light or dark blue, many shades of green, amber, ruby, yellow, cranberry, even purple. The colors were all delicate and gentle — never cheap and garish.

To reach the million-piece mark, Portland Glass made what the market wanted. For example, the bar trade was brisk. Maine — due to become the first bastion of Prohibition — in 1866 produced more than 100,000 whiskey, ale and wine glasses. Even in those days, advertising premiums were a sales gimmick; and so Portland Glass made glass jars as premiums for makers of pickles, jams, mustard and candy. Back 100 and more years ago, kerosene lamps were art features in many drawing rooms. So Portland Glass made a rather 'arty' line of chimneys, globes and lamps.

But the real glory and fame of Portland Glass was its superb work in vases, goblets, punchbowls, compote dishes, pitchers, ewers, epergnes — the whole galaxy of lavish glassware for the lavish tables of the Victorian era.

Listen to the names of some of the beautiful patterns. The names themselves have a quaint delight: Tree of Life, Shell and Tassel, Loop and Dart, Owl and Possum, Hobnail, Crackle, Roman Rosette, Jacob's Ladder, Powder and Shot, Thousand Faces, Witch Balls, Prayer Rug, Dirigo Pear and scores more.

One oddity about the Portland Glass Company is how quickly it rose to fame and prosperity and then how suddenly it collapsed. Its whole life was a mere 10 years. Begun in 1863, it shut down in 1873. But it left its important mark on American glassmaking. And its 10-year life was stormy.

Begun with $75,000 capital, it doubled its capital to over $150,000 in two years, and kept adding to its plant and to its production. The menace of fire is perpetual to any glass plant with a 70-foot-square furnace, but the Portland Glass Company escaped when the Great Fire of Portland burned down 1,500 buildings on the Fourth of July 1866. Its luck did not hold. The next year, on September 11, 1867, fire ravaged Portland Glass. But it was back in operation by the next spring, turning out glorious glass in mammoth quantities.

Yet it was soon to fall victim to bad financial troubles. Creditors took over and reorganized and renamed the company as the Portland Glass Works. Then the great Depression of 1873 hit hard. Banks closed. Businesses failed. And 10 years after it started, Portland's glass factory shut down. The plant was sold to a Boston firm making a cheap product called Terra Alba.

Today collectors and museums vie over the best pieces of Portland Glass. Thank Heaven, beautiful collections have been given to the Portland Museum of Art, where everyone can view them. And Frank H. Swan, a noted collector of 35 years ago, has written a book called "Portland Glass," which, oddly, is published in Des Moines, Iowa.

Camden, coastal jewel

CAMDEN — Barbara joined our boat "Steer Clear" here in Camden Harbor for a nine day mid-September cruise of the Maine coast. But we enjoyed Camden so much that we spent two nights and a day on a guest mooring in the inner harbor, fascinated by all the end-of-summer water traffic and delighting in the beauty of this town.

The harbor is crowded. But the great windjammers come through threading their way to berths so far up the harbor you think they are aground on Main Street.

Their thick stalwart masts fill the sky. Through their rigging lines you see old white clapboard ship captains' homes on the hillside and the tower of a church whence carillons ring out.

Down on their decks, men and women scurry back and forth carrying supplies from town stores to ships' holds or offloading passengers.

Sure, these are cruise ships. And the cargoes are mostly food and drink for a week of sailing around Penobscot Bay for vacationers.

Every minute all day and most part of the night some boat, big or small, sails by. Tiny kids in tiny boats dart across the harbor. Occasionally a lobster boat moves by, but seldom. Here is no fishing harbor like our homeport. Here in Camden the elegant yachts pass temptingly by. Lovely to look at but beyond our purse. That is why sitting in Camden harbor watching the passing hulls is a bit like sitting at a Paris cafe.

Camden began in 1769 when James Richards from Dover, N.H., who had sailed in to cut ship's timber a year earlier, returned with two brothers, Joseph and Dodiphar following him. They founded Camden. The name honors Charles Pratt, first Earl of Camden, who was a strong and outspoken friend of the American colonies in Parliament. By 1790 the population of Camden, which then included what are now Rockport and Glen Cove, rose to 331.

In 1791 Camden became Maine's 22nd town. The first town meeting was held at Peter Ott's Tavern (now a steakhouse on the harbor). German-born Peter Ott came from Waldoboro's German colony to start his tavern. One of those early town meetings voted to "build a Pound on Mr. Peter Ott's land and Mr. Peter Ott to be Pound Keeper. . . . The Pound to be 7 feet high and tight enough to Stop Pigs a Month old, a Dore with Iron Hinges, a lock and kee."

From The Owl and The Turtle Book Shop overlooking the harbor, I bought Gorham Munson's book "Penobscot — Down East Paradise" and read a bit of the colorful history of Camden. Important in the Revolutionary War, Camden became a fortified town in the war of 1812, with a population topping 920. Mount Battie became a command outpost. Later, hotels were built and burned atop Mount Battie. A great fire of Nov. 10, 1892 destroyed most of the business district. Thereafter all downtown had to be brick. Munson relishes the names of Camden citizens in the old town records . . . Banajah Barrows and Comfort Barrows, Peletiah Corthell and Deplura H. Bisbee, Manassa Spear and Bathsheba Thorndike. But most of all I like the Camden girls christened "Experience."

Camden is a tourist town now. But it stays beautiful and it stays its own self. Thanks in great part to the Cyrus Curtis clan of Boks and Zimbalists and the wealth generated by Satevepost and Ladies Home Journal, Camden has open spaces and parks, outdoor amphitheater, yacht club. Camden is a jewel of the Maine coast, seen at her best from the mooring which Steer Clear enjoyed.

Pulling horses of Maine

EDGECOMB — Half a dozen huge pulling horses — called "the gentle giants" by their owners — are grazing now on the hillside pastures of Bill and Helen Perry's Springhill Farm.

These are the lazy days of the year for pulling teams. From June until October they compete in Maine fairs. But the last fair of the season — Topsham — finished yesterday. Now people like Bill Perry get to go woodchuck and bird hunting; and then in November, deer hunting. And while they hunt, their pulling horses get to rest.

But for the Perry horses, that's just until December. "Then we all go into the woods for a hard winter's work, cutting and bringing in the timber," says Bill.

In an age of tractors, the Perrys stay horse people: he has dappled roans and bays weighing around a ton each which he uses for work and competition; Helen has Appaloosas — oldest breed known in America — for riding.

As a younger man, Bill Perry was a blacksmith. "We'd shoe 19 horses a day some days," he recalls. "The charge was only $16 a horse. And that wasn't long ago — just 1967. Now it's up to $80."

His worst job, he says, was shoeing a little Llama. "Llamas have split hooves and foul tempers. And this critter bit, spit and landed a solid kick. But I trimmed those toes."

He hasn't forgotten how to shoe either: He puts special shoes on his pulling teams, "new shoes every six weeks."

In the woods last winter, Bill Perry and his horses brought out 600 cords of wood, racing a friend who was using a $28,000 skidder nearby.

"Week after week, I brought out more wood than he did. Another thing: one day a horse of mine threw a shoe. In 20 minutes I had a new shoe on him. Next day my friend's skidder blew a tire — it cost him $400 for a new one and a three day wait to get it.

"You can also get more wood out by using horses," claims Perry. He says that a landowner asked him to clean up after some skidders had left behind a mess. "I went in and took out 90 more cords left to rot by skidders."

In many ways, Bill Perry is a tough man: Last year, he wrestled a seven-foot brown bear, "just for fun," at Portland's Expo. But he's a softie when it comes to horses — 14 altogether, including the Appaloosas.

He takes me to see Buster, a 20-year-old roan gelding, and plays with him until Buster prances and kicks and rears like a young stud. Then he goes to the top of a hillock and lets out some yells until another old horse comes trotting into sight.

Raven, also 20, is a Percheron, the only non-Belgium among Perry's pulling horses. Raven is not pulling at the fairs anymore — "Cracked a bone in his leg, had a fat, lazy summer," says Perry. But come December, he'll be back working with his owner in the woods.

Now Phoebe comes trotting across the pasture. Phoebe is an unlikely name for such an enormous horse, only three years old yet weighing close to a ton already. And she'll get lots bigger, says Perry, pointing out that Phoebe's sister already tops a ton and that her mother is 2,200 pounds. Phoebe's only green-broken now. This winter she'll start in the woods — "a beginner like in first grade. Probably harness her up with old Raven to teach her."

We walk down to the barn. "Helen and I start here at five every morning," Perry says. "Our last chore here is at about five in the evening, when we do a cleanup and a final feed . . . In the pulling season, we feed a ton of special feed every two weeks. The special feed costs $150 and includes oats and crushed sweet corn. We also feed extra vitamins all summer as a tonic."

Training for the fairs starts in March, as soon as Perry and his horses end their work in the woods. Then he and his team put in four hours a day of pulling exercise, dragging 1200 pounds. The fair

season begins with Pittston's in June and continues through to Topsham's in mid-October. "We compete in every one," says Perry
proudly.

The tack room at **Springhill** is ablaze with blue and red ribbons,
some won by Bill's pulling horses, some by his wife's Appaloosas.

While he can shoe his horses himself, he still has to buy horse
gear. A complete pulling harness costs $800, he says. Then pointing
to a collar on a rack he admits that it alone cost $105.

The steel hooks that Perry uses are expensive also — $42 each —
even though they are less than half the size of a man's hand. "Use

anything less than top quality, and you risk having the hook break and a chain snap and fly back. Fellow had his leg smashed up that way," says Bill Perry. Walking around the horse barn, Perry lands a loving smack on the rump of a roan named Big Bob, then tugs in a friendly way on Bob's tail. When the big horse turns his head, it becomes obvious that one eye is sightless: it's milky white.

"A woman from New York came climbing into the field this summer to see us exercising," says Bill. "When I showed her Bob's blind eye she said I ought to be prosecuted for letting a blind horse work, that a one-eyed horse ought to be shot. I said, 'Lady, if you'll shoot Sammy Davis, I'll shoot Bob.'

"Bob," adds Perry, "has been a champion for years, in Massachusetts, where they specialize in pulling the biggest weight just six feet, as well as here, where we go for distance. He pulled 832 feet in five minutes for one prize."

I sit down on the straw with Perry, while he tells me about one of his biggest peeves: the over-loading of pulling horses at Maine fairs.

Some people claim pulling is cruel, and Perry concedes that it can sometimes put an undue strain on the horses.

"Overloading by fair officials was terrible. They've loaded down my teams with 6,900 pounds plus a 100-pound drag — at least 7,000 pounds total. That's too much in the class for teams weighing 2,900 pounds. The weight in that class should be no more than 6,000 pounds.

"The proper test should be time and distance. The competition should be to see how far your 2,900 pound team can pull 5,800 pounds in five minutes. But fair officials are cutting down on distance by overloading."

The sun is down now and a chill is on the evening air as we walk through the ruts of the exercise ground, past the Appaloosas to the farmhouse.

"What separates a farm work horse from a top pulling horse is heart," explains Bill Perry. "Not size, not muscle, but heart. That's the difference. So when these officials overload a horse so he can't budge his load no matter how hard he tries — that takes the heart out of him. Sooner or later he'll lay back and give up trying."

The drinking days of Old Portland

PORTLAND — The great old drinking days of Port-
land might be a worthy topic next time the Legislature wrings its
hands about the legal drinking age.

The up-and-down drinking age has gone like a yo-yo, as I recall,
from 21 to 18 to 20, on premises and off premises. There may even
be proposals that 19-year-olds can drink only from non-returnable
bottles, 18-year-olds can drink only while dancing, and 20-year-olds
can drink anywhere provided they have a letter from their legislator.

Well, in Portland's good old days, anybody of any age could drink
darn near anywhere.

Every grocery store had the rum barrel and the gin keg out where
the cash customers could "take a little support," as they said then.

Stores didn't have green stamps as enticers in those days. They
had, instead, big bowls of rum flip and gin punch which sat invitingly
on store counters. They were the "come-ons" to grease the wheels of
commerce. Quite a comedown from flips to trading stamps.

The ubiquity of rum meant that men and women didn't have to
head for a tavern to get a drink when away from home. One was
always handy.

Rum-drinking was all in the day's work. A bell was rung in Portland at 11 in the morning and 4 in the afternoon to signal "rum-
break." Every workman put down his tools and headed for the rum.

There were, as best I can find out from old maps, about 23 places
where grog was served within a three-minute walk from where City
Hall stands today. I called the City clerk to find out how many
licensed drinking places Portland has now. He says about 140, all
told, including 70 beer taverns, as he described them. And that is
peanuts compared to the "good old days."

Alice Greele's tavern was the favorite watering hole in Revolutionary times. Portland men gathered there, say the history books,

to swap news of the war, to eat a plate of home-baked beans, and drink a few mugs of Greele's famous flip.

The day they got the news of Burgoyne's surrender, rum flip flowed faster than the tide. To celebrate the defeat of "Gentleman Johnny," the British general at the Battle of Saratoga, everybody bought rounds of flip. It was passed out the windows to crowds in the street. Portland celebrated just the way Portland celebrated V-E and V-J days: with joyful roistering in the taverns and the streets.

Wherever there was a cannon, somebody fired it and somebody else passed the flip. One celebrant was shot to death by a cannonball that went off a brick wall, took off his drinking arm and passed through his chest.

Then came molasses — rich, sweet, molasses from the West Indies. Portland was the biggest importer of molasses outside New York. Six million gallons in 1860. Molasses meant rum.

Portland boasted seven distilleries running day and night, and a grocery clerk named John Bundy Brown parlayed molasses into the immense Portland Sugar Company, turning out 250 barrels a day.

About this time Neal Dow, the famous prohibitionist son of Portland, declared Maine people drank more liquor per capita than the inhabitants of any other state in the union. And maybe he was right.

Dow, direct descendant of Hate Evil Hall and a devout Quaker, got the Maine Legislature to pass an "Act for the Suppression of Drinking Houses and Tippling Shops." When he was mayor of Portland, Dow led raids on "tippling shops" and poured casks of the demon rum into the open sewers.

Mad at being deprived of their rum, angry Portlanders stormed Military Hall, where Mayor Dow kept his "medicinal liquor" locked in the cellar. One good citizen was shot to death in the rum riot.

Maybe in some heavenly tippling house in the Great Beyond, some of those rum-loving, old Portlanders have been laughing as they saw our Legislature rule that 18-year-olds are too young to sip legal brew in today's equivalent to Alice Greele's tavern.

"Hey! you lawmakers!" they say. "Don't you know that two of the 12 apostles were 18?"

The Defence: Diving on history

STOCKTON HARBOR — The divers surface from their search in the murky, muddy waters off Sears Island. They are exploring the wreck of the 85-foot "Defence," a 16 cannon privateer, scuttled by her American crew in 1779 to prevent capture by the British.

The tall diver near me bends and off loads the heavy oxygen tank, peels off the black rubber helmet and, to my amazement, long blonde hair tumbles down. A sweep of the arms and the black clinging wet suit is peeled off. There in a vivid blue, tiny bikini stands Cynthia Orr, 22, team leader of five divers, and a new graduate in anthropology from the University of Pennsylvania.

The water is cold down where the Defence has been lying in her muddy bed for almost 200 years. Cynthia Orr takes a mug of hot chocolate and goes into consultation with Avery Stone and Betty Seiffert. They are in office clothes — halters and shorts, and their academic qualifications, too, are awesome. Miss Stone is the official Recorder for the American Institute of Naval Archeology.

Next, Cynthia talks with Betty Seiffert, who is the conservation technician from the Maine State Museum. From a steel card-index file, Betty takes a large card. First, she sketches the handle of a pottery jug recovered by Cynthia; gives it a catalogue number; measures and records its dimensions; and notes the precise location on the wreck where it was found.

Betty repeats the whole process with each find. She has catalogued 391 pieces recovered; 29 metal artifacts, such as spoons, cannonballs, grape shot; 52 pottery and glass items, such as jugs for oil and bottles for ale; 55 items of bones and textiles. Among these are barrels marked "pork" and "beef." They each contained 32 big pieces of meat. The bones are still preserved in good shape.

"The reason all the artifacts are so well preserved is cold mud," explains Betty Seiffert. "For 198 years the water temperature down there has been very cold. And the wreck has been covered in thick mud. The mud cover has stopped any oxygen getting to the ship. So, no underwater feeders, such as worms or fungi, have flourished and eaten away at the ship and her contents. What we cannot recover this season, we will bury again in a mud and sand mixture to preserve till the diving begins again next summer."

Director of this project is David C. Switzer, professor of history at the University of New Hampshire, and director of this project since 1975.

"The ship we are diving on, was part of the Penobscot expedition — the worst and biggest fiasco in joint naval and military operations of the Revolutionary War."

Switzer explains that in 1779, during the Revolutionary War, the British established a naval base at Castine.

To drive them out, Massachusetts sent a naval force of 40 ships, transporting over 1,000 troops in July of 1779.

Admiral Richard Saltonstall was in command overall; and commanding the militia troops, were Solomon Lovell and Peleg Wadsworth, who later came to live in Maine. The artillery was under the command of Paul Revere. But Saltonstall turned out to be a timid and inept commander. He had the British vastly outnumbered; but he stalled for a month while British reinforcements sailed on Castine.

Under the command of Admiral George Collier, the six British warships scared the daylights out of Saltonstall. He panicked. His fleet and soldiers fled up the Penobscot and Bagaduce Rivers. But the privateer gunboat "Defence" tried running for safety into Stockton Harbor. The British pursued. The crew then blew up the powder magazine and that explosion sank the ship in the 15 feet of water where she has lain ever since. The defeated Saltonstall was court martialed and stripped of the right to ever command forces again.

Paul Revere walked home to Boston and the American troops fled through the wilderness as best they could to the settlements along the Kennebec river and thence back to Massachusetts.

"The tremendous importance of this sunken Defence," says Switzer, lies in the fact that this is the only known war vessel of the Revolutionary War that is still almost intact. It is this fact which has led MIT, the AINA, the National Geographic, as well as the Maine State Museum, and the Maritime Academy to sponsor this archeological work. Our ultimate goal is to raise all or a very large section of Defence as it still exists on the bottom today. It might be raised, if possible, as a unit. Or more likely, we may bring it up piece by piece and reconstruct it. We have all the measurements of every detail."

The ship was built in 1778 at Beverly, Mass. Her first, and last, voyage, was to Castine. There were 16 cannon aboard which shot six pound cannonballs. Each cannon weighed over 1,000 pounds. Two of these cannon have been raised from the Defence.

The stones recovered from the ballast in the Defence match the stones found today on the beach at Beverly where she was built in 1778.

"The huge size of the cookstove is astonishing," says Switzer, displaying a detailed drawing. "It is made of brick, and measures four and one-half feet wide, four and one-half feet deep and almost five feet high. It weighs a ton. In its center is a big cavity, into which a huge copper cauldron fitted. We have recovered that cauldron. It is 32 inches long, and 32 inches across and almost two feet deep.

"The Defence carried 100 in crew, a huge crew for a ship about 85 feet long and 22 feet in the beam. But as a privateer, she carried extra men to take charge of the prize vessels she captured."

"Meanwhile," says Dave Switzer, director of the Defence project, "the privateer brig Defence is the most important wreck of any Revolutionary War vessel in North America."

Conflicts, Conflicts

DAMARISCOTTA — Conflict of interests, that political disease, is infecting thousands of Maine citizens — me among them.

Garden versus boat; trout stream versus flower bed; painting the porch furniture or playing baseball — which to do?

Conflicts of interest in May and June are a testing of personal priorities, thrust upon his chosen children by the Almighty, who is sometimes jealous of the people He lets live in Maine while He is stuck up in heaven.

The end of May - beginning of June, is the time when the disease reaches its most virulent stage.

Nowhere else in America does the time and weather fit for painting your boat or catching your trout or paddling your canoe run head-on into the time for getting in the garden.

Conflict. Conflict. We in Maine are sorely tested by the Almighty. It's His fault. He makes good paint-drying times coincide with good planting weather. Ditto with the time to go after trout in a secret stream, or go sailing in a spring-summer breeze.

The root of our conflict, of course, is winter. Winter likes Maine so well it won't leave. It sticks around here, hanging on long after it has been glad to leave other states. Why, down in the Carolinas, azaleas are blooming in February, just about the time our skiing is at its best. Bees are sniffing honey in Savannah just when snow bunnies are decorating Sugarloaf.

God so loves sprinkling green Maine pines with his white fluffy snowflakes that he keeps dumping them on us through April, even into May, when they have long since crowned the cherry blossom queens in Washington.

Winter hogs the Maine stage so long that spring and summer go crazy, waiting in the wings to make their entrance. Finally, when winter clears out, spring and summer come rushing in, almost tripping each other. Hardly is late spring on center stage than summer darts out to perform indecent hot and steamy dances for a moment, then runs off, promising to be back soon with the fog and humidity.

In other states, there is not this kind of competition. Winter doesn't stay long where the scenery is dull and the inhabitants thin-blooded. By February, winter is gone from there, and spring is in and stays for months.

In those run-of-the-mill states, people have all kinds of leisurely time to plant gardens, hit golfballs, catch trout (if they're lucky enough to have a few around) and paint and launch boats before summer comes.

Here you gotta be quick or you might miss spring altogether. Once frost is out of the ground in Maine, it's rush, rush, rush: to get the garden tilled, fertilized and planted before the black flies eat you up, and to get that boat overboard before summer folk grab all the moorings.

Take the garden. As a boat person, I do my duty by the garden — reluctantly.

The basic trouble with a garden is that virtue gets altogether too much reward. The more I virtuously till the soil, the more I virtuously spread that fertilizer, the more I bend and plant, the more I'm going to have to harvest.

Work begets work in a garden. Far better to leave it untended in May and June, so then you'll be free later when it's time to weed and harvest.

The conflicts of interest are unending. I can see it now . . . that lovely summer day when we are out among the islands, watching the hot sun sink toward the sea, anchored in a remote and soothing cove. Precisely then, Barbara will turn and say, "I know my tomatoes are rotting on the vine. And I hate to think of all those beans getting bigger and tougher while we're out here cruising."

Take a regular Saturday morning. You wake up and shout with joy to see a perfect day.

A perfect day for what? For the boat? The garden? Fishing?

Sneaking off in a canoe? Or is this the perfect day for putting in the screens, painting the porch, doing the lawn?

It's no laughing matter. The director of the state Bureau of Watercraft tells me that 110,779 boats with motors are registered in Maine. Probably another 100,000 may be motorless and therefore unregistered. So there are probably nearly quarter of a million people wanting to get their boats painted, launched and used today. Me among them. To say nothing of those who want to get out tossing a line at the fish or hitting a ball down the fairway.

My betting is there are nearly quarter of a million gardens sitting out there demanding attention also.

Conflicts. Conflicts.

Where Maine magic began

ABOARD STEER CLEAR — The most beautiful, most happy places in the world for me are the islands off the coast of Maine.

I have been saying that for years and every year I say it with more fervor, more conviction.

Perhaps these Maine islands and the Maine people who work among them, are no more wonderful than they were last year, or five years ago. But they seem so. Maybe it is just the contrast; the rest of the world seems more tarnished, more tawdry, more false.

To savor that contrast, lie at anchor in a sheltered cove on an uninhabited island along Merchants Row, in that spectacular span of islands and water between Isle au Haut and Deer Isle. Rise before six in the morning and watch the sun come up out of the sea and kiss, in turn, the green pines on dozens of sleepy islets. Soon the warm rays lift the veil of mist to let you see the first lobster boats at work. Hear gulls screech searching food; watch gay guillemots bob and dive. (In Canada they call them 'police birds,' because they are black and white like Canadian police cars.) Ospreys and yellow warblers and my new friends the ruddy turnstones are all at work early. (Those busy turnstones really do turn stones.)

Row ashore in the dinghy on the early tide. Look down through two fathoms of clear unpolluted water and drift over the life below, clearly visible. Big, encrusted scallops; heaps of blue mussels; crabs scurrying; fish slowly cruising; sand dollars by the hundreds; spiny sea urchins; whelks in beautiful trumpet shaped houses; seaweed with filigree branches of olive green, beautiful as any flower garden.

Pull the dinghy up on the beach, and then walk the shore. Jump your way among the rocks and boulders. Marvel at their colors, shapes, history. Some are burnt red, some ochre yellow, some mottled green, some pearl grey, some pitch black.

Some are round and smooth and polished as a billiard ball, thanks to being rolled for a thousand years in the tides. Others are contorted and tortured and misbegotten, scarred from terrible upheavals in the fiery bowels of the earth millions of year ago. Leaping from one stone to another, you may be leaping across millenia.

Leave the shoreline and scramble up the island, across a patch of meadow, a copse of wood and onto the granite ledge at this island's little summit, maybe 120 feet above the sea. As you climb, eat handfuls of wild raspberries. The night's dew hangs in wet silver webs on the fruit. It is a special nectar on the tongue, known to few.

Atop your island, alone, gaze slowly around 360 degrees. Cock your ear to the distant, neighborly noise of a lobster boat engine in the misty, unseeable distance. There is no wind yet. At this early hour, the sea is glassy calm. Traces of the night linger on, till the sun's warm rays drive them out. Under the climbing sun, the whole sky gradually turns clear light blue. Can it be the same heaven, which last night was deep velvet black, jewelled with a million stars? Last night those stars, which pressed close down from heaven onto your boat, shone beneath your boat too. So calm was the cove, so bright were the myriad stars, that the black sea reflected the bright stars hung in the black heaven above.

You feel a strange perspective about yourself and your universe here alone on this island at sunup. You feel tremendously happy, but very, very small; a mere fleeting speck of life, a barely noticeable

microcosm, which will leave no trace at all, even on this tiny island, where teeming life has been, is and will be. The eternity of it all engulfs you.

For example, this granite ledge atop the island on which you stand — is it one million, or 200 million years old? Now the summit, was it once part of the ocean bottom? More recently, a mere 15,000 years ago, did ice tens of thousands of feet thick cover this spot and all these islands? That ice buried Mount Desert, buried the Camden hills.

On shore, a man feels more in control, in a man dominated world, a mover and shaker in his daily chores. But out here, a man knows he will leave a lesser mark on this island than the golden lichen which grows on a rock. Yet out here this insignificance is no put-down, as it would be on land.

Here a man does not compete. He belongs. You fit in to an incomprehensibly huge scheme of nature; be it as only an infinitesimal cog — you fit. You may be overwhelmed or battered, or even killed out here; but not by any enemy. Stand on this ledge and look the full circle, you see barely a sign of man's puny work; and yet feel a benign sense of belonging, of being more at home here than in a manmade city.

In mankind's tiny time frame, this is where the New World first began. Some Indian may have led some European or some Viking to the summit of this same island four hundred or a thousand years ago, when those bold voyagers explored these seas.

What a breed of men, what a breed of sailors! In small boats, they sailed the Atlantic. No charts of these shores. No gimmicks of modern navigation. They came to a land no men knew, came on a course, which pointed to what? Explored in long boats with a lead line, measuring yard by yard to find where the ledges lurked, ready to rip out their boat's planking if they guessed wrong.

In a pinch today, a man could navigate by the charts those explorers drew 400 years ago. The depths are the same; the islands have the same contours; and the ledges below are as hard and sharp as when they marked those dangers.

Stand atop this island, and feel small. But feel also a comforting sense of continuum, or long roots, of the durability of mankind, if not of individual man. Feel the sense of endless time. Islands and seas and mountains alter and vanish; but there is everlastingness to their change. The form of earth alters; but the essence keeps on, different, but the same.

Stand atop this island and take comfort from this perspective; here, the worst disasters leave barely a scar; the most heroic acts are soon forgotten and leave no dent at all. Hates and feuds and wars which in their own short hour rent hearts, seem meaningless once spent. The world's calamities pass, leaving little mark.

But still the raspberries grow, still the gulls screech, still the guillemots dive and play and still the seals poke up their bulbous eyes and twitch their whiskers in astonishment at the world above the water. Still the sun rises and still the tides rise and the tides fall absolutely unaffected by Washington and Wall Street or presidents or principalities. What men do or don't do doesn't soften the island granite under my feet one iota.

Here is a spot which no president has ever seen and which no president will ever change. It pre-dated and it will outlast our Republic.

To Papa:
love ya.
Terri

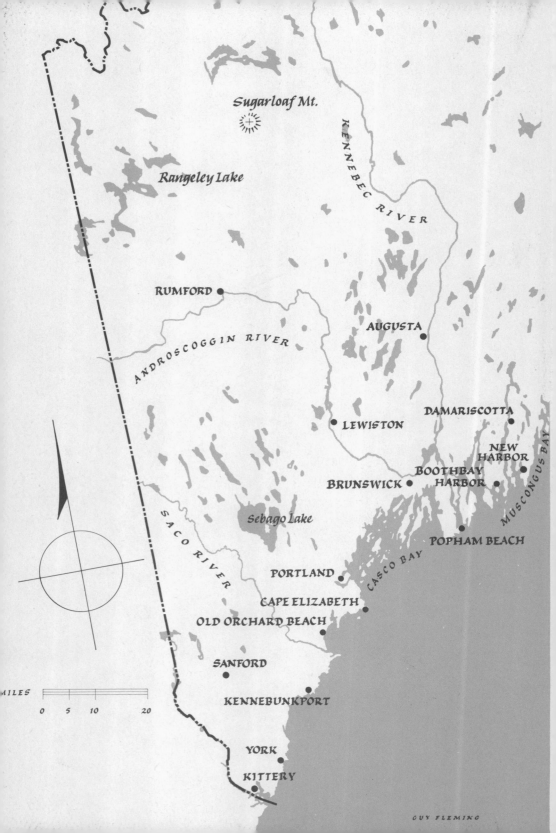

Sugarloaf Mt.

Rangeley Lake

KENNEBEC RIVER

RUMFORD

AUGUSTA

ANDROSCOGGIN RIVER

LEWISTON

DAMARISCOTTA

NEW HARBOR

BOOTHBAY HARBOR

BRUNSWICK

MUSCONGUS BAY

Sebago Lake

POPHAM BEACH

SACO RIVER

CASCO BAY

PORTLAND

CAPE ELIZABETH

OLD ORCHARD BEACH

SANFORD

KENNEBUNKPORT

YORK

KITTERY

MILES

0   5   10   20

GUY FLEMING